The Premises of International Criminal Procedure

Megumi Ochi

The Premises of International Criminal Procedure

Identifying the Principles in International Collaboration

Springer

Megumi Ochi
Graduate School of International Relations
Ritsumeikan University
Kyoto, Japan

ISBN 978-981-97-6785-4 ISBN 978-981-97-6786-1 (eBook)
https://doi.org/10.1007/978-981-97-6786-1

The translation was done with the help of an artificial intelligence machine translation tool. A subsequent human revision was done primarily in terms of content.

Cover photo: The entrance to the "permanent premises" of the International Criminal Court (ICC), also known as the "jewel box" (*Photo by* Theodora Jugrin).

This Springer imprint is published by the registered company Springer Nature Singapore Pte Ltd.
The registered company address is: 152 Beach Road, #21-01/04 Gateway East, Singapore 189721, Singapore

Foreword

International criminal law has undergone a spectacular development since the Nuremberg and Tokyo military tribunals, which was accelerated after the 1990s, due to the establishment of various international criminal tribunals, such as the ICTY, ICTR and ICC. The development, however, has been rather disorganized, if not fragmented, especially in the field of criminal procedural law.

Such disorganization stems from the imbalance between the international perception on the substantive and procedural aspects of international criminal law. It is possible, though not easy, to find a consensus among the nations on the definition of the core crimes, since they are crimes against the common values of international society and crimes under general international law. Agreeing on the procedural law to be applied to adjudicate them is quite a different matter. There are few procedural rules established under international customary law, and each State has different domestic criminal procedural laws firmly established in its own legal tradition. They differ significantly and it is almost impossible for the States to find a compromise.

As a multilateral treaty establishing a universal international criminal tribunal, the Rome Statute (and Rules on Procedure and Evidence adopted by the member States) contains provisions on judicial procedures, but the scope and content of such provisions are limited, because the negotiators could not agree on many crucial aspects of procedural law. For this reason, the ICC has sought to clarify and concretize its procedures through the accumulation of jurisprudence, depending on the law-making functions of the judges.

Similarly, in academia, research activities have been more focused on substantive aspects of the core crimes, while the theoretical analysis of procedural law is still in the development stage, except for some specific topics related to international human rights law. Moreover, procedural law is a living law with many court cases in different situations and its link to the practice of the courts must not be lost.

This book, *The Premises of International Criminal Procedure—Identifying the Principles in International Collaboration*, is one of the valuable products of such research, focused on the criminal procedural law employed in the ICC. As the title of the book shows, it presents not only a theoretical analysis of international criminal law but tries to identify the common principles/assumptions/values ("premises") applicable across that field of law, and to find the relationship between them in the dynamism of the actual trial process. While "seriousness of the core crimes" or "deterring illegal investigations" have traditionally been assumed to be the premises of international criminal procedure, current practice indicates that "speed and the first come, first served" and "consideration for national sovereignty" play crucial roles. It is fascinating to follow the author as she goes through all stages of the ICC judicial process—investigation and indictment, various challenges in international cooperation, trial *in absentia*, rights of the accused, examination of evidence, and reparation for victims—and examines the applicability of those principles. The study is highly theoretical and at the same time empirical. There is also an impressive and enlightening Addendum: The Premises in the Formation of an International Cooperative Framework for International Criminal Justice for the Russian–Ukrainian Situation.

The author, Dr. Megumi Ochi, is a promising Japanese scholar in international criminal law. It has been over ten years since I met her when she was as intern at the Pre-Trial Chamber of the ICC. She currently serves as an associate professor at the Graduate School of International Relations, Ritsumeikan University in Kyoto. Dr. Ochi's recent research has been dedicated to the examination of philosophical and procedural issues in international criminal law, transformative justice, sources and standards, as well as domestic war crimes trials and the utilization of digital evidence. Her work includes two monographs on international criminal procedure written in Japanese and articles published from peer-reviewed journals such as the *International Criminal Law Review* and the *Asian Journal of International Law*. Beyond her academic roles, since September 2014, Dr. Ochi has been an active participant in academic networking and cooperation, contributing as a member of the Young Penalist Committee and the Editorial Board of the International Association of Penal Law (AIDP). Additionally, she has held the position of senior fellow at Case Matrix Network (CMN) since October 2016.

Due to the involvement of the ICC in the serious situations in Ukraine and Gaza, the ICC is currently under unprecedented political and legal scrutiny. It is no exaggeration to say that the future survival of the ICC depends on how it responds to this challenge. In this context also, this book could not be timelier. It will be enjoyed by all those who are interested in the theoretical as well as pragmatic aspects of the ICC and will provide all students of international criminal law with a valuable resource and reference.

Kuniko Ozaki
Former Judge of the International
Criminal Court
Specially Appointed Professor
Chuo University
Tokyo, Japan

Preface to Original Japanese Edition

The International Criminal Court (ICC), an international organization that pursues the criminal responsibility of individuals for crimes under international law, has developed a unique criminal procedural law. It is unique and different from the criminal procedural laws of any State and reflects the various circumstances and values of international criminal justice, which is premised on international cooperation. What are the premises unique to international criminal procedures? In order to answer this question, this book examines the principles of international criminal procedure from the perspective of the circumstances and values (= premises) on which they are premised. Specifically, it examines the principles that govern international criminal procedures, especially the activities of the ICC, in the chronological order of the procedures (investigation → prosecution (indictment) → extradition → (prohibition of) trial (*in absentia*) → redress for the rights of accused persons → examination of evidence → reparation for victims) and highlights their characteristics by comparing them with the legal principles that govern similar phenomena domestically. This book also has the aspect of verifying the Premises Theory proposed in my previously published book *Kokusaikeijihou no Taikei: Premise Riron to Ichijihusairi no Gensoku (A System of International Criminal Procedure: Premise Theory and the Principle of Ne Bis In Idem)* (Shinzansha, 2020). In addition, in the Addendum, I have added the results of an analysis using the framework of the conclusions obtained in this book on the multilateral international collaboration system that has begun to be formed through the cooperation of the ICC and various States in the face of the situation caused by Russia's full-scale invasion of Ukraine, which began in February 2022.

Against the backdrop of Russia's invasion of Ukraine, interest in the ICC and international criminal justice has increased further. In this context, I would like to provide a new image of the ICC by describing the various circumstances that bind the ICC and the values that it holds dear. This is the pragmatist aspect of the ICC, in that while it adheres to human rights standards, it can only exercise coercive power within the scope permitted by national sovereignty, but sometimes it moves faster than any other State in a first-come, first-served manner, and if necessary, it will tolerate some human rights violations by other States.

It is my hope that this book will help readers develop a perspective on how to "use" the ICC system, while also suggesting the characteristics, limitations, and possibilities of the international legal system that lies behind it, and will in some way promote the investigation and prosecution of core crimes that occur in times of war and other situations, as well as the prevention of resulting crimes.

Kyoto, Japan
August 2022

Megumi Ochi

Preface to the English Edition

The original Japanese language edition of this current monograph was conceived in the hope that some parts of my original doctoral thesis submitted to Osaka University in 2015—namely, those concerning various principles other than *ne bis in idem*—could be revived and elaborated, in combination with the essays on various other principles that I had written during the ten years from my master's course to my post-doctoral period and to my current position. This volume substantially complements the previous book—*Kokusaikeijihou no Taikei: Premise Riron to Ichijihusairi no Gensoku (A System of International Criminal Procedure: Premise Theory and the Principle of Ne Bis In Idem)* (Shinzansha, 2020)— by empirically and sociologically depicting the state of "premises" in international criminal procedure, which is an element of Premise Theory— that I introduced in an article written and published in English—Megumi Ochi (2023), "The New Recipe for a General Principle of Law: Premise Theory to 'Fill in the Gaps'," *Asian Journal of International Law* 13(1) 169–187.

I believe that Japan is a State that is supposed to be in a leading position of international criminal justice from the perspective of its experience of the World War II and postwar war crimes trials and its monetary contributions in the modern world, discussions among Japanese scholars in international criminal law were hardly communicated to international scholarly circles. Since Japanese criminal justice system and academics have been administrating a complex mixed system between its old inquisitorial system and modernized adversarial system, their knowledges and ideas based on its thick comparative analysis efforts must contribute to the international criminal procedure. The discussions I had with my Japanese colleagues helped me to become aware of one of my roles and responsibilities to translate Japanese arguments for English readers. This book cites many academic articles and books written in Japanese. I have recorded all original Japanese language titles along with English translations of them to communicate that an active and deep discussion on the subject exists and is ongoing among Japanese academics.

In translating, some expressions and descriptions including the footnotes were modified to suit to the English edition and thus are not direct translations from the Japanese version. Due to the nuance gap between the Japanese and English versions, especially, the key word "*genri* (principle, rationale, axiom, doctorine)" was replaced with "premise" whenever this was more appropriate to communicate my intention. Other terms such as "*judaisei*" (seriousness/gravity) and "*hikiwatashi*" (extradition/surrender) are translated to both whenever it is impossible to make distinction.

I would like to express my gratitude to the Suntory Foundation for financially supporting this English translation. The original Japanese language book was translated into a rough draft English version with the help of DeepL, and later checked and modified with great effort for accuracy and elaborated further with the support of Dalia Haymov and Yuto Yokoyama. Special thanks go to Juno Kawakami and Springer Nature for supporting me with publication.

Finally, I would like to express my heartfelt gratitude to my beloved family and friends who have always supported me.

Kyoto, Japan
June 2024

Megumi Ochi

Contents

About the Author

Megumi Ochi is an academic and legal professional who specializes in International Criminal Law and currently serves as an associate professor at the Graduate School of International Relations, Ritsumeikan University, Kyoto, Japan. She obtained her Ph.D. in Law from Osaka University, Japan, and an LL.M. from Leiden University in the Netherlands. She has been a senior fellow at Case Matrix Network (CMN) (2016–2024) and an active member of the governing bodies of the International Association of Penal Law (AIDP) (2014–2024). She has published two monographs on international criminal procedure in Japanese and co-edited three books on international criminal justice in English.

Abbreviations

ACA	Atrocity Crime Advisory Group
CISA	Convention Implementing the Schengen Agreement
DRC	Democratic Republic of the Congo
EAC	Extraordinary African Chambers
ECCC	Extraordinary Chambers in the Court of Cambodia
ECJ	European Court of Justice
ECOWAS	Economic Community of West African States
FBI	Federal Bureau of Investigation
GoF	Group of Friends of Accountability
HRC	Human Rights Committee
ICC	International Criminal Court
ICCPR	International Covenant on Civil and Political Rights
ICJ	International Court of Justice
ICTR	International Criminal Tribunal for Rwanda
ICTY	International Criminal Tribunal for the former Yugoslavia
ILC	International Law Commission
IMT	International Military Tribunal
IMTFE	International Military Tribunal for the Far East
IRMCT	International Residual Mechanism for Criminal Tribunals
JIT	Joint Investigation Team
KSC	Kosovo Specialist Chambers
RPE	Rules of Procedure and Evidence
SCSL	Special Court for Sierra Leone
SFOR	Stabilisation Force
STL	Special Tribunal for Lebanon

List of Cases

1. International Criminal Justice Institutions

ICC

Prosecutor v. Al Bashir, Joint Concurring Opinion of Judges Eboe-Osuji, Morrison, Hofmański and Bossa (ICC-02/05-01/09-397-Anx1-Corr) Appeals Chamber (17 May 2019).

Prosecutor v. Al Hassan, Public redacted version of "Article 69(7) Application" (ICC-01/12-01/18-1346-Red2) Trial Chamber X (8 March 2021).

Prosecutor v. Al Mahdi, Judgment and Sentence (ICC-01/12-01/15-171) Trial Chamber VIII (27 September 2016).

Prosecutor v. Bemba, Decision on the "Prosecution Application for Leave to Submit in Writing Prior- Recorded Testimonies by CAR-OTP-WWWW-0032, CAR-OTP-WWWW-0080, and CAR-OTP-WWWW-0108" (ICC-01/05-01/08-886) Trial Chamber III (16 September 2010).

Prosecutor v. Bemba, Decision on the admission into evidence of materials contained in the prosecution's list of evidence (ICC-01/05-01/08-1022). Trial Chamber III (19 November 2010).

Prosecutor v. Bemba, Redacted Decision on the "Request for the conduct of the testimony of witness CAR-OTP-WWW-0108 by video-link" (ICC-01/05-01/08-947-Red) Trial Chamber III (12 October 2010).

Prosecutor v. Bemba, Dissenting Opinion of Judge Kuniko Ozaki on the Decision on the admission into evidence of materials contained in the prosecution's list of evidence (ICC-01/05-01/08-1028) Trial Chamber III (23 November 2010).

Prosecutor v. Bemba, Judgment on the appeals of Mr. Jean-Pierre Bemba Gombo and the Prosecutor against the decision of Trial Chamber III entitled "Decision on the admission into evidence of materials contained in the prosecution's list of evidence". (ICC-01/05-01/08-1386) Appeals Chamber (3 May 2011).

Prosecutor v. Bemba, Public redacted version of "Decision on 'Defence Motion for authorization to hear the testimony of Witness D-45 via video-link'" of 6 March 2013 (ICC-01/05-01/08-2525-Red) Trial Chamber III (7 March 2013).

Prosecutor v. Bemba, Decision on the "Second Further Revised Defence Submissions on the Order of Witnesses" (ICC-01/05-01/08-2644) and on the appearance of Witnesses D04-02, D04-09, D04-03, D04-04 and D04-06 via video-link (ICC-01/05-01/08-2646) Trial Chamber III (31 May 2013).

Prosecutor v. Bemba, Decision on the admission into evidence of items deferred in the Chamber's "First decision on the prosecution and defence requests for the admission of evidence" (ICC-01/05-01/08-2012) (ICC-01/05-01/08-2793) Trial Chamber III (3 September 2013).

Prosecutor v. Bemba, Partly Dissenting Opinion of Judge Ozaki on the Decision on the admission into evidence of items deferred in the Chamber's "First decision on the prosecution and defence requests for the admission of evidence" (ICC-01/05-01/08-2012) (ICC-01/05-01/08-2793-Anx) Trial Chamber III (3 September 2013).

Prosecutor v. Bemba, Judgment pursuant to Article 74 of the Statute (ICC-01/05-01/08-3343) Trial Chamber III (21 March 2016).

Prosecutor v. Bemba et al., Corrected public redacted version of Decision on 'Prosecution Submission of Evidence Pursuant to Rule 68(2)(c) of the Rules of Procedure and Evidence' (ICC-01/05-01/13-1481-Red-Corr) Trial Chamber VII (12 November 2015).

Prosecutor v. Bemba et al., Decision on Video-Link Testimony for Defence Witnesses (ICC-01/05-01/13-1697) Trial Chamber VII (4 March 2016).

Prosecutor v. Bemba et al., Decision on Requests to Exclude Western Union Documents and other Evidence Pursuant to Article 69(7) (ICC-01/05-01/13-1854) Trial Chamber VII (29 April 2016).

Prosecutor v. Bemba et al., Judgment pursuant to Article 74 of the Statute (ICC-01/05-01/13-1989-Red) Trial Chamber VII (19 October 2016).

Prosecutor v. Gaddafi and Al-Senussi, Public redacted-Decision on the admissibility of the case against Saif Al-Islam Gaddafi (ICC-01/11-01/11-344-Red) Pre-Trial Chamber I (31 May 2013).

Prosecutor v. Gaddafi and Al-Senussi, Decision on the admissibility of the case against Abdullah Al-Senussi (ICC-01/11-01/11-466-Red) Pre-Trial Chamber I (11 October 2013).

Prosecutor v. Gaddafi and Al-Senussi, Judgment on the appeal of Libya against the decision of Pre-Trial Chamber I of 31 May 2013 entitled "Decision on the admissibility of the case against Saif Al-Islam Gaddafi" (ICC-01/11-01/11-547-Red) Appeals Chamber (21 May 2014).

Prosecutor v. Gaddafi and Al-Senussi, Judgment on the appeal of Mr. Abdullah Al-Senussi against the decision of Pre-Trial Chamber I of 11 October 2013 entitled "Decision on the admissibility of the case against Abdullah Al-Senussi" (ICC-01/11-01/11-565) Appeals Chamber (24 July 2014).

Prosecutor v. Gbagbo, Decision on the "Corrigendum of the challenge to the jurisdiction of the International Criminal Court on the basis of articles 12(3), 19(2), 21(3), 55 and 59 of the Rome Statute filed by the Defence for President Gbagbo (ICC-02/11-01/11-129)" (ICC-02/11-01/11-212) Pre-Trial Chamber I (15 August 2012).

Prosecutor v. Gbagbo, Judgment on the appeal of Mr. Laurent Koudou Gbagbo against the decision of Pre-Trial Chamber I on the jurisdiction and stay of the proceedings (ICC-02/11-01/11-321) Appeals Chamber (12 December 2012).

Prosecutor v. Gbagbo and Ble Goude, Decision on the Prosecutor's application to introduce prior recorded testimony under Rules 68(2)(b) and 68(3) (ICC-02/11-01/15-573-Red) Trial Chamber I (9 June 2016).

Prosecutor v. Gbagbo and Ble Goude, Decision on the mode of testimony of Rule 68(3) witnesses (ICC-02/11-01/15-721) Trial Chamber I (11 October 2016).

Prosecutor v. Gbagbo and Blé Goudé, Decision on the mode of testimony of Rule 68(3) witnesses, Partially Dissenting Opinion of Judge Henderson (ICC-02/11-01/15-721-Anx) Trial Chamber I (18 October 2016).

Prosecutor v. Gbagbo and Ble Goude, Judgment on the appeals of Mr. Laurent Gbagbo and Mr. Charles Blé Goudé against the decision of Trial Chamber I of 9 June 2016 entitled "Decision on the Prosecutor's application to introduce prior recorded testimony under Rules 68(2)(b) and 68(3)" (ICC-02/11-01/15-744) the Appeals Chamber (1 November 2016).

Prosecutor v. Gbagbo and Ble Goude, Decision on the "Prosecution's application to conditionally admit the prior recorded statements and related documents of Witnesses P-0108, P-0433, P-0436, P-0402, P-0438, P-0459 and P-0109 under rule 68(3) and for testimony by means of video-link technology for Witnesses P-0436, P-0402, P-0438, P-0459 and P-0109 under rule 67(1)" (ICC-02/11-01/15-870) Trial Chamber I (4 April 2017).

Prosecutor v. Gbagbo and Blé Goudé, Decision on counsel for Mr. Gbabo's request for reconsideration of the 'Judgment on the Prosecutor's appeal against the oral decision of Trial Chamber I pursuant to article 81(3)(c)(1) of the Statute' and on the review of the conditions on the release of Mr. Gbagbo and Mr. Blé Goudé (ICC-02/11-01/15-1355-Red) Appeals Chamber (28 May 2020).

Prosecutor v. Katanga, Judgment on the Appeal of Mr. Germain Katanga against the Oral Decision of Trial Chamber II of 12 June 2009 on the Admissibility of the Case (ICC-01/04-01/07-1497) Appeals Chamber (25 September 2009).

Prosecutor v. Katanga, Judgment pursuant to article 74 of the Statute (ICC-01/04-01/07-3436-tENG) Trial Chamber II (7 March 2014).

Procureur c. Katanga, Jugement rendu en application de l'article 74 du Statut (ICC-01/04-01/07-3484) La Chambre De Première Instance II (23 mai 2014).

Prosecutor v. Katanga, Order for Reparations pursuant to Article 75 of the Statute (ICC-01/04-01/07-3728-tENG) Trial Chamber II (24 March 2017).

Prosecutor v. Katanga, Judgment on the appeals against the order of Trial Chamber II of 24 March 2017 entitled "Order for Reparations pursuant to Article 75 of the Statute" (ICC-01/04-01/07-3778-Red) Appeals Chamber (8 March 2018).

Prosecutor v. Katanga and Ngudjolo, Directions for the conduct of the proceedings and testimony in accordance with Rule 140 (ICC-01/04-01/07-1665). Trial Chamber II (20 November 2009).

Prosecutor v. Kenyatta, Decision on Defence request for excusal from attendance at, or for adjournment of, the status conference scheduled for 8 October 2014 (ICC-01/09-02-11-960) Trial Chamber V(B) (30 September 2014).

Prosecutor v. Lubanga, Decision concerning Pre-Trial Chamber I's Decision of 10 February 2006 and the Incorporation of Documents into the Record of the Case against Mr. Thomas Lubanga Dyilo (ICC-01/04-01/06-8-Corr) Pre-Trial Chamber I (24 February 2006).

Prosecutor v. Lubanga, Decision on the Defence Challenge to the Jurisdiction of the Court pursuant to article 19 (2) (a) of the Statute (ICC-01/04-01/06-512) Pre-Trial Chamber I (3 October 2006).

Prosecutor v. Lubanga, Judgment on the Appeal of Mr. Thomas Lubanga Dyilo against the Decision on the Defence Challenge to the Jurisdiction of the Court pursuant to article 19 (2) (a) of the Statute of 3 October 2006 (ICC-01/04-01/06-772) Appeals Chamber (14 December 2006).

Prosecutor v. Lubanga, Decision on the confirmation of charges (ICC-01/04-01/06-803-tEN) Pre-Trial Chamber I (7 February 2007).

Prosecutor v. Lubanga, Decision on various issues relating to witnesses' testimony during trial (ICC-01/04-01/06-1140) Trial Chamber I (29 January Trial Chamber I (29 January 2008).

Prosecutor v. Lubanga, Decision on the Admissibility of Four Documents (ICC-01/04-01/06-1399) Trial Chamber I (13 June 2008).

Prosecutor v. Lubanga, Decision on the consequences of non-disclosure of exculpatory materials covered by Article 54(3)(e) agreements and the Prosecutor v. Lubanga, Decision on the consequences of non-disclosure of exculpatory materials covered by Article 54(3)(e) agreements and the application to stay the prosecution of the accused, together with certain other issues raised at the Status Conference on 10 June 2008 (ICC-01/04-01/06-1401) Trial Chamber I (13 June 2008).

Prosecutor v. Lubanga, Judgment on the appeal of the Prosecutor against the decision of Trial Chamber I entitled "Decision on the consequences of the ICC having not yet made a decision on the application of the Article 54(3)(e) agreements and the application to stay the prosecution of the accused, together with certain other issues raised at the Status Conference on 10 June 2008" (ICC-01/04-01/06-1486) Appeals Chamber (21 October 2008).

Prosecutor v. Lubanga, Decision on the prosecution's application for the admission of the prior recorded statements of two witnesses (ICC-01/04-01/06-1603) Trial Chamber I (15 January 2009).

Prosecutor v. Lubanga, Decision on the Admission of Material from the "Bar Table" (ICC-01/04-01/06-1981) Trial Chamber I (24 June 2009).

Prosecutor v. Lubanga, Redacted Decision on the defence request for a witness to give evidence via video-link (ICC-01/04-01/06-2285-Red) Trial Chamber I (9 February 2010).

Prosecutor v. Lubanga, Redacted Decision on the Prosecution's Urgent Request for Variation of the Time-Limit to Disclose the Identity of the Intermediary 143 or Alternatively to Stay Proceedings Pending Further Consultations with the VWU (ICC-01/04-01/06-2517-Red) Trial Chamber I (8 July 2010).

Prosecutor v. Lubanga, Judgment on the appeal of the Prosecutor against the decision of Trial Chamber I of 8 July 2010 entitled "Decision on the Prosecution's Urgent Request for Variation of the Time-Limit to Disclose the Identity of Intermediary 143 or Alternatively to Stay" (ICC-01/04-01/06-2582) Appeals Chamber (8 October 2010).

Prosecutor v. Lubanga, Judgment pursuant to Article 74 of the Statute (ICC-01/04-01/06-2842) Trial Chamber I (14 March 2012).

Prosecutor v. Lubanga, First Report to the Trial Chamber on applications for reparations (ICC-01/04-01/06-2847) Registry (28 March 2012).

Prosecutor v. Lubanga, Decision on Sentence pursuant to Article 76 of the Statute (ICC-01/04-01/06-2901) Trial Chamber I (10 July 2012).

Prosecutor v. Lubanga, Decision establishing the principles and procedures to be applied to reparations (ICC-01/04-01/06-2904) Trial Chamber I (7 Trial Chamber I (7 August 2012).

Procureur c. Lubanga, Requête de la Défense sollicitant l'autorisation d'interjeter appel de la "Decision establishing the principles and procedures to be applied to reparation" rendue le 7 août 2012 (ICC-01/04-01/06-2905) La Chambre de Première Instance I (13 août 2012).

Procureur c. Lubanga, Acte d'appel à l'encontre de la "Decision establishing the principles and procedures to be applied to reparation" délivrée par la Chambre de première instance I le 7 août 2012 (ICC-01/04-01/06-2909) La Chambre D'appel (24 août 2012).

Procureur c. Lubanga, Acte d'appel contre la "Decision establishing the principles and procedures to be applied to reparation" du 7 août 2012 de la Chambre de première instance I (ICC-01/04-01/06-2914) La Chambre D'appel (3 septembre 2012).

Procureur c. Lubanga, Acte d'appel de la Défense de M. Thomas Lubanga à l'encontre de la "Decision establishing the principles and procedures to be applied to reparation" rendue par la Chambre de première instance I le 7 août 2012 (ICC-01/04-01/06-2917) La Chambre D'appel (6 septembre 2012).

Prosecutor v. Lubanga, Judgment on the appeals against the "Decision establishing the principles and procedures to be applied to reparations" of 7 August 2012 with AMENDED order for reparations (Annex A) and public annexes 1 and 2 (ICC-01/04-01/06-3129) Appeals Chamber (3 March 2015).

Prosecutor v. Lubanga, Redaction of Filing of Reparations and Draft Implementation Plan (ICC-01/04-01/06-3177-Red) Trial Chamber II (3 November 2015).

Prosecutor v. Lubanga, Annex A to Filing on Reparations and Draft Implementation Plan (ICC-01/04-01/06-3177-AnxA) Trial Chamber II (3 November 2015).

Prosecutor v. Ngudjolo, Judgment pursuant to article 74 of the Statute (ICC-01/04-02/12-3-tENG) Trial Chamber II (26 December 2012).

Prosecutor v. Ntaganda, Decision on Prosecution's request to hear P-0039's testimony by way of video-link (ICC-01/04-02/06-897-Red2) Trial Chamber VI (12 October 2015).

Prosecutor v. Ntaganda, Decision on Prosecution application under Rule 68(2)(c) of the Rules for admission of prior recorded testimony of P-0022, P-0041 and P-0103 (ICC-01/04-02/06-1029) Trial Chamber VI (20 November 2015).

Prosecutor v. Ntaganda, Reparation Order (ICC-01/04-02/06-2659) Trial Chamber VI (8 March 2021).

Prosecutor v. Ruto and Sang, Decision on Mr. Ruto's Request for Excusal from Continuous Presence at Trial (ICC-01/09-01/11-777) Trial Chamber V(A) (18 June 2013).

Prosecutor v. Ruto and Sang, Dissenting Opinion of Judge Herrera Carbuccia (ICC-01/09-01/11-777-Anx2) Trial Chamber V(a) (18 June 2013).

Prosecutor v. Ruto and Sang, Judgment on the appeal of the Prosecutor against the decision of the Trial Chamber V(a) of 18 June 2013 entitled "Decision on Mr. Ruto's Request for Excusal from Continuous Presence at Trial" (ICC-01/09-01/11-1066) Appeals Chamber (25 October 2013).

Prosecutor v. Ruto and Sang, Public Redacted Version of Corrigendum: Decision on Prosecution Request for Admission of Prior Recorded Testimony (ICC-01/09-01/11-1938-Corr-RED 2) Trial Chamber V(a) (19 August 2015).

Situation in the Republic of Kenya, Decision Pursuant to Article 15 of the Rome Statute on the Authorization of an Investigation into the Republic of Kenya (ICC-01/09-19-Corr) Pre-Trial Chamber II (31 March 2010).

ICTR

Barayagwiza v. Prosecutor, Decision (Prosecutor's Request for Review or Reconsideration (ICC-97-19-AR72) Appeals Chamber (31 March 2000).

Kajelijeli v. Prosecutor, Judgment (ICTR-98-44A-A) Appeals Chamber (23 May 2005).

Prosecutor v. Bagosora, Decision on The Application by the Prosecutor for a Formal Request for Deferral (ICTR-96-7-D) Trial Chamber I (17 May 1996).

Prosecutor v. Bagosora et al., Judgement and Sentence (ICTR-98-41-T) Trial Chamber I (18 December 2008).

Prosecutor v. Barayagwiza, Decision (ICTR-97-19-1) Appeals Chamber (3 November 1999).

Prosecutor v. Barayagwiza, Decision on Defence Counsel Motion to Withdraw (ICTR-97-19-T) Trial Chamber I (2 November 2000).

Prosecutor v. Hategekimana, Judgment (ICTR-00-55B-A) Appeals Chamber (8 May 2012).

Prosecutor v. Nahimana et al., Judgment (ICTR-99-52-A) Appeals Chamber (28 November 2007).

Prosecutor v. Ngirumpatse, Decision on the Defence Motion Challenging the Lawfulness of the Arrest and Detention and Seeking the Return or Inspection of Seized Items (ICTR-97-44-I) Trial Chamber II (10 December 1999).

Prosecutor v. Rwamakuba, Decision on Appropriate Remedy (ICTR-98-44C-T) Trial Chamber (31 January 2007).

Prosecutor v. Semanza, Judgement and Sentence (ICTR-97-20-T) Trial Chamber (15 May 2003).

Prosecutor v. Zigiranyirazo, Decision on Interlocutory Appeal (ICTR-2001-73-AR73) Appeals Chamber (30 October 2006).

Semanza v. Prosecutor, Decision (ICTR-97-20-A) Appeals Chamber (31 May 2000).

ICTY

Prosecutor v. Blaškić, Judgment on the Request of Croatia for Review of the Decision of Trial Chamber II of 18 July 1997 *(IT-95-14-AR108bis)* Appeals Chamber (29 October 1997).

Prosecutor v. Delalić, Judgment (IT-96-21-T) Trial Chamber (16 November 1998).

Prosecutor v. Karadžić, Decision on the Accused's Motion for Remedy for Violation of Rights in Connection with Arrest (IT-95-5/18-PT) Trial Chamber (31 August 2009).

Prosecutor v. Nikolić, Decision on Defence Motion Challenging the Exercise of Jurisdiction by the Tribunal (IT-94-2-PT) Trial Chamber II (9 October 2002).

Prosecutor v. Šešelj, Decision on Assignment of Council (IT-03-67-PT) Trial Chamber I (21 August 2006).

STL

Prosecutor v. Ayyash et al., Order to Seize the Trial Chamber Pursuant to Rule 105 Bis (A) of the Rules of Procedure and Evidence in Order to Determine Whether to Initiate Proceedings in absentia (STL-11-01/I/TC) Pre-Trial Judge (17 October 2011).

Prosecutor v. Ayyash et al., Decision to Hold Trial in absentia (STL-11-01/I/TC) Trial Chamber (1 February 2012).

2. Other

Permanent International Court of Justice

Affair relative à l'usine de Chorzow, CPJI Serie A, No. 9, p. 21.

ICJ

Legal Consequenes of the Construction of a Wall in the Occupied Palestinian Territory, Advisory Opinion, ICJ Reports 2004, p. 136.

Questions concernant l'obligation de poursuivre ou d'extrader (Belgique c. Sénégal), arrêt, CIJ Recueil 2012, p. 422.

Separate Opinion of Judge Yusuf in a case concerning *Questions concernant l'obligation de poursuivre ou d'extrader (Belgique c. Senegal)*, arret, CIJ Recueil 2012, p. 422.

HRC

A v. Australia, Communication No. 560/1993, UN Doc. CCPR/C/59/D/560/1993 (30 April 1997).

Mbenge v. Zaire, Communication No. 16/1977, UN Doc. CCPR/C/OP/2 at 76 (1990).

European Court of Human Rights

Colozza v. Italy, Application No. 9024/80 (12 February 1985).

Demebukov v. Bulgaria, Application No. 68020/01 (28 February 2008).

Van Geyseghem v. Belgium, Application No. 26103/95 (21 January 1999).

Jalloh v. Germany, Application No. 54810/00 (11 July 2006).

Krombach v. France, Application No. 29731/96 (13 February 2001).

Lala and Pelladoah v. The Netherlands, Application No. 16737/90 (22 September 1994).

Maleki v. Italy, Communication No. 699/2996 (27 July 1999).

Poitrimol v. France, Application No. 14032/88 (23 November 1993).

Sejdovic v. Italy, Application No. 56581/00 (1 March 2006).

Somogyi v. Italy, Application No. 67972/01 (18 May 2004).

T v. Italy, Application No. 14104/88 (12 October 1992).

Domestic Courts

Israel

Eichmann, in the District Court of Jerusalem, 36 ILR 5 (15 December 1961).

Australia

Levinge v. Director of Custodial Services (1987) 9 NSWLR 546.

The UK

R v. Preston (1993) 2 AC 130.

R v. Berry (1897) 104 LT Jo 110.

R v. Browne (1906) 70 JP 472.

R v. Jones (2003) 1 AC 1.

R. v. Horseferry Road Magistrates' Court, Ex parte Bennett (1994) 1 AC 42.

Switzerland

Adamov v. Switzerland, judgment (Application no. 3052/06) Second section (21 June 2011).

C v. Federal Police Department, 100 ILR 657 (16 September 1987).

Germany

BVerfG—Beschluß vom 17.07.1985 (2 BvR 1190/84)—DRsp Nr. 1994/2567.

BverfGE 75 (31 May 1987).

Japan

The Supreme Court, 7 September 1978, Penal Code, Vol. 32, No. 6, p. 1672.

France

Berbie, Cour de Cassation, 78 ILR 124, 148 (6 October 1983).

Re Argoud, Cour de Cassation, 45 ILR 90 (4 June 1964).

The US

Crosby v. United States, 506 US 255 (1993).

Diaz v. United States, 223 US 442, 455–59 (1912).

Frisbie v. Collins, 342 US 519 (1952).

Green v. United States, 355 US 184, 187–188 (1957).

Hopt v. Utah, 110 US 574, 28 L Ed 262, 4 S Ct 202 (1884).

Ker v. Illinois, 119 US 436 (1886).

United States v. Toscanino, 500 F 2d 267 (1974).

United States v. Alvarez-Machain, 112 S.Ct. 2188 (1992).

United States v. Lanza, 260 US 377 (1922).

South Africa

State v. Ebrahim, 1991 (2) SALR 553.

Chapter 1
Introduction: What Are the Premises Inherent in International Criminal Procedure?

Abstract This introduction explains why we need to understand the special characteristics of international criminal procedure and how this book attempts to understand them. Previous studies have provided insufficient explanation of how they differ from domestic legal principles and why they differ, and what premises of international criminal procedure give rise to such differences. Can we provide any unified account for the differences between the procedure of the ICC and of any States? This boils down to the question: what are the premises inherent in international criminal procedure? To find an answer, this book applies the Premise Theory of general principles of law and reviews the premises that have been proposed by previous research that adopted a mainly teleological or theoretical approach. This book is structured in the chronological order of the proceedings, examining the premises of the principles underlying the various issues that arise in the investigation, prosecution, and trial proceedings at the ICC.

1 Introduction

In 1998, the international community agreed to establish the International Criminal Court ("ICC") in The Hague, a city in the Netherlands, to try serious international crimes ("core crimes") that occur worldwide. Until 2015, the ICC was operating in a former KPN Telecom building, provided free of charge by the Dutch government. In December 2015, the ICC completed its move out of its previous temporary home and into new permanent premises on the seaward side of The Hague (the "permanent premises"). This enabled the ICC to become a complex of six buildings, including the Office of the Prosecutor and the Registry, and to pursue justice for core crimes in three spacious courtrooms equipped with IT equipment.

However, the mere existence of a trial facility does not make core crimes trials happen. The ICC process requires cooperation by the States in which the core crimes were committed, or by the State in which the accused is located, the United Nations ("UN"), and other relevant actors. In addition, because core crimes sometimes involve thousands of people, including the perpetrators and victims, they are addressed not

M. Ochi, *The Premises of International Criminal Procedure*,
https://doi.org/10.1007/978-981-97-6786-1_1

only by the ICC, but also simultaneously by various judicial institutions and alternative justice frameworks in the places where the crimes were committed. In other words, ICC proceedings are conducted in the context of international cooperation to address core crimes, which requires a law that considers the various circumstances that arise and the values of international criminal justice, which are assumed by the ICC system itself.

What are the premises inherent to international criminal procedural law? In what follows, I will discuss why this question is important and how it can be answered, and then introduce the structure and scope of this book.

2 The Problem

2.1 Attempts to Establish an International Criminal Justice System

A crime is an act that violates the morality of the community.[1] As the most basic "legal" system of human social life, the system for bringing justice has been shared, transcending time, place, culture, and religion, by human beings in various forms. Systems of punishment and atonement for those who break the rules of society have been constructed and operated along with the formation of communities, and their contents and methods vary according to the customs and beliefs of the community.[2] However, the so-called Western criminal justice system—in which crimes and punishments are first established by law, investigations are conducted in cases of alleged violations, and sentences are imposed after hearings and deliberations by public authorities[3]—reaches all continents through colonial rule or what is now called capacity building.[4] The Western system of criminal justice, in which sentences are imposed through a process of adjudication by the public authorities, has become universal, with the exception of some States and regions that have maintained customary systems.

Along with the spread of the Western criminal justice system, the system of State monopoly of penal power—on which it is premised—has also spread. The investigation, prosecution and trial of crimes have been considered one of the most important functions of State sovereignty. The first attribute of sovereignty is the "power to give law (*loy*)"[5] and the treatment of lawbreakers is fundamental to the governance of the State.

---

[1] Hart [68], p. 405.

[2] See, for example, Yamanaka [251], pp. 3–5.

[3] See e.g., Stern [204]; Tonry [227], p. 3. The "liberal premise" of international criminal law is juridification, criminalization and individualization; Stahn [199], p. 9.

[4] See, e.g., Cunneen [35], p. 386.

[5] Bodin [16], Chapitre IX.

However, the importance of international law—a supranational discipline based on past agreements between States—concerning the *ius puniendi* and the decision to exercise it has become increasingly important in recent years, not only because of the cross-border nature of crime, but also because of the internationalization of the meaning of crime.[6] In particular, the need for internationalization of criminal justice has been recognized for some crimes that have been shared by the international community with respect to their seriousness. In recent years, therefore, investigations, prosecutions, and trials for such crimes of international significance have been carried out by various actors in a variety of ways.

The attempt to build the international criminal justice system as we know it today,[7] after several partial successes and setbacks,[8] began with the worldwide prosecution of war crimes on a global scale immediately after the crimes were committed and recorded in the places where soldiers moved and were deployed. War crimes trials against tens of thousands of suspects alleged to have initiated World War II and to have been involved in crimes during the war were carried out by international courts such as the International Military Tribunal ("IMT"), also known as the Nuremberg Tribunal, and the military tribunals of an international nature by the occupying power, such as the International Military Tribunal for the Far East ("IMTFE"), also known as the Tokyo Trials, or by using national military commissions or military courts in Western States and Asia–Pacific States.[9]

After the UN was established, the UN International Law Commission ("ILC") began discussions towards the codification of the international criminal justice experience represented by the Nuremberg trials and the establishment of an international criminal court.[10] In the course of that debate, several serious crimes have been listed as crimes under international law or "crimes against the peace and security of mankind".[11]

In parallel with this movement, efforts were made by the international community to develop international laws for the prosecution of individuals who committed genocide and other serious violations of the laws of armed conflict. With the conclusion of the Convention for the Prevention and Punishment of the Crime of Genocide

[6] See e.g., Boister et al. [17].

[7] For the definition of international criminal justice, see Ochi [149], Footnote 5.

[8] The Hagenbach Trial, held in 1474 by judges appointed from the countries and cities of the Holy Roman Empire, is said to be the oldest example of international criminal justice. On the other hand, after World War I, legislation was sought for the prosecution of German Emperor Wilhelm II, but it did not materialize because of the lack of extradition. See *Ibid*., 34–35.

[9] For details, see *Ibid*., Chapter 1, Section 2.

[10] For more information, see ILC's Analytical Guide; ILC, "Formulation of the Nürnberg Principles" at https://legal.un.org/ilc/guide/7_1.shtml; ILC, "Question of international criminal jurisdiction" at https://legal.un.org/ilc/guide/7_2.shtml; ILC, "Draft code of crimes against the peace and security of mankind (Part I)" at https://legal.un.org/ilc/guide/7_3.shtml; ILC, "Draft code of crimes against the peace and security of mankind (Part II)—including the draft Statute for an international criminal court" at https://legal.un.org/ilc/guide/7_4.shtml (as of 27 December 2021).

[11] Articles 15–20, Draft Code of Crimes against the Peace and Security of Mankind 1996, *Yearbook of the International Law Commission*, 1996, Vol. II (Part II).

("Genocide Convention") in 1948 and the Geneva Conventions on the Protection of War Victims in 1949,[12] the development of national laws enabling the prosecution of genocide and war crimes as defined in these conventions was promoted by States.

It was not until the 1990s that there was a new development in international criminal justice efforts. In response to post-Cold War genocide, the International Criminal Tribunal for the former Yugoslavia ("ICTY") was established in The Hague, and the International Criminal Tribunal for Rwanda ("ICTR") was established in Arusha, Tanzania. These two specially established (*ad hoc*) international criminal tribunals ("*ad hoc* Tribunals") were established based on UN Security Council resolutions. These tribunals closed in 2017 and the International Residual Mechanism for Criminal Tribunals ("IRMCT") has taken over the remaining court proceedings and judicial cooperation activities for States.

The Rome Statute of the ICC ("ICC Statute"), a multilateral treaty, was adopted in Rome in 1998 and at the time of writing (18 August 2022) had 123 State parties. The ICC has jurisdiction over four crimes discussed at the ILC: genocide, crimes against humanity, war crimes and crimes of aggression, which have since received special treatment as "core crimes".[13] Soon after its establishment, the Court began investigating various cases through so-called self-referrals from several African States Parties to the ICC Statute, but was subsequently criticized by the African Union and others because of its image as a court targeting African States.[14] However, the scope of its activities has since expanded beyond the African continent, and at the time of writing, it is investigating 17 situations—Democratic Republic of Congo, Uganda, Sudan, Central Africa (2 situations), Kenya, Libya, Côte d'Ivoire, Mali, Georgia, Burundi, State of Palestine, Bangladesh/Myanmar, Afghanistan, the Philippines, Venezuela I, and Ukraine –,[15] and preliminary investigations into three situations—Guinea, Nigeria, and Venezuela II—are underway.[16] In particular, in response to the Russian invasion of Ukraine on 24 February 2022 and the numerous core crimes complained of as a result, the ICC has not only conducted its own investigations, but has also seen a completely new form of international collaboration, with a multifaceted investigative cooperation system involving several groups of States.

---

[12] The term is used collectively for four conventions: the Geneva Convention for the Amelioration of the Condition of the Wounded and Sick in Armed Forces in Time of War, 12 August 1949 (Convention I); the Geneva Convention for the Amelioration of the Condition of the Wounded, Sick and Shipwrecked Members of Armed Forces at Sea, 12 August 1949 (Convention II); the Geneva Convention relative to the Treatment of Prisoners of War, 12 August 1949 (Convention III); and the Geneva Convention for the Protection of Civilian Persons in Time of War, 12 August 1949 (Convention IV).

[13] ICC, "The States Parties to the Rome Statute" at https://asp.icc-cpi.int/en_menus/asp/states%20parties/Pages/the%20states%20parties%20to%20the%20rome%20statute.aspx (as of 18 August 2022).

[14] See Inazumi [80].

[15] ICC, "Situations under investigation" at https://www.icc-cpi.int/pages/situation.aspx# (as of 18 August 2022).

[16] ICC, "Preliminary examinations" at https://www.icc-cpi.int/pages/pe.aspx (as of 18 August 2022).

Core crimes trials are also conducted by institutions other than the ICC. Originally, the pursuit of responsibility for war crimes was supposed to be conducted by the parties to the armed conflict during the continuation of the conflict.[17] In addition, as represented by the *Eichmann* case, for example, cases related to the Nazi Holocaust have been conducted in the domestic courts of each State even decades after World War II. Since 2000, within States that experienced large-scale human rights violations during independence struggles, persecution by dictatorial regimes during the Cold War, or internal armed conflicts over resources, there have been various forms of international cooperation in dealing with core crimes, including the establishment of internationalized courts or hybrid courts, and the use of local procedures. Some examples are the Special Court for Sierra Leone ("SCSL"), Extraordinary Chambers in the Court of Cambodia ("ECCC"), Extraordinary African Chambers ("EAC"), Rwanda's Gacaca system, and Colombia's Special Jurisdiction for Peace. Such institutions are often established on a time-limited basis. In addition, an increasing number of States where core crimes have been committed domestically or based on universal or other jurisdiction are seeking to try core crimes using existing or newly established national judicial systems. National institutions have been established in States where core crimes were committed domestically, such as Bosnia and Herzegovina ("Bosnia"), Cambodia, Serbia, Iraq, Bangladesh, Central Africa and Kosovo, and their establishment has been successively confirmed in recent years.[18]

In this book, the individual units of authority that prosecute core crimes are referred to as "criminal jurisdictions", without distinguishing between international and domestic ones.[19] Criminal jurisdictions that prosecute core crimes do so through their own criminal justice institutions, which include their own trial courts and investigative and prosecution agencies.[20] Such criminal justice institutions include national criminal justice institutions and International Criminal Justice Institutions. The term "International Criminal Justice Institutions" refers to institutions that are independent of a particular State and are operated by a number of States, or semi-international institutions whose operation is partially entrusted to a particular State but in which a number of States also participate in their operation. In this book, International Criminal Justice Institutions such as the ICC that operate as international organizations completely independent of any nation state are referred to as "international criminal courts."

---

[17] Fujita [58], p. 197.

[18] For details, see Ochi [149], Chap. 1 and 2.

[19] The term "*shihoken* (criminal jurisdiction)" includes the authority to prosecute, including investigation and arrest, the authoirty to try and sentence, and the authority to enforce punishment. Such criminal jurisdiction include, for example, individual States, the ICC and specially established criminal tribunals. While the concept of "jurisdiction" here refers to a unit, jurisdiction is used as a concept that indicates the scope of authority possessed by such judicial power. In other words, criminal jurisdiction, which is an initiative of international criminal justice, represents a unit of authority that has jurisdiction over core crimes. See Ochi [149], at Note 22.

[20] On the concept of the judicial system as a "direct enforcement system" of comprehensive international criminal justice, see Bassiouni [11], p. 535.

2.2 Characteristics of International Criminal Procedure

International criminal procedure refers to the law governing the procedures of International Criminal Justice Institutions that prosecute core crimes.[21] Much of it has been conceived and developed on the basis of a long tradition of domestic law, in particular the two major models referred to as the Continental and Anglo-American systems of law.[22] Criminal procedure has developed in each State in its own elaborate way, closely related to the nature of its society, so that international parity is not easy to achieve, and this is the area in which the difficulties of developing international criminal law are most clearly expressed.[23]

The content of international criminal procedure may deviate from what has been pointed out in previous comparative criminal law as characteristics of the domestic legal principles from which it is seen to originate. Even though it is an international tribunal, its judicial framework itself is a Western criminal justice system in which individuals are tried by public authorities. For example, it was theoretically possible to choose to apply, *mutatis mutandis*, the domestic criminal procedure of the State where the international trial was held, or to try the accused in accordance with the domestic criminal procedure of the State where the accused or suspect was born and raised. However, this approach was not adopted due to two assumptions that arose during the procedural system-building phase of the IMT, which was the first step in the international criminal justice effort: one is that the procedure of an International Criminal Justice Institution must be different from the national law of any State.[24] The other premise was that the application of customary international law was mandatory at the time of the establishment of the *ad hoc* Tribunals in order to avoid the criticism of *ex post facto* law prosecution.[25]

Because of these—sometimes implicit—assumptions, international criminal procedure has developed as a unique one. In the course of its development, various procedural rules have been applied in judicial decisions as necessary, in addition to rules that have gone through the legislative process. What has made the approval of such new rules possible is the existence of various fundamental principles that undelie the entire system of procedure. In particular, when the applicable law is unclear from the existing rules or when it is unclear what rules should be applied in special circumstances, recourse to "general principles" has often been attempted. In conjunction with the conceptualization of international criminal procedure as international law, such general principles are understood as a form of "general principles of law" that constitutes a source of international law and ensures its existence.[26]

---

[21] Ochi [149], pp. 21–32.

[22] For an overview, see Higashizawa [75], pp. 138–139.

[23] Ozaki [157], p. 312.

[24] The IMT was reportedly structured to ensure the equal participation of the four Allied Powers in court proceedings as a basic principle. Ambos and Bock [2], p. 491.

[25] See, *Prosecutor v. Delalić*, Judgment (IT-96-21-T) Trial Chamber (16 November 1998), para. 414.

[26] See Ochi [149], p. 3.

The reason for the form of existence of international criminal procedure itself can be sought in the two assumptions mentioned earlier. It can also be said that it has been clarified to some extent how the general principles of individual specific international criminal procedures differ from the corresponding principles of domestic law.[27] However, when taking a comprehensive view of the various general principles of international criminal procedure, it is difficult to say that there is a sufficient unified explanation of how they differ from domestic legal principles and why they differ, and what premises of international criminal procedure give rise to such differences. Is there any unified theoretical explanation for the differences between the procedure of the ICC and the national legal principles that have developed in other States? These questions, in other words, boil down to the question: what are the premises inherent in international criminal procedure?

2.3 *Previous Research on What ICC Procedures Presuppose*

2.3.1 Purpose of the ICC's Procedure

Early systematic studies on international criminal procedure have been premised on a principled discussion of the aims and objectives of international criminal procedure. For example, according to Christoph Safferling, the first single author on international criminal procedure, the objectives of international criminal procedure include, as "direct procedural aims" linked to the realization of international criminal substantive law, identifying the perpetrators and proving their guilt allegations, and "translating" their guilt into just sentences.[28] And the "indirect aims" are to bring healing to the international community as a whole, to bring stability between parties to a conflict, to deter future deviance, to establish the rule of law, to give victims a voice, and to keep an official record.[29]

It was also the premise of a major collaborative study of international criminal procedure led by Göran Sluiter that international criminal procedure has both ancillary and inherent purposes in international criminal substantive law.[30] The objectives ancillary to substantive law include the admissibility of incriminating evidence, historical fact-finding, protection of due process rights, structured victim participation, standard-setting as a model for national systems, and the implementation of criminal substantive law through effective public trials.[31] On the other hand, as an

---

[27] See e.g., Carter and Pocar [27]; Safferling [172]; Sluiter et al. [195]. On the principle of equality of arms, see, for example, Fedorova [49], pp. 3–4 and 461.

[28] Safferling, *ibid.*, pp. 74–75.

[29] *Ibid.*, pp. 75–76.

[30] Ohlin [150], p. 55.

[31] *Ibid.*, pp. 61–67.

inherent objective, it is to fill a legal vacuum where core crimes have occurred and the rule of law has been lost, exemplified by the ICC's complementarity principle.[32]

On the other hand, Fausto Pocar and Linda Carter, who attempted to characterize international criminal procedure as a mixture of the Continental and Anglo-American models of criminal justice, argue that the goal of criminal justice in Continental law is to uncover the truth, whereas in the Anglo-American model, the emphasis is on protecting the rights of the accused and it takes precedence over the search for the truth.[33]

According to the recent comment of Jenia Turner, which is based on the pluralism of international criminal and procedural law, international criminal proceedings have objectives in common with ordinary criminal proceedings, such as truth-finding, effective enforcement of criminal law, and fairness in proceedings.[34] In addition to these, other objectives specific to international criminal justice include establishing a historical record of crimes, promoting peace, and serving as a model of respect for human rights.[35]

2.3.2 The "Environment" and "Aspiration" of International Criminal Procedure

While these previous studies have identified the purpose and goal of international criminal procedure in ideological terms, Frédéric Mégret proposed a paradigm shift, rejecting the view of international criminal procedure as a law that seeks a fair trial or as a point of conflict between Continental law and Anglo-American law, and focusing on its new "international" dimension.[36] He also proposed a paradigm shift to focus on the "internationality" of international criminal procedure, rejecting the view that international criminal procedure is a point of conflict between Continental law and Anglo-American law.[37]

Mégret pointed to the following. First, the fact that international criminal trials are conducted as part of, or at least significantly joined to, the international legal order provides difficulties such as (i) *ensuring the cooperation of States and access to evidence*.[38] Second, there are (ii) *elements of cultural diversity and value pluralism* and the resulting misunderstandings and incomprehension.[39] Third, international criminal justice is conducted in extreme circumstances, such as those involving the establishment of special tribunals, which may lead to (iii) *exceptionality, such as*

[32] *Ibid.*, pp. 67–68.

[33] Pocar and Carter [159], pp. 19–20.

[34] Turner [233], p. 997.

[35] *Ibid.*

[36] Mégret [122], pp. 5–6.

[37] *Ibid.*, pp. 23 and 25.

[38] *Ibid.*, p. 25.

[39] *Ibid.*, pp. 25–26.

deviations from human rights and normal rules.[40] Fourth, and related to this, the fact that it differs from the ordinary criminal system due to the fact that it was established to deal with particularly grave situations, means that it is expected to have not only judicial functions but also some (iv) *police functions*.[41]

In addition, according to Mégret, not only these restrictive factors, but also the positive "aspiration" of international criminal justice due to its being an international effort also operates.[42] First, in general, due to the urgency of the background of its establishment, an international criminal court can emphasize a certain (v) *autonomy and creativity* and create new procedural frameworks. It is also (vi) *expected to develop as unique* due to the problem of legitimacy caused by similarity with the domestic law of one of the States.[43] In addition, (vii) each court's institutional characteristics such as the *temporary and geographical jurisdictional characteristics*, (viii) *institutional characteristics* such as the experience and quality of judges, the court's mandate such as (ix) *victim protection* and establishing a (x) *historical record*, the fundamental goal of a (xi) *fair trial*, (xii) *prevention of harm by the international court itself*, (xiii) *specific legal system*, and (xiv) *alignment with the goals of transitional justice*.[44]

2.3.3 The Need for an Updated Empirical Verification

Mégret's focus on the "international character" of international criminal procedure and his analysis of in what sense it is "becoming international" is largely based on empirical or theoretical/ideological analysis, although it is based on a number of precedents. In addition, it does not specifically identify which procedural laws are affected by these "environments" or "aspirations". Furthermore,—although unsurprisingly in relation to the year of its publication: 2009—, many of the precedents rely on those of the ICTY and do not draw on recent ICC precedents.

To examine the principles inherent in international criminal procedure, this book will first focus on the general principles that form the basic structure of international criminal procedure. Then, based on the way these general principles are formulated in domestic law, which seems to be the origin of these principles, I compare them with those adopted by International Criminal Justice Institutions, especially the ICC, and examine how the circumstances and values on which international criminal procedure is premised are reflected in the content of these general principles. Through this, I aim to identify some of the principles inherent in the law of international criminal procedure. For this purpose, I will use Premise Theory, a theory for understanding the method of recognition of general principles.

---

[40] *Ibid*., p. 26.

[41] *Ibid*., p. 27.

[42] *Ibid*., p. 32.

[43] *Ibid*., p. 33.

[44] *Ibid*., pp. 34–40.

3 Methodology: Applying Premise Theory

Premise refers to "the various circumstances and values presumed by the legal field to which a general principle is to be applied".[45] The identification of the content of general principles requires certain methods. One explanation of such a method is Premise Theory. The theory is to explain the method of recognition of the general principles of international criminal procedure discussed in my previous book, *A System of International Criminal Procedure*. The contents of Premise Theory are explained as follows.

> General principles are recognized, taking into account the premise of the area of law to which they are intended to apply, through either modifying common elements of existing principles ("the modification approach"), selecting from existing principles ("the selection approach"), or modifying a selection from existing principles ("the two-step approach"), or by creating new principles that are compatible with such premise.[46]

Criminal proceedings in international courts have generally been viewed as a balancing point between the so-called Continental/inquisitorial model, which has its philosophical basis in the authority of the judges to discover the truth about the criminal case, and the so-called Anglo-American/adversarial model, in which guilt is determined through fair argument between the parties to the case. Which of several alternatives is adopted as a candidate for that equilibrium point, or whether one "invents" a specific rule not found in either legal system, is determined by the premise of the question at hand. In other words, premise is the determinant of the content of the general principle. This is the most concise account of Premise Theory.[47]

---

[45] Ochi [149], p. 122. However, premise is not only specific to the field of law but can be individualized to the circumstances and values underlying the premise of each system and individual case. Ochi [148].

[46] *Ibid.*, p. 402.

[47] Kazuya Sakamoto makes the following two points regarding the challenges of Premise Theory. First, he points out that the selection of "premise" taken into consideration in the recognition of the principle of *ne bis in idem* in the *System of International Criminal Procedure* "seems to have been specified ideologically rather than inductively derived from the analysis of judges' 'internal perspective' as expressed in judgments and other documents." Secondly, "if the 'normative premise' to be commonly considered by international criminal justice organizations is selected, and if they have content that conflicts with each other, it is important to determine their priority relationship and balance in identifying the general principle." The author raises the issue of "methodology, such as how to evaluate these factors affecting the 'internal perspective' of the judge in relation to the Premise Theory'." As pointed out, there are very few precedents on the principle of *ne bis in idem*, which was treated as an example in *A System of International Criminal Procedure*, and the material for analysis from the "internal perspective" of judges is extremely limited. Considering this point, this book follows the theoretical basis of the interpretations and results used in the precedents for the general principles for which there are ample precedents, and also discusses the "internal" reasons why certain premises were taken into consideration. There are some issues that fall outside the scope of this book and therefore must be addressed at another time. Sakamoto's third point raises questions such as, "Differences in the content of general principles may arise from differences in the 'premise' taken into account when approving general principles, but to what extent are such differences permissible, and what kind of unity is required of general principles

The task of drawing out the respective premises of the various general principles of international criminal procedure is also the task of verbalizing the inherent principles or rationales of international criminal procedure itself. In that sense, what this book seeks to achieve is not merely the elucidation of the premises that are taken into account in the recognition of individual general principles of international criminal procedure, but the identification of the inherent principles of international criminal procedure itself.[48]

---

in the first place?" Sakamoto [174], p. 132. It is difficult to provide a sufficient answer to this point because this book focuses its scope on the ICC. In addition, even within the same ICC, different situations and cases have emerged in recent years, leading to the phenomenon of different (sometimes diametrically opposed) general principles being adopted by different parts of the ICC (for example, the fragmentation of the system for the examination of witnesses has been highly controversial; see e.g., Karemaker et al. [96]). (Although space does not allow for a full examination of this point, I will conclude this book with a discussion of possible approaches to be taken in future research.).

[48] Shun Kaku points out, what is conducted in *A System of International Criminal Procedure* is "an inquiry into what are the principles inherent in international criminal procedure, and how it should be interpreted in accordance with them," and that Premise Theory is not an analysis from the external perspective of "recognition methods" but rather "a jurisprudential interpretive position." For this reason, he notes that "if one were to seek jurisprudential support for Premise Theory, it would be more appropriate to argue for Dworkin's argument against the Hart-Raz view." The reason for this is that "Premises Theory, which takes the 'recognition method' as its criterion, takes the particular jurisprudential position of 'compatibility with Premises'," while "the 'rule of recognition'," which Hart presents as the identification criterion of law, can be described from an external perspective by referring to the facts as the convention of a group of judges. Kaku [93], p. 56. In *A System of International Criminal Procedure*, while taking "systematics" as "the collectivity of operation" in Luhmann's system theory, the assumption that one legal system encompasses "all laws recognized by the law-applying institutions it establishes" is made by supporting Raz's theory of authoritative recognition. In addition, as an indicator of the systematics and independence of one legal system, he referred to the code of system in system theory or Hart's "rule of recognition" relied on by Raz as an indicator for the selection of applicable laws by the law-applying body in the theory of authoritative recognition, and adopted the term "recognition method" of applicable laws as a factual expression. In contrast, Kaku points out that Premise Theory is not an analysis from an external perspective of "recognition method" but a "legal hermeneutic position." However, he does not deny the validity of that research perspective itself. This point is also explained in the book review meeting of September 2020. Kaku [94], pp. 2–3. Rather, it seems to recommend an understanding of legal reasoning that rejects the question of whether judges find or invent law as an ancient and futile one; cf. Dworkin [45], pp. 225 and 352. Rather than focusing on general indicators to measure systematics and independence, it suggests the necessity and significance of shifting the perspective to the conflicting and related ideals that are weighed when trying to maintain the integrity of the legal system of international criminal procedure, assuming the existence of such a system (Dworkin's *Law's Empire* raises the issue of consistency regarding "justice and fairness." Dworkin, *ibid*, 225.) If I reconstruct the significance of Premise Theory in line with this suggestion, I can say the following. According to Dworkin's *Law's Empire*, "According to law as integrity, propositions of law are true if they figure in or follow from the principles of justice, fairness, and procedural due process that provide the best constructive interpretation of the community's legal practice." Dworkin, *ibid*. However, the cases discussed in *Law's Empire* are hard cases in domestic law, such as civil law including law of wills and emotional damages, administrative law such as injunctions against dam construction, or constitutional guarantees of racial integration, and it can be inferred that Dworkin's argument has these cases in mind. It is not clear whether the same principles would hold in a multiplicity of special fields of law, such as international law or (I argue)

Since the concepts of "environment" and "ambition" used by Mégret correspond to "circumstances" and "value" among the premises discussed in *A System of International Criminal Procedure,* the above 14 elements given by Mégret can be regarded as a list of premises in international criminal procedure. However, in light of the above-mentioned limitations of Mégret's list, this study will empirically analyse the premises of international criminal procedure. It takes several procedural principles as examples, using ICC relevant rules and precedents as materials.[49]

Based on the presumption that the various rules used in criminal proceedings at the ICC are examples of general principles of international criminal procedure, this book infers the inherent premises of international criminal procedure through the premises that are identified by a comparison with corresponding principles under national or relevant international law. The inference is based on the fact that the specific variation of specific preexisting principles is selected as a general principle of international criminal procedure.

4 Structure and Scope of this Book

This book is structured in the chronological order of the ICC's criminal proceedings, examining the premises of the principles underlying the various issues that arise in the investigation, prosecution, and trial proceedings at the ICC.

Criminal proceedings generally begin with an investigation by an investigating authority. Chapter 2 considers the legal principles governing parallel investigations

independent international criminal procedure, or whether a specific principle would follow. While the Premise Theory is a conceptual framework that presupposes the existence of a legal form of general principles and describes the methods of their recognition, the premises themselves identified by it, as Kaku points out, have the effect of pinching the principles of the field of law to which they are applied.

[49] In addition, in *A System of International Criminal Procedure,* I took up the principle of *ne bis in idem* and raised the premise of pursuit of justice, guarantee of criminal human rights, respect for the sovereignty of punishment, determination of the truth, and promotion of peace. However, as pointed out by Sakamoto above, these are only ideologically derived rather than based on an analysis of the internal perspectives of the judges, and they may need to be revised through the discussion in this book. See Ochi, *Kokusai Keiji Tetsuzukihō no Taikei,* Chap. 8. Furthermore, Kaku points out that what the book presents as the discussion of "*lex lata*" in *A System of International Criminal Procedure* appears to be a "*lex ferenda*" based on normative considerations (see Kaku [94], p. 58). This book does not provide room for a sufficient response to this question. However, in lieu of a brief response to this point, I will provide some explanation of my approach to the content of the principles treated in the preceding article and this book. What I have identified as "a law" in my previous book and in this book is understood as an interpretation that is valid from my internal perspective among several possible interpretations of the content of existing laws. In other words, for example, in the preceding article, regarding the exception rule to the application of the principle of *ne bis in idem,* I concluded that the exception rule that requires thorough trial, rather than the exception rule that requires thorough punishment, is the appropriate one (see Ochi [149], Chap. 8.). Although this interpretation is not in line with the precedents that have chosen the interpretation that requires thoroughness in punishment, it is what I consider to be the "correct" interpretation in terms of consistency with the various values that are valid in international criminal justice.

and prosecutions between the ICC and States. Parallel investigations and prosecutions have been governed in national law mainly by the principles of prosecutorial unity, the principle against double prosecution and the principles relating to the allocation of jurisdiction. This chapter examines how these broadly applicable disciplinary principles are applied in the context of the particularities of collaborative regimes in international criminal justice.

When a suspected perpetrator of a core crime is found somewhere in the world, the next question is where to extradite the person, especially if he or she has multiple charges against him or her and several States are seeking to try him or her in their own States. Chapter 3 provides an analysis of the development of the rules on the priority of extradition for core crimes and the provisions that would give priority to extradition to the ICC. In doing so, the concept of the "gravity" of the crimes will be important, and it will be clarified that this concept contains two different meanings: the gravity of the crime itself and the gravity of the nature of the crime.

Apprehension of suspect is important in international criminal justice as long as it basically follows the principle that a trial does not begin unless the accused is present. However, if a trial *in absentia* is possible, the custody of the accused is not necessary for the execution of the trial. Chapter 4 considers the state of the principle prohibiting trial *in absentia* in international criminal justice, which governs such a premise. The principle of no trial *in absentia* is also found in many States, but there are differences in its content. On the other hand, certain international standards have developed in international human rights cases and other cases. Through a review of international human rights cases and ICC precedents, this chapter will identify the procedural standards on which international criminal justice should rely and examine how they are balanced with the requirement to secure prosecution in international criminal justice.

During the period between when a case becomes the subject of ICC proceedings and when the suspect is handed over from the national criminal justice authorities to ICC officials, the suspect may be subjected to violations of his or her human rights. For example, they may be detained in poor conditions for longer than is reasonable, or they may be denied access to explanations of the facts of the alleged crimes in a language that they fully understand. The question is whether the ICC can and should provide redress for such violations of rights, even if they are committed by national authorities or by the actors who originally took custody—militias, UN peacekeeping forces, etc. Chapter 5 analyses the decisions of the ICC Chambers in cases that have arisen at the ICC in comparison with the redresses provided by States and previous International Criminal Justice Institutions, and examines the remedial approaches taken at the ICC and the premises underlying them.

Once the suspect is surrendered to the ICC, a pre-trial procedure begins: the ICC's so-called Document Containing the Charges ("DCC") is filed, and the facts of the crime are confirmed through the Confirmation of the Charges ("CoC") procedure. Once the facts of the crime are confirmed through the CoC procedure, the trial process commences. In general, the trial of a core crime case before an international tribunal involves testimony from dozens, or even hundreds, of witnesses. Particularly when witnesses are in the place where the crimes were committed, far from the Netherlands, where the ICC is located, the question arises of how to reconcile the orality principle that testimony should be given orally in court against the need to present evidence remotely using web conferencing systems or in the form of the previously recorded written statements. The other issue is how to use the norm on the exclusion of illegally collected evidence, which regulates that illegally collected evidence should not be used when there is a violation of human rights in the process of evidence collection by local authorities. Chapter 6 examines the characteristics of the law applied at the ICC in relation to these evidentiary principles through comparisons with systems in other States.

Once the trial of the case has commenced and a judgment has been delivered, the next stage is for the ICC to initiate victim reparation proceedings. Chapter 7 examines the contents of the first ICC reparation order in the *Lubanga* case, and the principles identified for reparations, through a comparison with the various victim reparations systems adopted and in operation in the States, to clarify how the ICC's reparations system has begun to be structured. In doing so, the chapter examines how the balance between the demands for restorative justice and victims' rights relief was achieved during the transitional period.

The *Concluding Discussions*, after summarizing the various premises identified in the general principles examined in the body of this book, discusses the premises inherent in international criminal procedure and provides future challenges and prospects for international criminal justice.[50]

This book contains, as an *Addendum*, an analysis of the multifaceted international cooperative framework that has begun to be formed by the ICC and the cooperation of States in response to the situation created by the Russian full-scale invasion of Ukraine, which began in February 2022, using the analytical framework of the various premises and inherent principles of international criminal procedure developed in the conclusions of the present book.

[50] This book does not discuss the issues prior to the commencement of an investigation, the issues of immunity and irrelevance of public qualification and the issues of jurisdiction and admissibility of a case. See, e.g., Nakazawa [135]; Ochi [144]; Takemura [212, 215, 217]. For the standard of gravity in the selection of the situation, see Murai [132]; Ochi [143]. For the issue of immunity and the irrelevance of official qualifications, e.g., Okada [151]; Takemura [214]. For the jurisdictional and admissibility issues, e.g., Kitano [102]; Takemura [213]. It does not cover various procedures and principles applied during trial other than the law of evidence. The most important ones are, for example, admission of guilt (plea bargaining), various procedures related to the progress of trial, and procedures for victim participation, for which there are precedents in various studies. See, e.g., Higashizawa [76]; Naruse [136]; Ozaki [156]; Suzuki [207]. Furthermore, the rules concerning prisoners were also excluded from the scope of this project.

Chapter 2
Principles Concerning Parallel Investigations and Parallel Prosecutions of Core Crimes

Abstract This chapter considers the general principles concerning parallel investigations and parallel prosecutions in international criminal justice and examines the impact of premises (circumstances or values) specific to international criminal justice on the validity and content of the said principles. It finds that, in international criminal justice, where multiple criminal justice agencies jointly investigate the same criminal case, parallel investigation is a prerequisite, and there are norms that prioritize the merits of joint investigation over the harms of parallel investigation in the domestic plane and inter-State relations. In addition, with regards to parallel prosecution, although norms for the allocation of jurisdiction are prevalent, their content is influenced by the institutional characteristics of International Criminal Justice Institutions. Although the issue of parallel prosecution is regarded as a problem to be avoided in the same way as in the domestic plane, the "first come, first served" rule is basically appropriate. In other words, in addition to the perspective of the litigation economy of the international community as a whole, it seems to be premised on the demand for speed: the normative premise that the sooner justice is done, the better.

1 Introduction

In various States, when an investigation or dual prosecution is conducted by several entities simultaneously, it is governed by principles and rules under national law, such as the principle of prosecutorial unity and the principle of prohibition of double prosecution, or the rules on the allocation of court jurisdiction. On the other hand, in international criminal justice, investigations and prosecutions are often conducted in parallel by multiple States and international courts, and thus require discipline under international law. Therefore, when a new criminal jurisdiction is established as a special court or an international court, respective rules have been provided to coordinate the relationship with national jurisdictions that may conflict with the investigative or prosecutorial powers held by the jurisdiction in question. While there have been many studies on the particular rules for each institution, the general characteristics of parallel investigations and parallel prosecutions in international criminal

M. Ochi, *The Premises of International Criminal Procedure*,
https://doi.org/10.1007/978-981-97-6786-1_2

justice and the general principles that deal with them have not been sufficiently examined.

This chapter considers the general principles concerning parallel investigations and parallel prosecutions in international criminal justice and examines the impact of premises (circumstances or values) specific to international criminal justice on the validity and content of the said principles.[1] In the following, first, I will review the theoretical basis of the general principles on the discipline of parallel investigations and parallel prosecutions and the disciplinary principles in the national laws of the States, and then discuss the general principles on the discipline of parallel investigations and parallel prosecutions in international criminal justice based on the characteristics of investigations and prosecutions by International Criminal Justice Institutions.

For the purposes of this chapter, "investigation" refers to the act of finding and securing the victim and collecting and preserving evidence by the investigating authority for the purpose of bringing or carrying out prosecution when it is believed that a crime has been committed. Thus, it is not a stage of a specific procedure, but represents an accumulation of dispositions of these characteristics.[2] On the other hand, the concept of "prosecution" varies from one legal system to another and is difficult to define in a unified manner, but it generally refers to the conduct of criminal proceedings by a prosecutor[3] based on information accumulated through an investigation.[4] The specific acts of prosecution include the filing of a public prosecution (indictment) and the maintenance of a prosecution. In some systems, the investigative and prosecuting authorities are separated, but in others the same authority conducts both. In addition, the issue of coordinating concurrent investigations and prosecutions is not always treated as a separate issue in some international and national laws.

[1] For more information on the concept of premise, see Ochi [149].

[2] Therefore, it does not refer only to "pre-indictment" or "pre-trial" proceedings. See Tamiya [220], pp. 39–40.

[3] The fact that the subject of prosecution is limited to the public prosecutor is called the prosecution monopoly principle. Hirano [77], p. 79.

[4] Generally, trial activity begins with the filing with the court of an accusatory instrument or indictment, which notifies the accused of the criminal facts (charge) that are the subject of the action and fixes the subject of the trial. Friman et al. [55], p. 383. See Stefani et al. [202], pp. 307–308. In Japan, prosecution refers to bringing an action for a decision by an umpire in a legal dispute. If a public (prosecutorial) body does this, it is called filing a public prosecution. Yamamoto et al. [248], p. 100.

2 Principles Concerning Parallel Investigations and Parallel Prosecutions in Domestic Criminal Justice Systems

2.1 Regulation Over Parallel Investigations

2.1.1 Rationale: Judicial Economy and Effective Prosecution

There are two rationales for disciplining parallel investigations. The first is the judicial economic reason. If an earlier investigation has been sufficiently conducted, it is contrary to judicial economy to investigate the same case at the same level of cost. In addition, when arrests and detentions are made by multiple investigative agencies at the same time, unnecessary investigations need to be restricted because they double the burden on the suspect.

Second, there is an adverse effect on the investigation itself. When multiple investigative agencies conduct parallel investigations into the same case, substantial adverse effects such as proliferation of evidence can be expected. For example, even if a State is requested to hand over certain evidence as part of international criminal justice cooperation, it may be necessary to refuse to cooperate if handing over the evidence would interfere with an ongoing investigation into another case in the State of origin. In addition, particularly in relation to witnesses, it is possible that witnesses may become exhausted by continuous interrogation and become reluctant to cooperate, thereby preventing them from giving necessary testimony. Furthermore, in the case of physical evidence, the problem of missing evidence due to diffuse storage of evidence in multiple investigative agencies and the risk of missing a limited opportunity to access important evidence are anticipated.

2.1.2 Principle of Prosecutorial Unity

In modern times, in the Continental legal systems, namely Germany and France, and the United States ("US"), criminal investigations are the province of the police, but it is the prosecutor who has the authority to direct them.[5] However, there are differences between the two with regards to conceptual foundations. In States with a Continental legal system, since the court's *ex officio* judgment is placed at the centre of the proceedings and the investigation is regarded as a supplementary means, the organizer of the investigation is the preliminary judge or prosecutor, rather than the police, and the investigation is controlled by the prosecutor.[6] On the other hand, it is said that Anglo-American law, especially from an American perspective, strongly recognizes that the person in charge of the investigation of individual cases is not the

---

[5] Feeney and Hermann [50], p. 225.

[6] *Ibid.*, 44. Shiratori [190], p. 185.

prosecutor as a nationwide bureaucratic organization but the police, which has the philosophy of local autonomy as its background.[7]

National laws governing the conduct of parallel investigations and prosecutions of the same case include, as a relevant principle, the principle of prosecutorial unity, commonly referred to in Germany, France and Japan.[8] This is the principle that prosecutors are organized in a unified and hierarchical manner throughout the State and conduct their work as one body.[9] Therefore, since prosecutors are legally regarded as forming only a single and identical personality, the actions of a single prosecutor are performed not in the name of each individual prosecutor but in the name of the prosecution as a whole. Thus, there is no need to renew the proceedings even if the person in charge is changed during the course of the trial. Under the principle of prosecutorial unity, even if individual prosecutors in the same State conduct separate investigations, they are encompassed as being the actions of the same prosecuting body and are hence not considered to be parallel investigations in the first place. Even in the case of investigations by the judicial police, although the prosecutor and the judicial police are independent of each other, they are related by virtue of the prosecutor's general directional power.[10]

On the other hand, criminal investigations in the US, which has a dual federal-state structure, are conducted at the federal level by the Federal Bureau of Investigation ("FBI") and federal prosecutors (US attorneys). At the state level, investigations are conducted by investigators from police agencies or district attorneys' offices, collectively referred to as "law enforcement agencies".[11] In cases where both the federal and state authorities have an interest in prosecution, such as the murder of a member of Congress, for example, conflicts of federal and state jurisdiction frequently arise, and investigations are usually conducted concurrently. However, no specific jurisdictional alignment is established, and in practice, the person who first secures custody of the suspect is the one who can try the case.[12]

---

[7] Tamiya [220], p. 44.

[8] Friman et al. [55], p. 80; Roxin [169], pp. 67–72; Shimaoka et al. [189], p. 137. However, as a French tradition, the prosecutor is considered to be the same magistrate as the judge. Shiratori [190], p. 181.

[9] Tamiya [220], p. 26.

[10] Feeney and Hermann [50], p. 225.

[11] Law enforcement agencies vary, including city police departments, county sheriffs, and State police agencies. Reed et al. [164], pp. 36–44. In Germany, criminal procedure falls under the jurisdiction of federal law, but police law is under the jurisdiction of State law, and the provisions of the relevant State also apply to specific police activities. Kim et al. [101], p. 119.

[12] Reed, *Ibid.*, p. 11.

2.2 Regulation Over Parallel Prosecution

2.2.1 Rationale: Judicial Economy and Avoidance of Double Judgment

The rule prohibiting two or more simultaneous prosecutions for the same case is widely recognized in Continental law as the concept of "prohibition of double prosecution". This concept is a major principle in litigation, whether civil or criminal, that a Party may not file a further suit on a matter that is already pending before the court.[13]

The rationale of this principle is three-fold. First, it imposes unnecessary duplication of burden (*doppelte Arbeit*) on the accused and the courts in the same case.[14] The entire process of filing a case, conducting a trial, and rendering a judgment involves human and financial costs for the judicial branch, as well as temporary and physical burdens for the accused. For these reasons, unnecessary prosecution needs to be limited to the extent absolutely necessary.

Second, double sentencing as a consequence of double prosecution must be avoided. In addition to the problem that the accused is punished twice for the same case, the credibility of the judgment will be decreased because of the existence of two contradicting judgments. Therefore, if, when a certain indictment is filed, there is a concurrent trial for the same subject matter of litigation, the case subject to such indictment cannot obtain a substantive judgment due to the effect of the first trial. The concept of process requirement (*Prozessvoraussetzung*) is that the absence of such a situation is a condition for the continuation of litigation. Process requirements are defined as the set of conditions, such as jurisdictional conditions and statute of limitations, which determine whether or not a substantive judgment can be obtained with respect to a certain subject matter in a certain lawsuit.[15] The prevailing theory in Germany is that if there are circumstances under which a substantive judgment cannot be rendered, or if circumstances are found that make it impossible to continue the proceedings with a view to a substantive judgment, the proceedings are terminated immediately.[16] For this reason, it is believed that a rule was needed whereby in the case of double prosecution, the conditions for litigation would not be met and the case would be inadmissible.

Another rationale for the parallel prosecution regulation is the protection of the accused. In Anglo-American law, the prohibition of double prosecution is regulated by the "double jeopardy" principle. Double jeopardy is the principle that prohibits the accused from bearing the burden of trial twice.[17] The jeopardy here is the danger

---

[13] Yamamoto [247].

[14] *Ibid*.

[15] Hirano [77], p. 97.

[16] Terasaki [254], p. 70.

[17] However, it does not necessarily prohibit a second trial that would benefit the accused. Kojima [106].

of a substantive trial—the danger of conviction.[18] If two or more prosecutions are carried out in parallel, the risk of conviction is double. The most obvious reason to protect an individual against repeated prosecution is because it would not be fair to do otherwise.[19] In other words, if a defendant can be prosecuted multiple times for the same conduct, the prosecutor can repeat the prosecution as many times as necessary until he/she convicts the defendant. In this view, the "risk" is of being tried under the law for a single incident and, if convicted, being sentenced to a substantial period of physical restraint or, in the most serious cases, to physical restraint for life or to the death penalty. It was therefore necessary to protect the accused from the risk of abuse of the penal power by the State.

2.2.2 Jurisdictional Rules and Prohibition of Double Prosecution

Regarding the discipline in cases where two prosecution proceedings are conducted simultaneously in the same State, in addition to the above-mentioned principle of prosecutorial unity, first, there is basically a system of allocation of court jurisdiction, such as subject matter jurisdiction and territorial jurisdiction, in national laws. Second, in addition to the basic jurisdictional discipline, many States have established a system to limit double prosecution by regarding the pendency of a case to another court as a deficiency in the terms of the case. On the other hand, the US, which has a federal system, has a dual court system between the federal and state courts, and the adjustment of jurisdiction between the federal and state courts is often governed solely by policy decisions.

First, with regards to jurisdiction, in Germany, for example, subject matter jurisdiction is regulated in Chapter 1 of the Court Constitution Act (*Gerichtsverfassungsgesetz*), while terrotiroal jurisdiction in criminal cases is regulated under Section 7 of the Code of Criminal Procedure. Jurisdictional issues that cannot be resolved by these jurisdictional concepts are explained by the concept of functional jurisdiction.[20] In France, on the other hand, there are detailed allocation rules such as personal jurisdiction in addition to territorial jurisdiction and subject matter jurisdiction, as different courts are assigned to different types and degrees of persons and crimes.[21] Moreover, in France, the most serious or most complex cases are tried before a pre-trial court before entering the main proceedings.[22] In Japan, as in Germany, the Court Act (*Saibansyoho*) stipulates about the subject matter jurisdiction,[23] and Article 2 of the Code of Criminal Procedure stipulates that the territorial jurisdiction of courts is

---

[18] Law Commission (United Kingdom), *Double Jeopardy and Prosecution Appeals* (Law Com No. 267, 2001), para. 2.6. See also, United States, *Green v. United States*, 355 US 184, 187–188 (1957).

[19] Van Den Wyngaert and Ongena [236], p. 707.

[20] Beulke [13].

[21] Stefani et al. [202], pp. 247–255.

[22] *Ibid.*, 233–247.

[23] Japanese Court Act Article 16 (High Court), Article 24 (District Court), Article 31 (Family Court) Article 33 (Summary Court), etc.

determined by the place where the crime was committed, the place where the domicile or the residence of the accused is located, or the place where the accused is at present.

Thus, the rules on court jurisdiction basically regulates to some extent which court is in charge of a case. However, if the prosecution is still duplicated for the same case, it is regulated by the prohibition of double prosecution as a process requirement. In Germany, for example, one of the conditions for a concrete case to be admissible is that it must be "untouched" (*unberührt*).[24] Therefore, if the same case is already pending before another court, between courts of different trial levels, the lower court transfers the case to the higher court, and between courts of the same levels, the court where the case was first pending has priority.[25] Under the Japanese Code of Criminal Procedure, when the same case is pending before several courts with different jurisdiction over the subject matter, the court of higher rank shall hear the case (Article 10 of the Japanese Code of Criminal Procedure), and when the same case is pending before several courts with the same jurisdiction over the subject matter, the court where the case was first prosecuted shall hear the case (Article 11). In addition, if a prosecution is filed again in the same court for a case in which a prosecution has already been filed, the prosecution must be dismissed [Article 338(3)].[26]

On the other hand, in the US, both federal and state court have jurisdiction.[27] The rule as to whether a public prosecution should be brought in federal or state courts is generally that violations of federal law are heard and determined in federal courts and violations of state law are heard and determined in state courts. However, due to the "doctrine of dual sovereignty", which indicates that the federal and state authorities each have sovereignty as an inherent right, if an act is alleged to violate both laws, it is possible to request a hearing in both, and it is not a matter of double jeopardy if the act is tried and punished in both courts respectively.[28] However, this jurisprudence is used in exceptional cases, and in fact the Federal Prosecutor's Manual provides for double prosecution only in cases of "compelling circumstances".[29]

---

[24] Roxin [169], p. 199.

[25] *Ibid.*

[26] Matsuo et al. [118], p. 953; Taguchi [208].

[27] Del Carmen [41], pp. 2–6.

[28] Some States have set up laws that prohibit state-overlapping prosecution for criminal acts that have been prosecuted under federal law. *Ibid.*, 9.

[29] *United States Attorney's Manual* (revised in 1997), 9-2.031: Dual and Successive Prosecution Policy.

3 Parallel Investigations and Parallel Prosecutions in International Criminal Justice

3.1 Characteristics of Investigations and Prosecutions in International Criminal Justice

3.1.1 Investigation and Prosecution Entities

The actors conducting investigations and prosecutions in the international criminal justice realm take different forms than those in domestic criminal justice systems.

Since the end of World War II, the method used for war crimes cases has been the establishment of commissions of inquiry to investigate, including the collection of evidence, and to report on various matters relating to the establishment of trial bodies. These commissions of inquiry served, in effect, as substantive investigative bodies, collecting evidence and conducting other investigations for criminal trials before the International Criminal Justice Institution.[30]

In addition, International Criminal Justice Institutions that prosecute core crimes in recent years have established a variety of investigative and prosecution entities. International Criminal Justice Institutions have a Prosecutor's Office, composed of multinational personnel, which cooperates with local investigative agencies in the investigation and evidence collection. Most International Criminal Justice Institutions have also adopted the principle of prosecutorial unity, whereby the chief prosecutor represents the entire "prosecutor" of the International Criminal Justice Institution concerned.[31]

3.1.2 International Cooperation

Investigations and prosecutions in international criminal justice require international cooperation. Core crimes are often committed on a large scale, both temporally and geographically. They are also characterized by the sheer number of perpetrators and victims. Frequently, the perpetrators flee to other States during or after the commission of a crime, or a large number of victims take refuge in other States. Therefore, international cooperation is necessary to secure the core perpetrators of crimes and to collect their testimonies.

In addition, although International Criminal Justice Institutions in particular often have their own prosecutorial bureaus, their prosecutors are not normally permitted to use coercive force within their respective States, which is essentially the public

[30] See e.g., Bassiouni [11], p. 544.

[31] The first chief prosecutors at the launch of the institution have been selected from core crime caseloads, including former members of the South African Truth and Reconciliation Commission and former prosecutors with domestic experience in large-scale organized crime prosecutions. See Crane et al. [34].

authority of the State.[32] Therefore, the securing of suspects and seizure of evidence, which are the basis of criminal prosecution, cannot be realized without the exercise of coercive power by domestic police and prosecutors, in principle. And it is usually the local judicial authorities who first come into contact with and arrest or detain suspects of core crimes.

The Statutes of the *ad hoc* Tribunals, such as the ICTY and the ICTR, set out the general obligation of States to cooperate with respect to the investigation and prosecution of suspects (Article 29(1) of the ICTY Statute and Article 28(1) of the ICTR Statute). It also provides that States shall comply without undue delay with any request for assistance or order issued by the Trial Chamber (para. 2 of each of the above). In addition, the *ad hoc* Tribunal prosecutor is entitled to question suspects, victims and witnesses and collect evidence, and to request the assistance of the authorities of the State concerned when conducting on-site investigations (Article 18(2) of the ICTY Statute and Article 17(2) of the ICTR Statute). In the *Blaškić* case, the ICTY Statute was established by a UN Security Council resolution, which confirmed that requests for cooperation from the ICTY are binding under Chapter VII and Article 25 of the UN Charter and Security Council Resolution 827, and that the ICTY has exceptional authority to issue orders to sovereign States.[33]

Even at the ICC, investigations are in principle conducted with the cooperation of the State (Article 99(4) of ICC Statute), and the ICC prosecutor can only do so directly in exceptional cases where there is no national authority capable of fulfilling its mandate (Article 57(3)(d)). The arrest of a suspect is triggered by the ICC Pre-Trial Chamber by issuing an arrest warrant at the request of the ICC prosecutor but is executed by a State as long as the judicial system of the charged State is functioning. The securing of personal and physical evidence is also achieved with the cooperation of States in accordance with various provisions of Part 9 of the Statute. States Parties have a general obligation to cooperate fully with the Court in investigations and prosecutions conducted by the ICC, except where their security interests may be threatened (Article 72), and to ensure that their national legal processes are available for cooperation (Articles 86 and 88). If immediate implementation is difficult, States Parties shall consult without delay with the Court to resolve the situation (Article 97). If a State Party fails to comply with a request for cooperation and prevents the Court from exercising its duties and powers, the Court may refer the matter to the Assembly of States Parties and, furthermore, if the situation is referred by the UN Security Council, the ICC may refer the matter to the Council (Article 87(7)).

The joint dissenting opinion attached to the *Al-Bashir* judgment advocated the so-called "Surrogation of Jurisdiction theory", which holds that States exercise ICC jurisdiction on behalf of the ICC, but the validity of this theory continues to be

[32] See, e.g., *Prosecutor v. Blaškić*, Judgment on the Request of Croatia for Review of the Decision of Trial Chamber II of 18 July 1997 (*IT-95-14-AR108bis*). Appeals Chamber (29 October 1997), para. 26.

[33] *Ibid.*

debated.[34] According to this theory, the execution of ICC arrest warrants and all investigative activities by judicial authorities of various States in response to requests for cooperation are considered to be carried out under the authority and control of the ICC. If a system of justice were envisaged in which investigators around the world would act as if under the control of the ICC prosecutor, then simultaneous investigations by the ICC prosecutor and investigators within States would no longer be considered parallel investigations from the point at which agents from different States began to act to fulfil requests for cooperation from the ICC.

3.2 Allocation of Jurisdiction in International Criminal Justice

The criminal jurisdiction of an International Criminal Justice Institution and the criminal jurisdiction of a State may exercise jurisdiction over the same case, and thus have competing jurisdictions. Therefore, how to coordinate the relationship between the investigation and prosecution by national jurisdictions that have jurisdiction over core crime cases was one of the difficult questions that accompanied the establishment of International Criminal Justice Institutions. Customary international law governing these relationships did not yet exist,[35] and the discipline of competing jurisdictions remained a problem with no uniform coordinating principle and a notable legal vacuum. Therefore, when individual International Criminal Justice Institutions were established, they had to address this issue in specific provisions.[36]

In the following, I will look at the disciplinary rules for parallel investigations and parallel prosecutions and the national legislation of the respective States, taking into account the characteristics of the jurisdictional rules, which differ significantly between the *ad hoc* Tribunals and the ICC.

---

[34] *Prosecutor v. Al Bashir*, Joint Concurring Opinion of Judges Eboe-Osuji, Morrison, Hofmański and Bossa (ICC-02/05-01/09-397-Anx1-Corr) Appeals Chamber (17 May 2019), paras. 441–445. See, Kawai [97].

[35] Cassese and Gaeta [28], p. 291.

[36] Because of the nature of the International Military Tribunal (IMT) and the International Military Tribunal for the Far East (IMTFE) in the immediate post-World War II period, in which the victorious powers collaborated in criminal prosecutions against the defeated powers, the issue of competing jurisdiction among the victorious powers was not considered, and the defeated powers were forced to accept the results of criminal prosecutions by the victorious powers. For this reason, little attention has also been paid to the issue of competing jurisdictions with the subject State. As a result, the Charters of the IMT and the IMTFE do not contain any provisions that explicitly regulate conflicts of jurisdiction with States.

3.2.1 *Ad hoc* Tribunal: Primacy

(a) Primary jurisdiction

The concept of the primacy of the jurisdiction of International Criminal Justice Institutions first emerged as a concept that governed the conflict between the jurisdiction of International Criminal Justice Institutions and that of States.

The ultimate goal of the ICTY and ICTR was to bring peace to the subject region, and in order to achieve this, simply ensuring parallel jurisdiction with the jurisdiction of the States was not effective enough.[37] Rather than leaving the prosecution to the conflict-torn States of the former Yugoslavia and Rwanda and their neighbours, it was argued that it was necessary to secure proceedings before an international tribunal, even if this meant interrupting the proceedings of the States. Therefore, under the authority of the UN Security Council, the primacy of the *ad hoc* Tribunals over the national courts of the Member States of the UN was recognized. According to Article 9 of the ICTY Statute and Article 8 of the ICTR Statute, which set out this principle of primacy, the ICTY or ICTR may request a national court to give priority to its own jurisdiction. The State receiving such a request must comply with the request of these *ad hoc* Tribunals when a case under the jurisdiction of the Court is pending before its national courts.[38] According to Rule 11 of the ICTY Rules of Procedure and Evidence ("RPE") and Rule 11 of the ICTR RPE, if a State receives a request from these *ad hoc* Tribunals to defer a domestic investigation or prosecution and fails to comply with the request within 6 months, the UN Security Council will be notified.

In the ICTR's *Bagosora* case, the Chamber requested Belgium to postpone the domestic investigation of the subject case, as the investigation was also ongoing in Belgium. In that case, the adverse effects of parallel investigations were examined. It was argued by the prosecutor that the multiple confusions and complications arising from parallel investigations, particularly in relation to witnesses, might present obstacles to the investigation at the ICTR.[39] The Trial Chamber accepted the same arguments and requested Belgium to postpone the parallel national proceedings.[40]

(b) Cooperation Laws of States

After the establishment of the ICTY and the ICTR, national laws were actively enacted to establish criminal justice cooperation with these *ad hoc* Tribunals. Twenty-three States including the States of the former Yugoslavia, European States and the US had established cooperation laws for the ICTY as of 2000, while 13 States including

---

[37] Brown [21], p. 394.

[38] The conditions for embodying primacy differ between the ICTY and the ICTR; see Rule 9 of the ICTY's Rules of Procedural Evidence and Rule 9 of the ICTR's Rules of Procedural Evidence.

[39] *Prosecutor v. Bagosora*, Decision on the Application by the Prosecutor for a Formal Request for Deferral (ICTR-96-7-D) Trial Chamber I (17 May 1996), para. 6.

[40] *Ibid.*, para. 12.

African States, European States and the US, established cooperation laws for the ICTR.[41]

However, not many States have national laws in place regarding the procedures to be followed in the event of a request from the ICTY or ICTR to postpone an investigation or prosecution in their State.[42] For example, Article 2 of the German "Law on Cooperation with the International Criminal Tribunal for the former Yugoslavia" ("German ICTY Cooperation Law") and Articles 3–6 of French Law No. 95-1 ("French ICTY Cooperation Law") provide that the national courts of a State shall determine whether the crimes subject to the ICTY's request for a deferral are crimes under the jurisdiction of the ICTY, and whether provisions are put in place to hear if the request relates to the subject of ongoing proceedings in the State.[43]

3.2.2 ICC: Complementarity

(a) Complementary jurisdiction

The ICC was established on the basis of a multilateral treaty, unlike *ad hoc* Tribunals based on UN Security Council resolutions. During the treaty negotiations, it was decided that the ICC would not be given primacy, and that the principle of complementarity would be adopted in relation to the State jurisdiction (Preamble, para. 10, Article 1 of the ICC Statute). According to this principle, the ICC is complementary to the criminal jurisdiction of the States and the ICC cannot continue criminal proceedings in a case where there is a genuine State investigation, prosecution, or trial (Article 17). This complementarity is embodied by the admissibility review of cases at the ICC.

For the sake of the complementarity principle, Article 17 of the Statute stipulates cases that the ICC cannot admit a case regardless of the way the situation was referred to it. Admissibility reviews have been conducted in almost all ICC cases at various stages of the proceedings.[44] The cases have indicated that the admissibility review uses a two-step test: the existence of domestic proceedings and the State's willingness and ability.[45] The three issues that have been considered important in the admissibility review are, first, the identity of the substantive conducts; second, the identity of the crimes; and third, the State's ability and willingness to investigate or prosecute.[46]

---

[41] On the other hand, Russia, China and others saw no need for domestic legislation. UN Doc. A/55/273-S/2000/777 (7 August 2000), para. 248. *See also*, Stroh [205], p. 271, notes 60, 61.

[42] For example, Germany, France, England, Austria, etc. *Ibid.*, p. 276.

[43] De la Cuesta [39], p. 729.

[44] For example, ex officio review at the time of issuance of an arrest warrant, petition for admissibility, and criminal fact-finding procedures.

[45] *Prosecutor v. Katanga*, Judgment on the Appeal of Mr. Germain Katanga against the Oral Decision of Trial Chamber II of 12 June 2009 on the Admissibility of the Case (ICC-01/04-01/07-1497) Appeals Chamber (25 September 2009), paras. 1, 75–79.

[46] See Ochi [145].

On the other hand, the ICC Statute also contains provisions to consider cases where cooperation with the ICC may affect another case within a State Party. According to Rule 94, if the immediate implementation of a request from the ICC could interfere with an ongoing domestic investigation or prosecution of another case, the implementation of that request may be postponed for a period agreed with the Court. However, such postponement shall not exceed the period necessary to complete the investigation or prosecution of the case in the requested State.

(b) Cooperation laws of States

Although the States that were required to cooperate with the ICTY and ICTR were mainly limited to European and African States, with the adoption of the ICC Statute in 1998, more States started to enact ICC cooperation legislation. Among them, several legislations concerning cases in which ICC investigations or prosecutions were concurrent with investigations or prosecutions in their own States can be found.

For example, Section 28 of the German ICC Cooperation Act provides that where criminal proceedings are being conducted in Germany for a crime under ICC jurisdiction and the ICC requires the extradition of a suspect unless the German proceedings are continued, the German prosecutor may refrain from conducting the prosecution if it appears to be in the public interest according to the special grounds in a domestic criminal prosecution. Article 2(2) of Part 21 of the Annex to the United Kingdom ("UK")'s ICC Cooperation Act provides that, irrespective of the scope of the subject case, if the ICC requests arrest and extradition and there are pending or ongoing proceedings against the person before a national court, the court may take measures such as suspending national proceedings if necessary.

On the other hand, Article 6 of Japan's ICC Cooperation Act stipulates that, with respect to the provision of evidence, if it is deemed that responding to a request for cooperation from the ICC may impede an investigation in Japan or the trial of a case pending before a court with respect to a crime other than the crime for which the request from the ICC is made, and it is not appropriate to respond immediately to such a request, Japan will consult with the ICC without immediately responding to the request. In addition, Article 19 of the Japan's ICC Cooperation Act stipulates that Japan will not surrender the suspect to the ICC when the case is pending before a Japanese court, except when admissibility is recognized under Article 17 of the ICC Statute.

4 The Significance and Methods of Discipline in International Criminal Justice

4.1 Significance of the Discipline of Parallel Investigations and Parallel Prosecutions in International Criminal Justice

In the following, the applicability of the principles governing parallel investigations and parallel prosecutions in international criminal justice will be discussed. To do so, this section will examine whether the rationales for the principles governing parallel investigations, namely, judicial economy and ensuring effective investigations, and the rationales for the principles governing parallel prosecutions, namely, judicial economy and avoidance of double sentencing, are also applicable to investigations and prosecutions in the international criminal justice realm.

4.1.1 Significance of Parallel Investigation Discipline

(a) Judicial economy

In general, the judicial economy of parallel investigations between two or more different criminal jurisdictions in the international criminal justice domain can be an issue. However, the features of International Criminal Justice Institutions that make cooperation of States indispensable would rather seem to require the concurrent conduct of multiple investigations. It is not necessary to prohibit parallel investigations from the outset, since the investigations of International Criminal Justice Institutions are usually conducted on the premise that they are shared by the State in which the crime was committed and the State in which the suspect is located. In the prosecution of core crimes, it is expected that the number of persons involved in other related crimes will also be enormous. Therefore, even if the most serious cases are dealt with by International Criminal Justice Institutions, it is expected that other cases will be subject to prosecution at domestic courts. Sooner or later, many of the core crime cases will require the prosecution of the related crimes in the State of origin or the State where the suspect is located, so that the parallel investigations will not be in vain and will not be considered an excessive burden on those cooperating in the investigation. In many cases, investigations into core crime cases involve more than one State, or the suspect and evidence are located in more than one State, so that it is even desirable that the investigation be conducted on a global scale by the judicial authorities of the State closest to the evidence.

Therefore, it can be concluded that the judicial economy reasons—the primary rationale supporting the principle of parallel investigation discipline—are not a sufficient basis for applying the principle of disciplining parallel investigations in the international criminal justice sphere.

(b) Effective investigation

As for the second concern, the possibility that parallel investigations may hinder effective investigations, the importance of preventing such investigations is relatively low due to the characteristics of international criminal justice.

When multiple investigative agencies conduct parallel investigations into the same case at the same time, adverse effects can be assumed, such as a decline in the reliability of testimony obtained and deficiencies due to the diffusion of evidence. Even in the case of international criminal justice, these adverse effects can naturally be expected. However, it was pointed out that core crime cases are characterized by the fact that there are multiple investigative entities and that they depend to a large extent on the cooperation of national investigative agencies. Except in exceptional cases where International Criminal Justice Institutions are allowed to conduct free investigative activities within the State, it is basically envisaged that the prosecution will be conducted through the accumulation of parallel investigations by multiple investigative organs. Naturally, an effective investigation for trial in a criminal jurisdiction that prosecutes core crimes requires a system of cooperation in which the domestic authorities of several relevant States conduct investigative activities and transfer the information obtained to the criminal jurisdiction concerned. However, this cannot be considered to imply a prohibition on parallel investigations.

Therefore, it can be concluded that the orientation towards effective investigations, which was the second rationale supporting the principle of parallel investigation discipline, is also not a sufficient basis for applying the principle against parallel investigations in the international criminal justice domain, as long as those investigations are both aimed at the prosecution of the same core crime.

4.1.2 Significance of Concurrent Prosecution Discipline

On the other hand, the principle of parallel prosecution discipline in the international criminal justice area is seen as an important one, as will be confirmed below. The two rationales given as the principle of discipline of parallel prosecution were judicial economy and avoidance of double sentencing, and I will discuss whether these rationales can be the basis of discipline of parallel prosecution in the international criminal justice area as well.

(a) Judicial economy

The first rationale for the concurrent prosecution rule, the procedural and economic reason, is valid in international criminal justice as well. First, from the standpoint of the accused, the problem may be that it would double the procedural burden on the accused. If prosecutions are conducted in parallel for the same case in different criminal jurisdictions, the accused is burdened with multiple procedures for the same case. Even in the international criminal justice area, where multiple criminal jurisdictions coexist and each jurisdiction can prosecute based on overlapping jurisdictions in order to prevent the escape of core crimes perpetrators, unnecessary repetition of the custody and prosecution of the accused should be avoided. The logic that parallel prosecutions should be prohibited for such procedural and economic reasons is also valid in the international criminal justice field.

In addition, the logic that parallel prosecutions for the same core crimes are contrary to judicial economy, even if they are the activities of other States or other international organizations, can be valid in the international criminal justice area from the perspective of the international community's efforts to collaboratively pursue the common goal of prosecuting core crimes, in terms of the effective use of its resources.

Possible cases where the prosecutions may be parallel include cases where the identity of the subject matter of the prosecution and the preceding prosecution is clear, and cases where it is not clear whether the subject matter of the prosecution and the scope of the preceding prosecution overlap. In the former case, if, because of the prosecution, the judgment of one criminal jurisdiction has the finality of a single case, there is no need to conduct a parallel prosecution in its own criminal jurisdiction at the stage when prosecution activities have been initiated or are about to be initiated in another criminal jurisdiction. Therefore, the necessity of daring to carry out unnecessary prosecution is not considered to be recognized in either jurisdiction. In the latter case, however, even if the earlier prosecution is terminated and a final judgment is entered as a result, it is not clear at the prosecution stage whether the effect of the single event would render the subsequent prosecution meaningless, and the possibility remains that the issue of judicial economy would not arise as a result.

In light of these considerations, the judicial economy reasons for the principle of discipline of parallel prosecutions would seem to be strong reason in the international criminal justice realm when it is clear that the subject matter of the earlier prosecution and subsequent prosecution are identical.

(b) Avoidance of double sentencing

The second principle of the discipline of parallel prosecutions, the avoidance of double sentencing, can be viewed in relation to the principle of *ne bis in idem*.[47] In other words, if two parallel prosecutions of the same case are expected to ultimately result in the application of the principle of *ne bis in idem*, then the substantive judgment in a jurisdiction that was initiated or adjudicated later becomes meaningless. It is difficult to envisage that a parallel prosecution would result in a valid final judgment in a subsequent prosecution after a previous prosecution in another criminal jurisdiction had become final. Therefore, a case in which such a result can be expected is a case in which no substantive judgment can be obtained, and the prosecution of such a case cannot be considered as fulfilling the so-called process requirement.

[47] On the scope and applicable exceptions to the prohibition of double trial in international criminal justice, see, Ochi [146, 147].

4.2 The Manners to Regulate Parallel Prosecution in International Criminal Justice

From the above review, it can be concluded that ensuring parallel prosecution discipline is significant in the international criminal justice area. On the other hand, as for the general prohibition of parallel investigations, its significance cannot be recognized due to the characteristics of investigations and arrest procedures in the international criminal justice area. Therefore, what can be recognized as a general principle of law applicable to international criminal justice is limited to the principle of parallel prosecution discipline. For this reason, the following discussion will focus on the principle regulating concurrent prosecution.

The final issue to be discussed is what approach is appropriate to ensure regulating of parallel prosecution. A comparative study of the various laws and regulations suggests two manners: first, the allocation of jurisdiction, or second, the prioritization of prior investigations and prosecutions. The following section discusses which of these methods of discipline is available in the field of international criminal justice.

4.2.1 Allocation of Jurisdiction

Rules for the allocation of jurisdiction have been established to govern the relationship between International Criminal Justice Institutions and States. Some of those rules have been seen to give priority to the International Criminal Justice Institutions, while others have been seen to be complementary. Which of these methods of allocating jurisdiction is chosen depends on the basis on which the organs are established. In the case of an institution established by a UN Security Council resolution or directly based on an international agreement between a State and the UN, the former may be accorded priority over a UN Member State and the latter over a subject State. On the other hand, in the case of the ICC established by multilateral treaties, the principle of complementarity was adopted so as to give priority to the jurisdiction of the States. These differences were also manifested in the national cooperation laws of the States *vis-à-vis* the International Criminal Justice Institutions, where differences were found between the cooperation laws for organizations with primary jurisdiction and those for institutions with complementary jurisdiction.

The individual rules governing investigations and prosecutions in the relationship between International Criminal Justice Institutions and States reflect the nature and characteristics of each criminal jurisdiction. The rules governing the relationship of International Criminal Justice Institutions with national jurisdictions are the fruit of negotiations between the actors involved in the creation of such institutions and are the result of a balance between the powers of the States concerned and the effectiveness of criminal justice. For example, the *ad hoc* Tribunals, grounded in the effect of UN Security Council resolutions, were able to establish rules that gave priority to States, while the ICC regulates its relationship with States Parties through rules that embody the principle of complementarity.

The criminal jurisdiction to prosecute core crimes was created, so to speak, on a variety of legal grounds in a circumstantial manner, and the legal options of disciplining the relationship of jurisdiction with other criminal jurisdictions differ depending on the institution's legal basis. In view of these considerations, it seems difficult to find a universal principle of allocation of jurisdiction. However, priority and complementarity are, in a sense, two sides of the same system. The principle of institutional design may be generally valid that it should be decided in advance which of the International Criminal Justice Institutions or the State is to have priority, and which is to have complementarity.

4.2.2 Primacy of Earlier Prosecution

The rule that where two or more prosecutions are being conducted simultaneously, the earlier prosecution takes precedence and the prosecution commenced subsequently is terminated is found in a number of international and domestic legal instruments.

For example, in the various treaties on international criminal justice cooperation, priority is given to investigations and prosecutions that have already begun in the State or in a foreign State. Article 4 of the Model Treaty on Extradition provides for the possibility of refusing extradition on the basis of the fact that a prosecution for the offence for which extradition is requested is underway in the requested State. However, this is not an obligatory ground for refusal of extradition and refusal is optional. In fact, Article 8 of the European Convention on Extradition and Article 4(1)(2) of the Japan–US Treaty on Extradition contains provisions to the same effect. In addition, Article 4(2) of the US-Russia Treaty on Extradition provides that extradition may be refused if the same crime is likely to be prosecuted in the requesting State.

In the treaties on mutual assistance in criminal justice, we have seen in recent years a provision to the effect that the execution of a request for assistance may be withheld if the assistance would interfere with an ongoing investigation in the home State, regardless of whether it is the same case or a different case. A provision to the same effect is placed in Article 4 of the Model Treaty on Mutual Assistance in Criminal Matters. The Commentary states that in such circumstances it is important for the investigating and prosecuting authorities to consult on their respective domestic procedures, leading to a satisfactory allocation of jurisdiction, which may result in either Party withdrawing its requests in favour of the other Party.[48] As an example of such consultation suggested in the Commentary, Article 10(3) of the EU-Japan Treaty on Mutual Assistance in Criminal Matters provides that

> If the execution of a request is deemed to interfere with an ongoing investigation, prosecution or other proceeding, including judicial proceeding, in the requested State, the requested

[48] United Nations Office of Drugs and Crimes, *Revised Manuals on the Model Treaty on Extradition and on the Model Treaty on Mutual Assistance in Criminal Matters* (8 December 2002), at https://www.unodc.org/pdf/model_treaty_extradition_revised_manual.pdf (as of 27 December 2021), para. 99.

> State may postpone the execution. The requested State shall inform the requesting State of the reasons for the postponement and consult the further procedure. Instead of postponing the execution, the requested State may make the execution subject to conditions deemed necessary after consultations with the requesting State. If the requesting State accepts such conditions, the requesting State shall comply with them.

The recognition of an ongoing investigation or prosecution in the home State as grounds for refusing extradition or assistance is, in another view, a prioritization of the preceding investigation or prosecution. While extradition and assistance were at the discretion of the State, the effective progress of a domestic investigation or prosecution was in the vital interest of that State and, in the absence of special reasons, the investigation or prosecution in that State would naturally have taken precedence. Even if extradition or assistance is made obligatory by treaty, recent treaties on criminal judicial cooperation have established exemptions from the obligation to cooperate, either as grounds for refusal when the investigation or prosecution of the same crime as that which is the subject of extradition is being conducted by the State concerned, or as grounds for postponement when the investigation or prosecution of a different crime is conducted by the State concerned and extradition or assistance would affect it.

The prohibition against double prosecution, which is well-established in the domestic laws, as a way of putting this principle into practice, took the way to continue proceedings in the court where the case had been first prosecuted, and to terminate proceedings that had been started later. Moreover, even between competing federal and state jurisdictions in the US, proceedings were conducted under the jurisdiction of whichever jurisdiction secured custody of the accused first.

Moreover, this trend is reflected, albeit to a limited extent, in the various provisions on State cooperation with International Criminal Justice Institutions. For example, at the ICC, if a prior domestic prosecution is pending against a case that the ICC intends to prosecute, the prior domestic prosecution will be given priority if the domestic prosecution does not lack genuine willingness or ability. However, once the case has been received by the ICC first and the criminal fact-finding procedure has been conducted and the prosecution initiated, the State cannot challenge the jurisdiction or admissibility of the case at the ICC on the grounds that it has initiated the investigation or prosecution in its own State (Article 19 of the ICC Statute), and as a result, once the ICC initiates the prosecution, the admitted case cannot be terminated. Thus, the ICC has also adopted a mechanism whereby the prosecution in the criminal jurisdiction that preceded the prosecution is given priority. However, there is an exception in relation to institutions with priority, such as the *ad hoc* Tribunals, where a rule was used to defer domestic proceedings even if domestic prosecution had already been initiated.

Considering these examples, it is effective to give priority to the preceding prosecution as a method to ensure the discipline of parallel prosecution, except in cases with an institution which has priority. Therefore, when there are concurrent prosecutions, a practical mechanism to ensure the principle regulating concurrent prosecution could be presented, in which the proceedings of the entity that initiated the prosecution first are given priority, and the prosecution initiated later cannot be continued.

However, it is important to note that this "first come, first served" rule may lead to the deterioration of the quality of trial due to hasty prosecution without sufficient investigation, or to the abusive securing of the accused. The principle regulating concurrent prosecution may promote criminal proceedings in a manner that places excessive emphasis on the pursuit of justice, which is a universal value of international criminal justice, and not enough on other values, such as the search for the truth and the guarantee of due process.[49] Although this point may seem to be a criminal policy issue, there remains the possibility that an important issue concerning the balance of values in jurisdiction and procedural law in international criminal justice may be latent.

Moreover, the regulation of parallel prosecution in the manner of giving priority to the preceding prosecution presupposes that when a prosecution is to be initiated, there must be a means of ascertaining whether a prosecution has already been initiated in another criminal jurisdiction. This can be ensured not only by international information sharing, but also, and more fundamentally, by another discipline that a prosecution cannot be initiated unless the accused is in custody. In other words, the principle of parallel prosecution discipline can be reinforced by the principle that a prosecution cannot be commenced in the absence of the accused (the principle of no trial *in absentia*).[50]

5 Conclusion

In this chapter, I have discussed various principles concerning the discipline of parallel investigations and parallel prosecutions in international criminal justice, and examined how the premise of international criminal justice affects the content of these principles. In international criminal justice, where multiple criminal justice agencies jointly investigate the same criminal case, parallel investigation is a prerequisite, and norms that prioritize the merits of joint investigation over the harms of parallel investigation in the domestic plane and inter-State relations are found. In addition, with regards to parallel prosecution, although norms for the allocation of jurisdiction can be found, their content is influenced by the institutional characteristics of International Criminal Justice Institutions. Although the issue of parallel prosecution is regarded as a problem to be avoided in the same way as in the domestic plane, the "first come, first served" rule is basically appropriate. In other words, insofar as "the sooner the better" is appropriate, in addition to the perspective of the litigation economy of the international community as a whole, it seems to be premised on the demand for speed—the normative premise that the sooner justice is done, the better.

I conclude that the disciplines on parallel investigations and parallel prosecutions in international criminal justice have different characteristics from those in the

[49] On the evils of rushing to domestic prosecution, see Chap. 4 of this book.

[50] See Chap. 3 of this book for a discussion of the principle of non-absenteeism in international criminal justice.

domestic plane and in inter-State relations. However, the implementation of international criminal justice in recent years has not only been carried out by international organizations independent of individual States, such as *ad hoc* Tribunals and the ICC. There has been an increase in hybrid models in which special courts specialized in dealing with core crimes are established within states with the support of international organizations, existing domestic criminal justice systems are strengthened, and national and international officials work together to investigate and prosecute. With regards to such tribunals and courts, the traditional issue of parallel investigations and parallel prosecutions in international criminal justice is considered to have entered a new phase.

Chapter 3
Principles Concerning Priority of Extradition for Core Crimes

Abstract This chapter examines the rules on the conflict and priority of extradition/surrender obligations in relation to international crimes and considers how the seriousness/gravity of the crimes in question is considered in determining the destination of extradition/surrender. The international system based on extradition treaties can be classified into four types of systems: bilateral, regional, universal, and vertical, from the viewpoint of the relationship with the other Party of the obligation. Since these extradition systems impose multilayered obligations, States may receive extradition requests from several other States under separate extradition systems. Conflicting extradition requests for the same offence have been disciplined mainly by placing provisions giving discretion to the requested State. On the other hand, conflicts between extradition requests for different offences are regulated by priority provisions, such as giving priority to earlier requests or extradition requests for more serious offences, and by discretionary provisions giving the requested State the discretion to decide. The gravity of the crime contained in these coordination provisions is debatable in various situations and can have two meanings: the gravity of the criminal act in terms of the scale, nature, manner and impact, and the seriousness of the nature of the concept of the crime.

1 Introduction

The extradition system in recent international law is made up of multiple treaty obligations that are intricately intertwined. Traditionally, extradition was often based on treaties concluded on a case-by-case basis or for the extradition of a particular suspect or based on courtesy or reciprocity.[1] In recent years, however, there has been a shift away from such *ad hoc* systems to a stable system based on more general and enduring treaty obligations, including a number of procedural rules.[2] First, treaties have been concluded that establish bilateral extradition obligations for certain crimes between two States and multifaceted extradition obligations for

[1] Bassiouni [10], p. 2. On the formation process of the extradition system, see Nishii [138].

[2] Yamamoto [250], p. 190; Yanagawa [252].

M. Ochi, *The Premises of International Criminal Procedure*,
https://doi.org/10.1007/978-981-97-6786-1_3

smoother international cooperation within the region. In addition, multilateral treaties on the prevention of certain crimes, such as drug trafficking, torture, and various terrorist offences, contain provisions requiring "*aut dedere aut judicare*" ("prosecute or extradite") for the crimes in question. These treaties oblige States to respond effectively to crimes of common concern in States where globalization has led to a significant increase. Furthermore, the establishment of an international criminal court for the prosecution of particularly serious core crimes has added a new dimension to the system of international cooperation on criminal matters. States are now also obliged to respond to vertical surrender requests from international courts. States can now be said to be subject to a complex system of extradition/surrender, consisting of multiple layers of treaty systems—horizontal bilateral and multilateral obligations, and vertical obligations before international courts.

As the system becomes more complex, the possibility of conflict of obligations within it increases. Customary law has not been established such that priority is automatically given to a particular State on some basis when extradition requests are made by more than one State.[3] Many extradition systems have included provisions to coordinate competing extradition requests ("coordination provisions"). One of the most frequently used of these is the standard of seriousness/gravity of the offence. As will be seen later, the criterion of giving priority or consideration to extradition for the more serious offence among competing extraditions is used in many coordination provisions, but the specific criteria for its application are not clear. In particular, the question of how the seriousness of the core crime should be reflected is likely to be problematic.

Among the international crimes,[4] four core crimes in particular—genocide, crimes against humanity, war crimes and crimes of aggression—are called "the most serious crimes of concern to the international community as a whole".[5] The core crimes have received special response by the international community, such as being subject to codification by the ILC as "crimes against the peace and security of mankind" and being considered crimes under the jurisdiction of the ICC, which was established based on a multilateral treaty. These facts are indicators of the seriousness of the core crimes. In previous discussions, there have been attempts to characterize extradition for war crimes committed during World War II as different from the existing system because they are crimes under international law.[6] However, until recently there has been little research on the rules governing priority in the apparent conflict between extradition obligations in respect of core crimes and extradition obligations in respect of other international crimes.

The conflict between extradition for core crimes and extradition for other international crimes may arise, first, when the same person commits a series of crimes and

---

[3] Sadoff [170], p. 289.

[4] The definition of the term "international crime" varies from one commentator to another, but in this book, it is used to mean "a crime as defined by international law" See e.g., O'Keefe [142], p. 56.

[5] It is generally agreed that the "core international crimes" include these four crimes, but there is some debate as to what their shared characteristics are. See e.g., Guilfoyle [67], p. 185.

[6] Ko [105], p. 274.

different extradition requests are received in relation to them, second, when virtually identical acts, in combination with different contextual elements, constitute multiple core crimes, and third, when virtually identical acts constitute both core crimes and other international crimes. In the third case, when there is a conflict between, for example, an extradition request by the State of the suspect's nationality for the core crimes and an extradition request by the State where the crime occurred for other international crimes against the State in which the suspect was found, the question arises as to which crime should be given priority. If the core crimes are the most serious type of crimes, they should be given priority over the prosecution of other crimes. On the other hand, there is also the issue of the need to balance this with other circumstances such as the jurisdictional basis of the requesting State and the strength of its prosecution interest.

The purpose of this chapter is to examine the rules on conflict and priority of extradition obligations in relation to international crimes and to consider how the gravity standard is applied in determining the destination of extradition. The term "conflict" is used in this chapter in the strict sense that "a party to the two treaties cannot simultaneously comply with its obligations under both treaties."[7] In other words, a conflict refers to a state of lack of law that resolves the apparent (*prima facie*) state of conflict. When there is a *prima facie* state of conflict, which cannot be resolved by Article 30 or 41 of the Vienna Convention on the Law of Treaties,[8] the two treaties are in conflict. This suggests that it is a situation which leaves room for the development of customary law to govern such conflicts—"...disputes will be left unsolved until a customary rule develops in the matter concerned."[9] The approach of this chapter is therefore to begin with a *prima facie* finding of whether there is an apparent state of conflict and then to examine whether it is possible to harmonize the apparent state of conflict through interpretation or to identify priorities between rules that appear to be in conflict.[10]

The scope of this chapter is limited to marshaling and analysing the structure of the relationships between extradition obligations in relation to international crimes under various treaties through treaty interpretation, and it may not be sufficient to elucidate the structure of obligations in the entire extradition system that has been built up through the accumulation of State practice. However, first, by organizing the treaty relations, it deduces an indication to the issue of gravity which is generally considered to be one of the premises of international criminal justice. It focuses on how the rules determining priority in the apparent conflict relationship reflect the core and allegedly serious nature of the core crimes. Much work has been done on

---

[7] Jenks [86], p. 426.

[8] 1969 Vienna Convention on the Law of Treaties, 1155 UNTS 331.

[9] Tammelo [221].

[10] See, Martti Koskenniemi, *Fragmentation of International Law: Difficulties Arising from the Diversification and Expansion of International Law* (Report of the Study Group of the International Law Commission), UN Doc. A/CN.4/L.682 (13 April 2006), para. 36.

the concept of core crimes from a substantive law perspective.[11] This chapter, on the other hand, considers this issue from a procedural perspective.

The first section gives an overview of today's extradition system, which consists of four types of systems: bilateral, regional, universal, and vertical. Next, the rules governing the coordination of competing extradition requests for the same offence in this multilayered system are reviewed. Furthermore, it examines how the rules for coordinating conflicts and considerations are provided for when there are competing extradition requests for different crimes. In light of these considerations, it discusses how the rules for determining priority in apparent conflict situations reflect the core and allegedly serious nature of the core crimes. Finally, pointing out that the system of international cooperation, which has evolved for different crimes, has therefore been unable to determine the primacy of extradition obligations in some cases without determining the relationship of priority between the crimes, it adds a few remarks on how the indicators for determining that relationship of priority should be pursued.

2 Multi-Layered System of Extradition

International systems based on treaties on extradition can be classified into four types of regimes from the viewpoint of the relationship with the other Party: bilateral, regional, universal, and vertical. First, the system based on bilateral treaties is a system between the home State and the other State. If there is a request for extradition from the other State, the subject must basically be handed over unless there are grounds for refusing extradition. The advantage of the bilateral system is that the State with which a treaty is concluded can be selected, and the conditions for extradition can be set individually by the other State. In most cases, provisions are in place to ensure that the subject offence is criminalized in both States, and rules are in place such as giving priority to criminal proceedings in the home State. Japan has concluded bilateral treaties with only two States, the US and South Korea,[12] but the US has concluded bilateral treaties with over 100 States.[13]

Second, there is a regional instrument consisting of extradition obligations for States within the region. The nine States of the Americas signed the Convention on Extradition in 1879, the first regional treaty dedicated to extradition.[14] The Americas subsequently deposited the Convention on Extradition in 1981 with the Organization

[11] For example, Bitzilekis [14]; Chouliaras [32]; DeGuzman [40]; Heller [70]; Hiéramente [73]; Mayama [119]; Sakamoto [175]; Simon [193].

[12] 1978 Treaty on Extradition between the United States of America and Japan, 1203 UNTS 225; 2002 Treaty on Extradition between Japan and the Republic of Korea, 2737 UNTS 177. Korea, 2737 UNTS 177.

[13] US Department of State, "Extradition Treaties" at https://www.state.gov/s/l/treaty/faqs/70138.htm (as of 27 December 2021).

[14] Zanotti [256], p. 1.

of American States.[15] European States concluded the European Convention on Extradition in 1957 and the Economic Community of West African States ("ECOWAS") concluded the Extradition Convention in 1994.[16] The regional system is characterized by the fact that the Parties are limited to States belonging to the region.[17] The extradition system is established against the background of the proximity of criminal justice systems and cultural values within the region, and the ease of movement of persons. Parties to a regional extradition treaty are basically obliged to respond to any request from any other Party.

Third, there is a universal system in which the States Parties are not limited to a region. While it is open to many States without regional limitations, it is limited in the crimes it covers. The universal extradition system is characterized by the fact that, except for the Genocide Convention,[18] it does not directly establish extradition obligations *per se*, but basically mandates the addition of certain crimes to the existing system, as we will see later. However, the universal extradition system places a so-called *aut dedere aut judicare* obligation, so that, as we will see in more detail later, extradition must be undertaken if not prosecuted in the home State. For States whose extradition requires the existence of a treaty, the relevant treaty instrument is directly available under the provision that the treaty establishing the universal extradition regime may be used as the basis for extradition. The multilateral treaties establishing universal extradition systems set the obligation *aut dedere aut judicare*, including the International Convention for the Suppression of Counterfeiting of 1929,[19] the Convention for the Suppression of Illicit Traffic in Dangerous Drugs of 1936,[20] the Convention for the Prevention and Punishment of Terrorism of 1937,[21] the Four Geneva Conventions for the Protection of Victims of War of 1949 and subsequent additional protocols,[22] the Convention for the Suppression of the

---

[15] 1981 Inter-American Convention on Extradition, 1752 UNTS 190.

[16] 1957 European Convention on Extradition, 359 UNTS 273; ECOWAS Documentation on-line, "Convention A/P.1/8/94 on Extradition" at http://documentation.ecowas.int/wpfb-file/convention-on-extradition2-pdf/ (as of 27 December 2021).

[17] For example, according to Article 29(1) of the Inter-American Convention on Extradition, the Convention is "open to accession by the States of the Americas" but according to paragraph 2, States that have obtained permanent observer status through the General Assembly approval may also join.

[18] 1948 Convention on the Prevention and Punishment of the Crime of Genocide, 78 UNTS 277.

[19] 1929 International Convention for the Suppression of Counterfeiting Currency and Protocol, 2623 LNTS 371.

[20] 1936 Convention for the Suppression of Illicit Traffic in Dangerous Drugs, 198 LNTS 299.

[21] World Digital Library, "1937 Convention for the Prevention and Punishment of Terrorism" at https://www.wdl.org/en/item/11579/ (as of 27 December 2021).

[22] 1949 Geneva Convention for the Amelioration of the Condition of the Wounded and Sick in Armed Forces in the Field, 75 UNTS 31; 1949 Geneva Convention for the Amelioration of the Condition of the Wounded, Sick and Shipwrecked Members of the Armed Forces at Sea, 75 UNTS 85; 1949 Geneva Convention relative to the Treatment of Prisoners of War, 75 UNTS 135; 1949 Geneva Convention relative to the Protection of Civilian Persons in Time of War, 75 UNTS 287; 1977 Protocol Additional to the Geneva Conventions of 12 August 1949, and relating to the Protection of Victims of International Armed Conflicts (Protocol I), 1125 UNTS 3; 1977 Protocol Additional

Traffic in Persons and of the Exploitation of the Prostitution of Othersof 1950,[23] and the Convention against Torture and Other Cruel, Inhuman or Degrading Treatment or Punishment of 1984.[24] The 1948 Genocide Convention and the 2006 Convention against Enforced Disappearances[25] envisage the existence of an international criminal tribunal. Since the 1970s, the initiative of relevant international organizations has facilitated the conclusion of various conventions to deal with various types of international crimes. With regards to aviation offences, the Convention against the Unlawful Seizure of Aircraft ("Hague Convention")[26] was deposited with the International Civil Aviation Organization ("ICAO") in 1970, and the Convention against Unlawful Acts against the Safety of Civil Aviation ("Montreal Convention")[27] in 1971. In 1979, the Convention on the Physical Protection of Nuclear Material[28] was deposited with the International Atomic Energy Agency ("IAEA"), and in 1988 the Convention for the Prevention of Unlawful Acts against the Safety of Maritime Navigation[29] was deposited with the International Maritime Organization ("IMO"). UN-sponsored treaties include the Narcotics Conventions—1961 Single Convention on Narcotic Drugs, 1971 Convention on Psychotropic Substances and 1988 Convention on Illicit Traffic in Narcotic Drugs and Psychotropic Substances,[30] as well as various conventions on the prevention of terrorist acts—1973 Convention on the Prevention and Punishment of Crimes against Internationally Protected Person,[31] 1979 Convention on the Prevention of Hostage-Taking,[32] 1994 UN Convention on the Safety of UN Personnel,[33] 1997 Convention against Terrorist Bombings,[34] 1999

to the Geneva Conventions of 12 August 1949 and relating to the Protection of Victims of Non-International Armed Conflicts (Protocol II), 1125 UNTS 609.

[23] 1950 Convention for the Suppression of the Traffic in Persons and of the Exploitation of the Prostitution of Others, 96 UNTS 271.

[24] 1984 Convention against Torture and Other Cruel, Inhuman or Degrading Treatment or Punishment, 1465 UNTS 85.

[25] 2006 International Convention for the Protection of All Persons from Enforced Disappearance, 2716 UNTS 3.

[26] 1970 Convention for the Suppression of the Unlawful Seizure of Aircraft, 860 UNTS 105.

[27] 1971 Convention for the Suppression of Unlawful Acts against the Safety of Civil Aviation, 974 UNTS 177.

[28] 1979 Convention on the Physical Protection of Nuclear Material, 1456 UNTS 124.

[29] 1988 Convention for the Suppression of Unlawful Acts against the Safety of Maritime Navigation, 1678 UNTS 221.

[30] 1961 Single Convention on Narcotic Drugs, 520 UNTS 151; 1971 Convention on Psychotropic Substances, 1019 UNTS 175; 1988 United Nations Convention 1988 United Nations Convention against Illicit Traffic in Narcotic Drugs and Psychotropic Substances, 1582 UNTS 95.

[31] 1973 Convention on the Prevention and Punishment of Crimes against Internationally Protected Persons, 1035 UNTS 167.

[32] 1979 International Convention against the Taking of Hostages, 1316 UNTS 205.

[33] 1994 Convention on the Safety of United Nations and Associated Personnel, 2051 UNTS 363.

[34] 1994 International Convention for the Suppression of Terrorist Bombings, 2149 UNTS 256.

Convention on the Prevention of the Financing of Terrorism[35] and 2005 Convention on the Prevention of Nuclear Terrorism,[36] 2000 Convention against Organized Crime,[37] and 2003 Convention against Corruption.[38] The Optional Protocol to the Convention on the Rights of the Child on the Sale of Children, Child Prostitution and Child Pornography of 2000[39] also established a universal extradition system for the offences concerned. As deposited with the Council of Europe, the European Convention against Terrorism of 1977[40] and the Cybercrime Convention of 2001[41] established universal extradition systems for these offences.

Fourth, there is a vertical system of extradition to international courts. There are multiple reasons why it is called vertical,[42] but it is particularly noteworthy that the State that is obliged to extradite is unilaterally obliged to extradite to the international court concerned, while the international court is not obliged to extradite to the State concerned. For extradition to an international court, the word "surrender" is used instead of "extradition" between States.[43] UN Member States were obliged to respond to extradition requests for suspects to the *ad hoc* Tribunals established by UN Security Council resolutions in the 1990s. In 1998, the ICC adopted the ICC Statute, and States Parties to the Statute are obliged to respond to requests for the surrender of suspects by the ICC (Part 9 of the ICC Statute).

Thus, through the establishment of bilateral, regional, universal, and vertical extradition systems, States have been able to confirm their extradition obligations with certain partners and to ensure fair extradition procedures for suspects, as well as to share a common definition of the crimes that define the target offences and to ensure multifaceted cooperation for the effective prosecution of such crimes. On the other hand, these extradition systems have created a multi-layered obligation, so that States have sometimes been expected to receive multiple extradition/surrender requests for the same person under separate systems.

---

[35] 1999 International Convention for the Suppression of the Financing of Terrorism, 2178 UNTS 197.

[36] 2005 International Convention for the Suppression of Acts of Nuclear Terrorism, 2445 UNTS 89.

[37] 2000 United Nations Convention against Transnational Organized Crime, 2225 UNTS 209.

[38] 2003 United Nations Convention against Corruption, 2349 UNTS 41.

[39] 2000 Optional Protocol to the Convention on the Rights of the Child on the Sale of Children, Child Prostitution and Child Pornography, 2171 UNTS 227.

[40] 1977 European Convention on the Suppression of Terrorism, 1137 UNTS 93.

[41] 2001 Convention on Cybercrime, 2296 UNTS 167.

[42] See Takemura [216].

[43] The term "transfer" was also considered in the drafting process of the ICC Statute, and the conclusion as to which word would be used was deferred until the final stage of drafting. Some delegations suggested the adoption of a unique concept of surrender to the ICC, as the use of the word extradition would appear to be influenced by restrictions on extradition between States (in particular, non-extradition of nationals). Ultimately, there was agreement to define each term as far as the purposes of the ICC Statute were concerned, and a definition of the terms "surrender" and "extradition" were placed in Article 102 of the ICC Statute. Machochoko [115], pp. 309–310.

3 Conflicting Extradition Requests for the Same Offence

Conflicting extradition requests for the same offence are not uncommon events. For example, in the case of the bombing of Pan American Airways Flight 103 over Lockerbie, Scotland, which killed passengers, including an American, and residents of Lockerbie, the US and the UK requested the extradition of two Libyans, who were alleged to be suspects, to Libya.[44] In addition, competing extradition requests are often made by the national State of the suspect in response to an extradition request from the State where the crime was committed, particularly in cases where political issues may arise.[45]

A comparative review of the relevant extradition treaties reveals various coordination provisions, as seen below. Basically, competing extradition requests for the same offence are governed by a provision that gives discretion to the requested State ("discretionary provision"). However, there are also treaties that have a specific priority rule ("priority provision").

3.1 Basic Bilateral and Regional System

The principle of the supremacy of *lex posterior* cannot be used to reconcile extradition treaties between two or more States which, by their very nature, are essentially between different parties; if a State concludes bilateral treaties on the same matter with more than two States, these two treaty obligations are necessarily in conflict. If two States demand extradition of the same person, there must be a rule as to which of these two obligations to extradite takes precedence over the other. When a treaty between State A and State B conflicts with a subsequent treaty between State A and State C, the treaty with State B is not affected by the treaty with State C, so State A has a choice between modifying or terminating either treaty or risking a breach of either or both.[46] When concluding treaties, States are encouraged to avoid such risks, often by placing coordination provisions in bilateral or regional extradition treaties.

Many of the relatively early treaties between the two States did not contain special provisions for the case of competing extradition requests[47] and Anglo-American law States understood the theory of the primacy of the principle of territoriality as

44 See, Placha [158], p. 126.

45 For example, in a case concerning Colombian drug cartels, it is reported that Colombia sometimes filed competing extradition requests in response to extradition requests from the US; See Bassiouni [10], p. 953 (note 7).

46 Aust [6], p. 193.

47 E.g., 1904 Extradition Treaty between Austria-Hungary and Greece, 2 LNTS 174; 1923 Extradition Treaty (the United States of America-Turkey), 153 LNTS 71.

customary international law and relied on this theory in their decisions.[48] The coordination provisions found from the 1870s until around the 1940s were, as will be discussed in the next section, provisions regarding extradition requests in respect of different offences relating to the same person. The extradition treaty between Brazil and Uruguay of 1916, which can be seen as an early example of coordination provisions applicable to competing requests for the same offence, contained a discretionary provision that the requested State was free to decide when there were competing extradition requests against the same person from several States.[49] Since then, similar discretionary provisions have gradually spread[50] and the majority of bilateral treaties concluded since the 1950s have such discretionary provisions, regardless of the legal system to which each Party belongs.[51] Some have included relative seriousness as a consideration in discretionary provisions. The earliest examples of this are the bilateral treaties that the newly established State of Israel concluded with other States in the 1950s.[52] Since the 1960s, bilateral extradition treaties have incorporated, in addition to gravity, such considerations as the place of commission of the crime, the date of the request, the nationality of the subject and the possibility of subsequent extradition to another State in the discretionary provision.[53]

In contrast, some bilateral treaties to which the States of the Americas are parties have adopted a distinction between cases in which the crimes are the same and those in which the crimes are different, with specific priority provisions for each. Article

---

[48] See Bassiouni [10], p. 953. Anglo-American law States insisted on the primacy of the principle of territoriality in criminal jurisdiction, while Continental European law States generally concluded bilateral extradition treaties in the first half of the nineteenth century. Yamamoto [249].

[49] 1916 Treaty on the Extradition of Criminals (Brazil-Uruguay), 1031UNTS 255, Article 11.

[50] E.g., 1928 Convention relating to Extradition and Judicial Assistance in Criminal Matters (Austria-Finland), 89 LNTS 69, Article 9; 1931 Convention E.g., 1928 Convention relating to Extradition of Criminals and Judicial Assistance in Criminal Matters (Austria-Finland), 89 LNTS 69, Article 9; 1931 Convention relating to the Extradition of Criminals and Judicial Assistance in Criminal Matters (Czechoslovakia-Sweden) 134 LNTS 135, Article 11.

[51] E.g., 1956 Extradition and Judicial Assistance in Criminal Matters (Israel-Italy), 316 UNTS 97, Article 13; 1956 Extradition Convention between Belgium and the State of Israel, 260 UNTS 3, Article 7; 1961 Treaty of Extradition between the United States of America and the United States of Brazil, 532 UNTS 177, Article 10; 1973 Treaty of Extradition (Australia–Italy), 1020 UNTS 71, Article 39; 1976 Extradition Treaty (Indonesia–Philippines), 1031 UNTS 225, Article 18; 1981 Treaty relating to Extradition (Philippines–Thailand), 1394 UNTS 3, Article 17; 1984 Treaty concerning Extradition (Australia–Finland), 1411 UNTS 320, Article 10; 1985 Treaty between Canada and Italy concerning Extradition, 1467 UNTS 3, Article 11; 1987 Extradition Treaty between the Kingdom of Belgium and the United States of America, 2093 UNTS 263, Article 13; 1988 Treaty on Extradition (Australia–Philippines)1641 UNTS 331, Article 10; 1989 Treaty concerning Extradition (Italy–Brazil) 1904 UNTS 70, Article 20; 1997 Convention 1997 Convention between the Kingdom of Belgium and the Kingdom of Morocco on Extradition 2317 UNTS 563, Article 15.

[52] Extradition and Judicial Assistance in Criminal Matters (Israel–Italy), *ibid*; Extradition Convention between Belgium and the State of Israel, *ibid*. The prosecution interest at the time suggests that the aim was to prioritize extradition for war crimes. See, Lube and Reed [114].

[53] E.g., 1963 Extradition Treaty (UK–Sweden), 590 UNTS 117, Article 14; 1971 Convention concerning Extradition and Judicial Assistance in Criminal Matters (Belgium-Yugoslavia [Socialist Federal Republic of Yugoslavia]), 872 UNTS 3, Article 15; 1972 Treaty on Extradition (Denmark–the United States of America), 952 UNTS 29, Article 15.

6 of the extradition treaty between Brazil and Peru of 1919 provides that in case of competing extradition requests for the same offence, priority shall be given to extradition to the State where the offence was committed.[54] Similar provisions can be found in treaties between States of the Americas, such as between Colombia and Costa Rica and between Bolivia and Brazil.[55] A similar provision is also adopted in bilateral extradition treaties with Western States, where Brazil is a Party.[56]

Regional systems also provide for cases where extradition is requested by two or more States, but they adopt different provisions. Article 17 of the European Convention on Extradition is a discretionary provision that the requested State shall decide in the case of competing extradition requests for the same offence. However, in making such a decision, the State must consider, *inter alia*, the relative gravity of the offences and the circumstances of the place of commission, the date of each request, the nationality of the subject person and the possibility of subsequent extradition to another State. On the other hand, Article 15 of the Inter-American Convention, reflecting the practice of the States of the Americas as seen earlier, adopts a priority provision that, in the case of requests for the same crime from two or more States, the request of the State where the crime was committed shall prevail, thus maintaining the priority of the principle of territoriality.

The Model Treaty on Extradition ("Model Treaty"), first adopted in 1990 and amended in 2002,[57] has been used as a model for newly concluded extradition treaties, reflecting previous treaty practice.[58] Not only does the Model Treaty reflect much previous State practice, but many bilateral treaties concluded after the Model Treaty, such as the 2002 extradition treaty between Japan and South Korea, have adopted very similar rules to it, and thus the coordination provisions in the Model Treaty reflect customary international law to some extent. Article 16 of the treaty provides for the case where there is a conflict between a request by a State Party to the extradition treaty in question and a request by a third State. It states that a Contracting State which

---

54 1919 Treaty on the Extradition of Criminals (Brazil–Peru), 1031 UNTS 277, Article 6.

55 1928 Treaty on Extradition between the Republic of Colombia and the Republic of Costa Rica, 2411 UNTS 12, Article 21; 1938 Extradition Treaty between Brazil and Bolivia, 54 UNTS 333, Article 13.

56 1953 Extradition Treaty between Belgium and Brazil, 272UNTS 157, Article 11; Treaty of Extradition between the United States of America and the United States of Brazil, 2093 UNTS 263, Article 10.

57 The Model Treaty is presented as an "important tool that should be carefully reviewed by States as part of their examination of their extradition relationships, to ensure that such relationships they are up to date." United Nations Office of Drugs and Crimes, *Revised Manuals on the Model Treaty on Extradition and on the Model Treaty on Mutual Assistance in Criminal Matters* (8 December 2002) at https://www.unodc.org/pdf/model_treaty_extradition_revised_manual.pdf (as of 27 December 2021), para. 4.

58 While the principles of extradition law established in the nineteenth century were based on the Continental legal systems, globalization has made it necessary to facilitate extradition to and from States with different legal systems, such as Anglo–American, Islamic and Socialist legal systems. Therefore, it has been pointed out that the Model Treaty reflects the need to establish commonly accepted principles of extradition law while at the same time allowing for flexible arrangements that consider the special circumstances of each of the Contracting States. Morishita [129].

is requested by the other Contracting State and a third State for extradition in respect of the same person shall, at its own discretion, determine which State the person shall be handed over to. However, the commentary to this discretionary provision, reflecting previous practice, recommends that the article specify the matters that the requested State must consider in adopting the article in practice.[59] Indeed, for example, Article 11(2) of the 2002 Extradition Treaty between Japan and the South Korea provides that, in determining which State to extradite, the State shall consider such matters as the time and place of the commission of the offence, the gravity of the offence, the date of the request, the nationality and place of residence of the person subject to extradition, and whether the request is under a treaty.

The considerations in the discretionary provision serve as a guideline in the determination of the destination of extradition by the requested State in competing extradition requests. In the *Adamov* case, in which there were competing extradition requests relating to embezzlement from Russia and the US, the Federal Court of Switzerland, the requested State, decided in a 2005 judgment to give priority to the Russian extradition request on the grounds that the person subject to extradition was a Russian citizen and that the acts complained of took place mainly in Russia.[60] Both Switzerland and Russia are parties to the European Convention on Extradition,[61] although an extradition treaty between Switzerland and the US was concluded in 1990.[62] Both Article 17 of the European Extradition Convention and Article 17 of the Extradition Convention between Switzerland and the US state that the requested State shall take into account various relevant matters in making its decision, but both of these discretionary provisions include the place of the crime and the nationality of the subject person as considerations.

As discussed above, the most common coordination provision found in bilateral and regional extradition treaties is the discretionary provision that the State receiving the competing requests may decide which of the two States to hand over to. Thus, if either of the bilateral or regional treaties on which the competing requests rest is left to the discretion of the requested State, the apparent conflict condition is resolved by the relevant treaty provision and that the treaty obligation of the one that does not provide for discretion prevails. In 1987, the Swiss Federal Court of Justice held that, in the case of two competing treaty requests, where one treaty contains a discretionary provision and the other does not, there is a lacuna which must be filled based on treaty

[59] *Revised Manuals on the Model Treaty*, 61.

[60] *Adamov v. Switzerland*, judgment (Application no. 3052/06) Second Section (21 June 2011), para. 29. However, the amounts of embezzlement covered by the two extraditions differ. BBC News, *Former Russian Minister Deported* (30 December 2005), at http://news.bbc.co.uk/2/hi/europe/4570716.stm (as of 27 December 2021).

[61] Council of Europe, "Chart of signatures and ratifications of Treaty 024" at https://www.coe.int/en/web/conventions/full-list/-/conventions/treaty/024/signatures?p_auth=KkrqPhLG (as of 27 December 2021).

[62] 1990 Extradition Treaty between the Government of the United States of America and the Government of the Swiss Confederation, 2934 UNTS (No. 51039).

law or principles of national law, and Switzerland determined the place of extradition at its own discretion.[63]

Problems may also arise where there is no discretionary provision in either of the several treaties underlying the competing requests, or where both have adopted different priority provisions. If there is no discretionary provision in either treaty, the treaty obligations are in conflict. It would be desirable for customary law to be established to resolve this conflict, and it would appear from the Swiss Federal Court's implementation in the above-mentioned case, and many extradition treaty provisions, that the discretionary provisions identified in the Model Treaty would play a coordinating role as customary international law. However, if both parties adopt different priority provisions, even if the discretionary provision is customary international law as confirmed by the Model Treaty, the priority provision would be considered to constitute *lex specialis* by its nature and any priority provision would prevail over the discretionary provision under customary law. When two conflicting priority provisions in an extradition treaty are both valid, there appears to be no customary law rule as to which priority provision prevails.

However, this is not a problem when the relationship of priority between treaties, rather than the relationship of priority of extradition, is expressly stipulated. The rules governing the relationship between a regional extradition treaty and a bilateral treaty already concluded between the parties to that treaty are completely different between the European Convention and the American Convention. The European Convention on Extradition clearly provides in Article 28(1) that the European Convention shall prevail over the provisions of any bilateral treaty or agreement governing extradition between the Parties to the European Convention. Bilateral treaties can be concluded between the parties to the European Convention only to supplement the provisions of the European Convention or to facilitate the application of the principles contained in the European Convention (Article 28(2) of the European Convention). The Inter-American Convention, on the other hand, states in Article 33(1) that the Inter-American Convention applies to the States that have ratified it but does not supersede any multilateral or bilateral treaty already in force, unless expressly declared or agreed to by the Parties.

3.2 Universal Systems

The universal extradition system essentially takes the form of a supplement to the bilateral system, with the provision that the crimes covered by the system are added to the crimes covered by the existing bilateral system. For example, Article 36(2)(b)(1) of the 1961 Single Convention on Narcotic Drugs, as amended, provides that the offences covered by the Convention are to be regarded as extradition offences in all

---

[63] The case concerned competing extradition requests from Belgium, which has a bilateral extradition treaty with no coordination provisions, and Italy, a Party to the European Convention on Extradition. *C v. Federal Police Department*, 100 ILR 657 (16 September 1987), 661.

existing and future extradition treaties between the Parties. Thus, if there is a bilateral extradition treaty between the States Parties to a treaty establishing a universal system, the obligation to respond to extradition requests in respect of such crimes would arise because the crimes covered by that instrument would be included in the crimes covered by the existing bilateral treaty. Similar provisions exist in the Convention against Torture and Other Cruel Treatment and the Convention against Enforced Disappearances.[64] The Convention on Aviation Related Offences, the Convention on the Physical Protection of Nuclear Material, the Convention against Unlawful Acts of Maritime Navigation, the Narcotics Related Conventions, the Convention on Terrorism, the Convention against Organized Crime, the Convention against Corruption and relevant Council of Europe Conventions also ensure a universal extradition regime for each crime by adding these crimes to the existing crimes covered by the bilateral system.[65]

The treaties establishing the universal extradition system provide that, for those cases between Contracting Parties for which the existence of a treaty is not a condition for extradition, it must be mutually recognized as an extradition offence in accordance with domestic law.[66] However, even if it is included as an extradition offence under domestic law, it is only under domestic law and does not create an obligation under international law of extradition. On the other hand, if there is no bilateral treaty between the contracting Parties that makes the existence of a treaty a condition for extradition, a multilateral treaty establishing a universal extradition regime may be regarded as the legal basis for extradition in respect of the offences governed by that

---

[64] Article 8(1) of the Convention against Torture and Other Cruel Treatment and Article 13(2) of the Convention against Enforced Disappearances.

[65] Article 8(1) of the Hague Convention, Article 8(1) of the Montreal Convention, Article 11(1) of the Convention on the Physical Protection of Nuclear Material, Article 11(1) of the Convention against Unlawful Acts of Maritime Navigation, Article 36(1)(b)(1) of the Single Convention on Narcotic Drugs, Article 22(2)(b) of the Convention on Psychotropic Substances, Article 6(2) of the Convention on Punishment of Illicit Traffic in Narcotic and Psychotropic Substances, Article 8(1) of the Convention against Crimes against International Representatives and Others 1; Article 10(1) of the Convention against Hostage Taking; Article 15(1) of the UN Convention on the Safety of United Nations Personnel; Article 9(1) of the Convention against Bombings; Article 11(1) of the Convention against the Financing of Terrorism; Article 13(1) of the Convention against Nuclear Terrorism; Article 16(3) of the Convention against Organized Crime; Article 44(4) of the Convention against Corruption; and Article 24(1) of the Convention on Cybercrime.

[66] Article 8(3) of the Convention against Torture, Article 13(5) of the Convention against Enforced Disappearances, Article 8(3) of the Hague Convention, Article 8(3) of the Montreal Convention, Article 11(3) of the Convention on the Physical Protection of Nuclear Material, Article 11(3) of the Convention against Unlawful Acts of Sea Navigation, Article 36(1)(b)(3) of the Single Convention on Narcotic Drugs, Article 22(2)(b) of the Convention on Psychotropic Substances, Article 6(4) of the Convention on the Punishment of Illicit Traffic in Narcotic and Psychotropic Substances Article 6(4) of the Convention against Illicit Traffic in Narcotic Drugs and Psychotropic Substances, Article 8(3) of the Convention against Transnational Organized Crime, Article 10(3) of the Convention against Hostage Taking, Article 15(3) of the UN Convention on the Safety of United Nations Personnel, Article 9(3) of the Convention against Terrorist Bombings, Article 11(3) of the Convention against the Financing of Terrorism, Article 13(3) of the Convention against Nuclear Terrorism, Article 16(6) of the Convention against Organized Crime, Article 44(7) of the Convention against Corruption Article 24(4) of the Convention on Cybercrime.

treaty.[67] This provision provides a mechanism by which the universal system can be used for certain crimes covered by the universal system in a complementary manner in the absence of a bilateral system. However, the provision is a permissive provision and does not provide a basis for obligation in lieu of a bilateral extradition treaty in cases where there is an extradition request.

The universal extradition systems under the Genocide Convention and the Geneva Conventions also complement bilateral or regional systems, but unlike the above systems, they do not mandate the inclusion of the targeted crimes as extradition offences. Article 7 of the Genocide Convention provides that in relation to extradition, States Parties "pledge themselves"[68] to extradite the offender. It is said that this provision establishes an obligation to respond to extradition requests from the Parties to the Genocide Convention. However, it states that this provision is "in accordance with existing national legislation or treaties" and envisages that extradition procedures are subject to existing bilateral or regional systems. Therefore, in the event of competing requests by Parties to a Genocide Convention under a bilateral or regional treaty, the priority of the extradition State is determined in accordance with the coordination provisions of that treaty. The priority of the extradition State would be determined in accordance with the coordination provisions of the relevant Convention. On the other hand, Article 49 of the first Geneva Convention states that each State Party "may", if it so wishes, in accordance with the provisions of its own legislation, hand the person over for trial to another relevant State Party. This provision merely provides that extradition may be an option notwithstanding the Geneva Conventions' obligations to investigate and prosecute, and that existing national laws shall govern whether a request for extradition by another State for a serious violation of the Geneva Conventions shall be complied with. Article 88 of Additional Protocol I to the Geneva Conventions expressly provides that the provisions on mutual assistance in criminal matters under the Conventions do not affect obligations under other bilateral or multilateral treaties currently governing the same matters.

[67] Article 8(2) of the Convention against Torture, Article 13(4) of the Convention against Enforced Disappearances, Article 8(2) of the Hague Convention, Article 8(2) of the Montreal Convention, Article 11(2) of the Convention on the Physical Protection of Nuclear Material, Article 11(2) of the Convention against Unlawful Acts of Sea Navigation, Article 36(1)(b)(2) of the Single Convention on Narcotic Drugs, Article 22(2)(b) of the Psychotropic Substances Convention, Article 6(3) of the Convention on the Prevention and Punishment of the Illicit Trade in Narcotic Drugs and Psychotropic Substances Article 6(3) of the Convention against Illicit Traffic in Narcotic Drugs and Psychotropic Substances, Article 8(2) of the Convention against Transnational Organized Crime, Article 10(2) of the Convention against Hostage Taking, Article 15(2) of the UN Convention on the Safety of United Nations Personnel, Article 9(2) of the Convention against Bombings, Article 11(2) of the Convention against the Financing of Terrorism, Article 13(2) of the Convention against Nuclear Terrorism, Articles 16(4) and (5) of the Organized Crime Convention, Articles 44(5) and (6) of the Convention against Corruption and Article 24(3) of the Convention on Cybercrime.

[68] The wording has been described as merely emphasizing that they are bound by the treaty provisions on extradition. Schiffbauer [182], p. 266. However, in response to the extradition request from Ethiopia on the count of genocide, as Zimbabwe does not have an extradition treaty between the two States, they refused the request. Tiba [224], p. 517.

Although the treaties establishing universal extradition systems generally all contain provisions providing for an obligation to "prosecute or extradite", with the exception of the Genocide Convention, the obligation contained in many recent treaties is not strictly an extradition obligation. The way in which the "prosecution or extradition" obligation is provided for varies, but it is understood that it can be divided into four types.[69] The first type is typified by the International Convention against Counterfeit Currency of 1929. A feature of this type, which has been incorporated into relatively old treaties, is that it provides for prosecution in the home State if the subject is not extradited on the grounds of nationality.[70] The second type is found in regional treaties, which ensure the prevention of crime in the region by requiring extradition to be requested in the region, regardless of the crime for which extradition is requested, but requiring prosecution in the home State if extradition is not carried out for any reason.[71] The third type is found in the Geneva Conventions, which provide that the State in which the suspect is located is obliged to bring a prosecution against the subject, but may extradite him/her to the requesting State if it so desires and if the requesting State provides sufficient *prima facie* evidence in the case.[72] The fourth type is the so-called "Hague Formula", which was provided for in the 1970 Hague Convention and has been incorporated into many subsequent multilateral treaties.[73] In this type, the State Party in whose territory a suspect is found is obliged, without any exception, to refer the case to its competent authorities

[69] *The Obligation to Extradite or Prosecute (aut dedere aut judicare), Final Report of the International Law Commission*, Yearbook of the International Law Commission II (Part Two), 2014 (hereinafter "*The Obligation to Extradite or Prosecute*"), para. 6.

[70] Article 8 of the International Convention for the Prevention of Counterfeit Currency; Article 7 of the Convention for the Prevention of Illicit Traffic in Dangerous Drugs; Article 9 of the Convention for the Prevention and Punishment of Terrorism; Article 9 of the Convention against Trafficking in Persons and Exploitation of the Prostitution of Others; Article 36(2) of the Single Convention on Narcotic Drugs; Article 22(2) of the Psychotropic Substances Convention; Article 22(2) of the Convention on the Sale of Children, Child Prostitution and Optional Protocol to the Convention on the Rights of the Child on Child Pornography (Article 5).

[71] For example, Articles 1 and 6 of the European Convention on Extradition, Articles 1 and 2 of the Inter-American Convention on Extradition, and Articles 2 and 10 of the ECOWAS Extradition Convention.

[72] Geneva Convention I, Article 49; Convention II, Article 50; Convention III, Article 129; Convention IV, Article 146; Additional Protocol I, Articles 85(1), (3) and 88(2).

[73] Article 7 of the Hague Convention, Article 7 of the Montreal Convention, Article 6(9) of the Convention on Illicit Traffic in Narcotic Drugs and Psychotropic Substances, Article 7 of the Convention on the Prevention and Punishment of Crime by International Representatives and Others, Article 8 of the Convention against Hostage Taking, Article 14 of the UN Convention on the Safety of Personnel, Article 10 of the Convention on the Physical Protection of Nuclear Material, Article 10 of the Convention against Unlawful Acts of Maritime Navigation, Article 8 of the Convention against Terrorist Bombings, Article 10 of the Convention against the Financing of Terrorism Article 8 of the Convention against Terrorism, Article 11 of the Convention against Nuclear Terrorism, Article 7 of the Convention against Torture, Article 16(10) of the Convention against Organized Crime, Article 24(6) of the Convention on Cybercrime, Article 44(6) of the Convention against Corruption, and Article 11 of the Convention against Enforced Disappearances.

for prosecution if it does not extradite the person concerned.[74] These four types can be broadly classified as those that place extradition as mandatory and prosecution as complementary (types 1 and 2) and those that place prosecution as mandatory and extradition as complementary (types 3 and 4).[75]

Most recent treaties establishing universal extradition systems have adopted the fourth type. In this type, extradition only serves to discharge the obligation to prosecute, not the extradition obligation to comply with the extradition request for the crime in question.[76] Therefore, even if a person does not respond to an extradition request for a target crime, he/she can still be prosecuted in his/her own State, and failure to prosecute would only constitute a breach of the obligation to prosecute, not a breach of the extradition obligation.[77] The Geneva Conventions adopt the third type, as mentioned above. As for the Genocide Convention, it is the "competent court of the State in whose territory the act was committed" or the "International Criminal Court" that is supposed to try the case, so the "prosecution or extradition" of the Hague Formula is not adopted.[78]

3.3 *Vertical Systems*

The ICC has a vertical surrender system for State Parties to the Statute, but there may be conflicts between surrender requests from the ICC and extradition requests from State Parties to the Statute or from non-State Parties using the bilateral, regional, or universal extradition system for crimes under ICC jurisdiction (Article 5 of the ICC Statute). A competing surrender/extradition request for the same crimes under ICC's jurisdiction is one in which the perpetrator of the core crime is located in the territory of the requested State, and the following three types of surrender/extradition requests may be filed: (i) by the ICC through the vertical system; (ii) by a State that has concluded a bilateral or regional extradition treaty with the requested State, using that treaty; and (iii) a request for extradition solely on the basis of the universal extradition

[74] The obligation to engage in prosecution arises from the fact of the suspect's whereabouts alone, and only after a request for extradition is made does the requested State have the option of adopting an alternative means of transferring the suspect to another State for prosecution in that other State. Kumagai [111].

[75] Separate Opinion of Judge Yusuf in a case concerning *Questions concernant l'obligation de poursuivre ou d'extrader (Belgique c. Senegal)*, arret, CIJ Recueil 2012, 422, at pp. 567–568, paras. 19–22. No link between the wording used and the nature of the offence is observed, but rather it is noted that for some fairly serious offences relatively weak or that far-fetched language is used. Bassiouni [9], p. 9.

[76] See, for example, Yamamoto [249], pp. 26–27.

[77] See, *Questions concernant l'obligation de poursuivre ou d'extrader (Belgique c. Sénégal), arrêt*, CIJ Recueil 2012, 422, p. 456, para. 95.

[78] This view is also consistent with the drafting process. There was a proposal by Iran to amend the Convention to impose an obligation to prosecute in a State other than the State of origin of the perpetrator in the absence of an extradition request, but the proposal was rejected by a majority of the opposition. Roth [168], p. 305.

regime from a State that has not concluded a bilateral or regional extradition treaty with the requested State.

If the requesting State is a Party to the ICC Statute, the vertical surrender request from the ICC (request type (i)) shall, in principle, prevail.[79] Article 90 of the ICC Statute provides for the case where an ICC State Party that has received an surrender request for a person from the ICC also receives an extradition request for that person from another State with respect to "the same conduct which forms the basis of the crime" that are the subject of that request. The provision is clear. If the requesting State is a State Party, the requested State gives priority to a request from the ICC if the ICC has decided to accept the case (Article 90(2) of the ICC Statute); extradition does not take place until the ICC has decided that the case is admissible (*Ibid.*, (3)). During the drafting process of the Statute, the issue was whether the obligations of the requested State towards the ICC are heavier, lighter or equal to those owed to other States.[80] As a result, it was decided to characterize the obligations under the ICC Statute as paramount by Article 90 of the Statute.

If the requesting State making the competing request is not a State Party to the ICC Statute, the extradition request from the ICC will prevail if there is no "international obligation to extradite" (*Ibid.*, (4)). If there is an international obligation under a bilateral or regional treaty to the requesting State which is not a State Party to the Statute, as in the case of request type (ii), then the requested State will determine, considering the requesting State's interests—such as the place of commission of the crime and the nationality of the victims and extradition subjects—and relevant considerations such as the possibility of subsequent surrender by the requesting State to the ICC (*Ibid.*, (6)). In this way, Article 90 of the ICC Statute has been described as attempting to preserve respect for existing obligations under international law and the institutional effectiveness of the ICC for States facing two competing requests.[81] In any event, some have argued that, as a basic principle, priority must be given to obligations under the ICC Statute.[82]

The status of extradition requests based on universal systems such as request type (iii) differs for each type of crime: for crimes under ICC jurisdiction, there is a universal extradition system under the Genocide Convention for genocide and under the Geneva Conventions for war crimes. Article 7 of the Genocide Convention, as mentioned above, creates an "international obligation to extradite" within the meaning of Article 90 of the ICC Statute in the Genocide Convention alone, as it establishes an extradition obligation as "an undertaking to extradite the offender in accordance with existing national legislation or treaties." On the other hand, Article 49 of the first Geneva Convention only provides that each State Party may, if it so

---

79 In the case of a request for extradition from a specially constituted court, uncontested priority was given due to its superiority, Rule 58 of the ICTY/ICTR RPE. The legal precedents and academic theories are being elaborated. See Takemura [214], pp. 22–27.

80 Kress and Prost [108], p. 2060.

81 Kuc [110], p. 267. It is also recommended that in the case of competing requests, measures such as deferring one of the requests, if necessary, after consultation with the ICC and the requesting State (Article 90(9)(a) of the ICC Statute).

82 Sluiter [196], p. 630.

chooses, extradite a person for trial to another relevant State Party in accordance with the provisions of its own laws and regulations, and thus only provides that extradition is an option even though there are search and prosecution obligations under the Geneva Conventions. As such, the Geneva Conventions by themselves do not create an "international obligation to extradite" within the meaning of Article 90 of the ICC Statute; the draft Convention on Crimes against Humanity, which the ILC completed a first reading of in 2017, also proposes to include an obligation to "prosecute or extradite". As the draft does not establish an extradition obligation for the State where the accused is located,[83] even if the Convention were adopted and entered into force, extradition requests for crimes against humanity to a ratifying State under the Convention by itself would be subject to Article 90(4) of the ICC Statute, which would give priority to extradition to the competing ICC.

So, it has been revealed that when there are two or more competing extradition requests for the same offence, they are coordinated by giving the requested State the discretion to decide while presenting issues to consider. This is done through coordination or priority provisions in bilateral or regional instruments or prioritization of the obligations to the ICC, except for the Inter-American Convention and bilateral treaties with provisions on the priority of the principle of territoriality. However, competing requests against the same person do not necessarily relate to the same offence. In fact, when the same person is charged with more than one crime, extradition requests may be filed for each of the different crimes. I will therefore consider cases where there are competing extradition obligations for different offences in the following section.

4 Conflicting Extradition Requests for Different Offences

4.1 Coordination Provisions in Bilateral and Regional Systems

Prior to the frequent occurrence of cases in which a single crime had cross-border effects and was the subject of prosecution interest in more than two State, conflicting extradition requests would arise primarily with respect to separate crimes in different States by the same person moving between States. The first priority rule was that prior requests would take precedence. For example, Article 12 of the Extradition Treaty between France and the UK of 1876 and Article 10 of the Extradition Treaty between Spain and Colombia of 1892 provide that a person whose extradition is requested by another Party shall be handed over to the first Party that made the request even if a third State in which another offence has been committed requests extradition

[83] Text of the Draft Articles on Crimes Against Humanity adopted by the Commission on First Reading, *Report of the International Law Commission*, Sixty-ninth session (1 May–2 June and 3 July–4 August 2017), UN Doc. A/72/10, pp. 14–16, Articles 10, 13.

in respect of that person.[84] Such provisions can be found in many bilateral treaties to which the UK or the US was party until the 1940s,[85] and in bilateral treaties between Spain and the Americas.[86] Also, in treaties where discretionary provisions have been adopted, the 1928 extradition treaty between Austria and Finland and the 1931 extradition treaty between Czechoslovakia and Sweden contain a provision that, when the requested State makes a discretionary decision on a conflict of extradition requests for different offences, extradition may be conditional only if the receiving State promises to extradite the person to the other requesting State subsequently.[87]

Some treaties use the gravity of the crime as a criterion of priority. Article 14 of the 1946 Extradition Convention between Iraq and Turkey provides that in the event of competing extradition requests for different crimes, extradition shall be granted to the State in which the most serious crime was committed.[88] However, the same article provides that if the subject is not a national of the State and the crimes are of equal gravity, the person is to be handed over to the State that filed the request first. Article 11 of the Extradition Treaty between Czechoslovakia and Italy of 1922 provides that if there is a conflict between extradition requests from one of the Parties to the treaty and a third State, extradition for the crime considered the most serious shall prevail, but if the crimes are of equal gravity, extradition shall be given to the State that filed the request first.[89]

In the Americas, when there are competing requests for different crimes, there is a hierarchy of elements for considerations. Article 6 of the extradition treaty between Brazil and Peru of 1919 provides that in the case of competing requests for different crimes, priority is given to extradition to the State where the most serious crime was committed, but if the two are of equal gravity, extradition will be granted to the State which requested first, and if the two requests were issued on the same date, the

[84] 1876 Treaty on Extradition between the French Republic and the United Kingdom of Great Britain and Northern Ireland, 1324 UNTS 327, Article 12; 1892 Convention on Extradition (Colombia-Spain), 1721 UNTS 418, Article 10.

[85] 1889 Treaty between Great Britain and Northern Ireland and the Argentine Republic for the Mutual Extradition of Fugitive Criminals, 1212 UNTS 253, Article 13; 1901 Treaty for the Mutual Surrender of Fugitive Criminals (Belgium-United Kingdom of Great Britain and Northern Ireland), 997 UNTS 378, Article 10; 1923 Extradition Convention between the United States of America and Estonia, 43 LNTS 277, Article 7; 1924 Treaty for the Extradition of Criminals (Finland-United Kingdom of Great Britain and Northern Ireland), 34 LNTS 79, Article 13; 1931 Extradition Treaty between the United States of America and Great Britain and Northern Ireland, 163 UNTS 60, Article 10; 1947 Treaty between the United States of America and the Union of South Africa 1931 Extradition Treaty between the United States of America and Great Britain and Northern Ireland, 163 UNTS 60, Article 10; 1947 Treaty between the United States of America and the Union of South Africa, 148 UNTS 85, Article 9.

[86] 1919 Extradition Treaty between Spain and the Republic of Paraguay, 2181 UNTS 599, Article 7.

[87] Convention relating to Extradition and Judicial Assistance in Criminal Matters (Austria-Finland), 1411 UNTS 320, Article 9; 1931 Convention regarding the Extradition of Criminals and Judicial Assistance in Criminal Matters (Czechoslovakia-Sweden), 134 LNTS 135, Article 11.

[88] 1946 Extradition Convention between the Kingdom of Iraq and the Republic of Turkey, 37 UNTS 369, Article 14.

[89] 1922 Extradition Convention (Czechoslovakia-Italy), 55 UNTS 171.

requested State determines the priority.[90] Similar provisions found in treaties between States of the Americas, such as those between Colombia and Costa Rica and between Bolivia and Brazil, treat the situation slightly differently when the two requests are of equal gravity.[91] Similar provisions are also adopted in bilateral extradition treaties with Western States to which Brazil is a Party, with the difference that if the crimes covered by the two requests are of equal gravity, the extradition treaty between Brazil and Belgium provides that extradition will be granted to the first request, while the extradition treaty between Brazil and the US stipulates that it will be decided by the requested State.[92]

The coordination provisions in most recent bilateral extradition treaties do not distinguish the expected responses between when the subject offences are the same and when they are different. As seen above, Article 16 of the Model Treaty, in the event of a conflict between a request by a State Party to an extradition treaty and a request by a third State, provides that the requested State shall decide at its own discretion to which State the person shall be extradited. Article 11(1) of the Extradition Treaty between Japan and South Korea provides that "in relation to the same or different offences", the response does not vary depending on whether the two offences are the same or different. However, Article 11(2) includes the gravity of the offence as a factor to be taken into consideration in deciding to which State to extradite the person, and it is envisaged that priority will be given to extradition requests for more serious offences.

Among regional extradition treaties, Article 17 of the European Convention on Extradition and Article 23 of the ECOWAS Extradition Treaty similarly make no distinction between the crimes covered "in respect of the same or different offences" and only mention the relative importance of the offences as a matter of consideration. On the other hand, the Inter-American Convention changes the consideration of the matter when the subject crimes of the competing requests are the same or different. Article 15 of the Inter-American Convention, reflecting the practice of the States of the Americas, gives priority to the State requesting extradition "for the crime punishable by the most severe penalty" when competing requests are made for different crimes, as is the case when the subject crimes are the same. It also provides that if the requested State considers that the different crimes are of equal gravity, priority shall be given in the order in which the requests are received.

Thus, discretionary or priority provisions in cases of competing extradition requests for different offences may include gravity of the offences as a ground for priority or discretionary consideration, but the standard to be applied in practice is unclear.

---

[90] *Ibid.*, *Treaty on the Extradition of Criminals*, 1031 UNTS 277, Article 6.

[91] Treaty on Extradition between the Republic of Colombia and the Republic of Costa Rica, *supra* note 56, Article 21 (next to gravity and order of request, the place of birth of the subject is the criterion); Extradition Treaty between Brazil and Bolivia, 54 UNTS 333, Article 13 (stating that the requested State shall decide in cases of equal gravity).

[92] Extradition Treaty between Belgium and Brazil, 272 UNTS 157, Article 11; Treaty of Extradition between the United States of America and the United States of Brazil, 532 UNTS 17, Article 10.

4.2 The Obligation to "Prosecute or Extradite" and the Obligation to Extradition for the Crime of Genocide in the Universal System

In the universal systems, no coordination provision, such as priority or discretionary provision, is found. Unlike bilateral or regional treaties, the objective of a multilateral treaty establishing a universal extradition regime is to ensure the prosecution of the specific offences covered by that treaty. Therefore, in a universal system of extradition for the prevention of specific crimes, avoidance of prosecution by extradition for crimes other than those covered by the said system may be a problem. The so-called "prosecute or extradite" or *aut dedere aut judicare* obligation is considered to have the function of constraining such State action. This obligation gives priority to all extradition requests relating to crimes covered by the universal system, not because of the priority of the extradition obligation itself, but in relation to the "prosecute or extradite" obligation as one not to extradite with respect to other crimes.

The 2012 International Court of Justice ("ICJ") decision in the Case Concerning the Question of the Obligation to Prosecute or Extradite implied that extradition relieves the obligation to prosecute only when it is committed in respect of a crime covered by the Convention in question. In other words, according to the ICJ, "The purpose of these treaty provisions is to prevent alleged perpetrators of acts of torture from going unpunished, by ensuring that they cannot find refuge in any State party. The State in whose territory the suspect is present does indeed have the option of extraditing him to a country which has made such a request, but on the condition that it is to a State which has jurisdiction in some capacity, pursuant to Article 5 of the Convention, to prosecute and try him".[93]

The handing over of a torture suspect to another State for an offence other than torture would, in fact, remove the obligation to do so, as the situation of "territory the suspect is present" would be terminated. However, this action may contribute to the fact that the person remains unpunished and may be considered as an act contrary to the purpose of the Convention against Torture. Therefore, if the obligation to "prosecute or extradite" is interpreted in light of the purpose of the Convention, the content of the obligation to "prosecute or extradite" is the obligation to prosecute or extradite for the very offence covered by the Convention that establishes the obligation, and it is not assumed that prosecution or extradition for any other offence would, by itself, discharge the obligation.[94] Under the universal extradition systems, which is established on a crime-by-crime basis, it is important for the obligation to

[93] See, *Questions concernant l'obligation de poursuivre ou d'extrader*, para. 120. The ILC's final report also states that extradition here cannot be replaced by extradition. See, *The Obligation to Extradite or Prosecute*, para. 22.

[94] In the Lockerbie case, there are cases where the extradition request was not filed in the US or the UK or in Libya, the State where the suspect was located, but in a court applying Scottish law at a Dutch airbase in accordance with a Security Council resolution, and it has been pointed out that "delivery" to a third State was a third way to fulfil the "prosecute or extradite" obligation. See Placha [158], p. 136.

"prosecute or extradite" not just to prosecute or extradite for some crime, but to prosecute or extradite for the specific crime that they define.[95]

The importance of which offence to extradite for seems to be a point that has been overlooked. No express rule or theory has been established as to how to govern the case of competing extradition requests for several different offenses for which a duty to "prosecute or extradite" has been established.

However, this does not mean that there is a conflict of obligation to extradite between treaties that establish a "prosecute or extradite" obligation. It is only this obligation that conflicts, which is primarily the obligation to "prosecute"—to submit the case to its competent authorities—in the event of non-extradition for the offence in question. The obligation under the universal extradition regime that establishes the "prosecute or extradite" obligation is therefore an obligation not to extradite in respect of other offences, and not an extradition obligation to comply with an extradition request for the subject offence. The direct extradition obligation is only a bilateral or regional one that is supplemented by these universal extradition systems. The apparent conflict between these obligations is then reconciled by the coordinating provisions of the bilateral or regional extradition system. However, where there are competing "prosecute or extradite" obligations, the State concerned is obliged to submit the case to its own authorities for both offences, so that a request for extradition for one of the offences does not relieve it of its obligation to prosecute the other offence by complying with that request. Thus, in this case, it is the obligation to prosecute, not the obligation to extradite under the treaty creating the "prosecute or extradite" obligation, that is in apparent conflict with the extradition obligation under other treaty. The primary requirement on the requested State is to prosecute in its own State all crimes covered by the "prosecute or extradite" obligation. If it does so, it may refuse extradition requests from any State, for example, by raising legitimate grounds such as the principle of double jeopardy.

Some treaties have coordination provisions expecting the overlap of acts subject to regulation between universal instruments. For example, the Convention against Hostage-Taking has explicit coordination provisions with the Geneva Conventions. The taking of civilians as hostages during armed conflict could theoretically constitute hostage-taking as a grave breach of the Fourth Geneva Convention as a war crime,[96] and hostage-taking as referred to in the Convention against Hostage-Taking [97] at the same time. Although these are different types of crimes and require different

---

[95] Although the ICJ decision referred here concerns the implementation of a specific treaty, the Convention against Torture, it is understood to be modelled on the so-called Hague Formula, which may also be helpful in explaining the meaning of the obligation to "prosecute or extradite" under other treaties that adopt the same formula. See, *The Obligation to Extradite or Prosecute*, para. 15.

[96] Article 147 of the Fourth Geneva Convention "Grave breaches to which the preceding Article relates shall be those involving any of the following acts, if committed against persons or property protected by the present Convention: …taking of hostages…".

[97] Article 1(1), of the Convention against the taking of hostages (hereinafter referred to as "hostage"): "Any person who seizes or detains and threatens to kill, to injure, or to continue to detain another person (hereinafter referred to as the "hostage") in order to compel a third party, namely, a State, an international intergovernmental organization, a natural or juridical person, or a group of persons, to do or abstain from doing any act as an explicit or implicit condition for the release of the

legal evaluation of the same acts by the same person, they are in fact based on the same acts and give rise to the possibility of competing extradition requests under the ICC Statute, the Fourth Geneva Convention and the Convention against Hostage-Taking respectively. However, Article 12 of the Convention against Hostage-Taking provides that in the case of hostage-taking committed during an armed conflict, the Fourth Geneva Convention or its Additional Protocols apply to such acts, and that the Hostage-Taking Convention does not apply to such acts to the extent that a State Party to the Convention is obliged by those Conventions to prosecute or extradite those who committed such acts. Article 4(2) of the Convention on the Prevention of Nuclear Terrorism also provides that the activities of armed forces regulated by international humanitarian law and in the performance of their official duties, which are regulated by other rules of international law, shall not be regulated by the said Convention. It is not clear what specific acts the provision has intended, but it is believed that the conflict with the Geneva Conventions is also reconciled in the same paragraph with regards to nuclear terrorism.

As noted above, only the Genocide Convention establishes extradition obligations with respect to genocide for the Parties to the Convention. Moreover, since there is no provision in the Genocide Convention for cases where there are competing extradition requests, it follows that, as between the Parties to the Genocide Convention, when there is a competing extradition request in respect of another crime, the extradition request in respect of genocide always takes precedence, although such an extradition obligation is considered to conflict with other universal institutional "prosecute or extradite" obligations under other universal systems.

4.3 Coordination Provisions in the ICC Statute

4.3.1 Distinction Based on Conduct

Article 90 of the ICC Statute organizes the applicable provisions not into a division between competing requests relating to the "same offence" and "different offences", but into a division between competing requests relating to the "same conduct" and "different conduct". Therefore, under the ICC Statute, if the conflicts relating to "different offences" are only different assessments of the "same conduct", the provisions on conflicts of requests relating to the "same conduct" will apply. On the other hand, if the conflicts are between requests for completely "different conduct", they are treated differently.

As mentioned above, most paragraphs in Article 90 of the ICC Statute provide for cases where extradition is requested from another State in respect of "the same conduct which forms the basis of the crime for which the Court seeks the person's surrender". Article 90(7) of the ICC Statute, on the other hand, provides for cases

hostage commits the offence of taking of hostages ("hostage-taking") within the meaning of this Convention.".

where extradition is requested by another State in respect of "conduct other than that which constitutes the crime for which the Court seeks the person's surrender".

"Conduct (*comportement*; *conducta*) which constitutes the crime" is the benck-mark of the scope of application of Article 90(2) to (6) of the ICC Statute and Article 90(7) thereof. Why the distinction by "offense/crime" was not used, as in the traditional bilateral and regional extradition regimes, is not explicitly stated, but is presumably for the sake of consistency with other provisions. In the drafting process, at the stage when Article 90 (originally Article 87(6)) was drafted on 26 June 1998, the corresponding wording was "offense", as in the previous extradition treaties.[98] But it was amended and changed to the word "conduct" at an additional session on 13 July of the same year.[99] The reason for this change was not specified. However, within the same article of the draft, there are references to other provisions on admissibility review[100] and the phrase "conduct which constitutes the crime" is adopted in Article 20(1) of the current ICC Statute, which provides for *ne bis in idem* principle. Considering the above, the adoption of the current wording is considered to reflect the adoption of the word "conduct" in the examination of the identity of the subject of the domestic investigation. Therefore, it is considered that the interpretation of the same concept in the admissibility of the ICC can be referred to for the interpretation of "conduct which constitutes the crime" as an indicator of the scope of application of each provision of Article 90.

In ICC case law, "the same conduct" for the purposes of admissibility review has been understood as referring to "substantially the same conducts by the same person".[101] Therefore, it seems that the case of overlapping conducts as a fact by the same person who is the subject of competing requests, but where the legal evaluation is different, is subject to the application of Article 90(2) to (6). On the other hand, when the subject matter of the request is for different conducts, Article 90(7) would apply even if the acts are related to each other. Thus, Article 90(7) would apply to proximate but substantially different conducts, while Article 90(2) to (6) would apply when substantially identical conducts constitute multiple core crimes or when substantially identical conducts constitute both core crimes and other international crimes.

---

[98] *Chairman's discussion paper regarding article 87*, UN Doc. A/CONF.183/C.1AVGIC/L.6 (26 June 1998), in *United Nations Diplomatic Conference of Plenipotentiaries on the Establishment of an International Criminal Court, Rome, 15 June–17 July 1998, Official Records, Volume 3, Reports and Other Documents* (United Nations, 2002) (hereinafter "*United Nations Diplomatic Conference*"), p. 323.

[99] *Draft Articles*, in *United Nations Diplomatic Conference*, p. 327.

[100] *Note regarding part 9 and articles 86, 87 bis, 90, 90 (a), 90 (b), 91 and X contained in the transmittal letter from the Chairman of the Committee of the Whole to the Chairman of the Drafting Committee dated 14 July 1998*, in *United Nations Diplomatic Conference*, p. 334.

[101] See Ochi [145].

4.3.2 Conflicting Extradition Requests as Different Offences for the Same Act

Conflicting surrender/extradition requests for the same conduct from the ICC and a third country for different crimes may result in cases where the same conduct is considered to be different core crimes, or where the same conduct simultaneously constitutes both a core crime and another international crime. For example, an act of genocide, such as murder committed with the intent to destroy a particular group, may constitute a crime against humanity when it was committed against civilians in a systematic and large-scale manner, while also constituting a serious violation of the Geneva Conventions because it occurred in the course of an armed conflict. The universal extradition system includes those under the Genocide Convention and the Geneva Conventions. As noted above, it can be problematic in cases where, pursuant to an existing extradition treaty or national law, a State requests the extradition of a person under obligations under the Genocide Convention or its "prosecution or extradition" obligations under the Geneva Conventions for the same conduct for which the ICC has requested surrender for crimes against humanity. In addition, since crimes under ICC jurisdiction are distinguished from other crimes by so-called contextual requirements, the underlying criminal conduct overlaps with other crimes. For example, torture, which constitutes a crime against humanity and a war crime, is also covered by the Convention against Torture. In addition, acts of terrorism committed with discriminatory intent can constitute genocide.

As we have already seen, under the Statute, any apparent conflict of extradition obligations between ICC State Parties for the same conduct is resolved by the coordination provisions of Article 90(2), (4) and (6) of the ICC Statute, which give priority to the request from the ICC. However, it is noteworthy that in cases where the same conducts constitute different crimes, the gravity of the subject crimes is not listed as a criterion for consideration in paragraph 6 when the State making the competing extradition request is not a State Party to the ICC Statute and an "international obligation to extradite" exists. In other words, even if an ICC State Party receives an surrender request from the ICC for the crime of genocide against a person who, for example, committed incitement to genocide, it is not prohibited to extradite the person for a crime that is generally regarded as less serious, such as defamation, which has been constituted by a statement of intent to commit genocide, to a non-State Party that has an extradition treaty with the requested State without considering the gravity of the crimes.

On the other hand, competing requests for offences which are the subject of an obligation to "prosecute or extradite" would be covered by paragraph 4. Paragraph 6 expressly provides for cases where there is an international obligation "to extradite" and cannot be interpreted as intended to apply that provision where there is an obligation to "prosecute or extradite" for other offences. Since the "prosecute or extradite" obligation establishes an obligation to prosecute rather than an obligation to extradite, it is the obligation to prosecute for offences covered by the "prosecute or extradite" obligation under the Geneva Conventions that conflicts with the obligation to respond to surrender request from the ICC. If it is reasonable to interpret such an obligation as an obligation not to extradite for other crimes, then there would appear to be a conflict between the obligation from the ICC to respond to surrender request for genocide and crimes against humanity and the obligation not to extradite for other than war crimes. However, the obligation to "prosecute or extradite" is only an obligation "not to extradite". Therefore, if there is an obligation to "prosecute or extradite" core crimes that are different from the crimes for which extradition is sought from the ICC, they fall within the scope of Article 90(4) of the ICC Statute, and it is reasonable to rule that surrender to the ICC takes precedence, but they are in conflict with the obligation of the requested State to prosecute them in its own State.

4.3.3 Competing Requests for Different Conducts

An example of a conflict between an surrender request from the ICC for different conducts and an extradition request relating to a non-core crime would be, for example, a case in which the accused is a leader of a terrorist organization that committed both genocide and terrorism bombings, and in which the ICC surrender request for incitement to genocide and the extradition request from another State for abetting a bomb attack may be in conflict. The provisions in the ICC Statute regarding competing surrender/extradition requests for different conducts are applicable regardless of whether the requesting State is a State Party to the Statute.

Article 90(7)(a) of the ICC Statute provides that a request from the ICC shall prevail if the requesting State does not have an international obligation to extradite in respect of the person concerned. As noted earlier, because the "prosecute or extradite" obligation establishes a duty to prosecute rather than an obligation to extradite, it is the obligation to prosecute crimes covered by the "prosecute or extradite" obligation, such as bombings and torture, that conflict with the obligation to respond to surrender request from the ICC. Since the "prosecute or extradite" obligation is only an obligation not to extradite and not an obligation to extradite, it is reasonable to rule that if there is an obligation to "prosecute or extradite" for a crime different from the crimes subject to surrender request from the ICC, Article 90(7)(a) of the ICC Statute applies and surrender to the ICC takes priority. Therefore, there is a conflict between the obligation to give priority to surrender to the ICC and the obligation to prosecute for bombings and torture in one's own State.

Secondly, according to Article 90(7)(b) of the ICC Statute, in the case of competing requests for extradition in respect of different conducts and when the requested State is subject to an international obligation to extradite, the requested State shall consider all relevant matters in addition to those listed in paragraph 6, namely, "the relative nature and gravity of the conduct in question". As we have already seen, extradition obligations under bilateral or regional extradition treaties and under the Genocide Convention are "international obligations to extradite". Thus, when extradition is requested for the crimes under ICC jurisdiction or other international crimes based on a bilateral or regional instrument or the Genocide Convention, the requested State decides at its discretion, but there are statutory considerations to be taken into account.

Under the ICC Statute, since the Statute gives the requested State the discretion to decide, the obligations under these provisions are not in conflict.

5 Reflection of the Gravity of Core Crimes

As the extradition system has become more multi-layered and complex, the relationship between the rules when multiple extradition requests are made against the same person has also become more complex. In examining the cases of competing extradition requests for the same offence and competing extradition requests for different offences, it was found that, although there were some situations where there was a possible conflict of obligations, the coordination provisions providing for priority and discretion generally functioned to resolve the conflict. However, in the actual application of the priority and discretionary provisions, in addition to the elements of the location of the crime and the determination of nationality, the content of the standard of gravity of the crime, which is particularly vague, can be problematic. In what follows, I focus on the standard of gravity in the application of these coordination provisions and consider how the consideration of the seriousness of the extradition offence, and in particular the gravity of the core crime, is considered in the determination of the destination of extradition.

5.1 Gravity in Priority Provisions

Among the various coordination provisions, some treaties mention gravity as an express prioritizing condition. Conflicts of obligation could become an issue when there is a conflict with a request for extradition from a State that is Party to an extradition treaty that has a priority provision other than gravity.

As we have seen above, the priority provisions that prioritize the first request and that prioritize the request for a more serious crime conflict when the first extradition request is for a lesser offence. For example, Article 10 of the Extradition Treaty between Spain and Colombia of 1892 provides that the person shall be handed over to the State where the request was first made,[102] while Article 21 of the Extradition Treaty between Colombia and Costa Rica of 1928, to which Colombia is also a Party, provides that priority is given to extradition to the State where the most serious crime was committed.[103] Unless one or both of these treaties have been terminated

[102] Convention on Extradition (Colombia-Spain), 1721 UNTS 418, Article 10.

[103] Treaty on Extradition between the Republic of Colombia and the Republic of Costa Rica, 2411 UNTS 12, Article 21.

or amended, the obligations under the priority provisions of these two treaties may conflict.[104]

Although there are no reported actual cases in which a situation where a prior extradition request was made for a lesser offence, in theory, a *prima facie* conflict of law does exist that would warrant the development of customary law reconciling the priority provisions for prior extradition requests with the priority provisions for extradition requests for the more serious offence. If the customary law is that the requested State determines the destination of extradition at its discretion, taking into account various circumstances, and if this customary law has been formed since as early as the 1940s, then it is reasonable under the principle of *lex posterior* that, when there is a conflict of obligations under the priority provisions, the requested State has the discretion to decide which priority provision is to be taken into account in determining the destination of extradition. However, if that were the case, the significance of the priority provision, which was placed as a special law different from customary law, would be lost. As an interpretation of customary law to reconcile these issues, it seems reasonable to consider that, where there is a priority provision, the requested State is required to give special consideration to matters particularly specified in the priority provision when exercising its discretion.

A particular potential problem in relation to the core crimes is when there is a conflict between an extradition request from a Party to an extradition treaty with a priority provision for grave crimes and a surrender request from the ICC. In the case of a conflict between a request for extradition based on a treaty with a priority provision and a request based on a treaty with a discretionary provision, the latter grants discretion and the requested State will make a decision in accordance with the priority provision of the former, provided that the decision does not amount to an abuse of discretion so as not to violate the priority provision with the former Party. Article 90(7)(b) of the ICC Statute gives the requested State the discretion to determine the destination of surrender/extradition in cases where a request for extradition is made by a non-State Party to the Statute to which the requested State has an international obligation to make extradition to that State. Therefore, if the State which is requested to surrender by the ICC is a Party to the Inter-American Convention on Extradition and another Party to the Convention requests extradition from that State for an offense different from the offense for which the ICC surrender request was made, the requested State must determine the destination of surrender/extradition based on the priority provision of Article 15 of the Convention, namely for the gravity of two possible sentences. The ICC statutory penalty for all crimes under its jurisdiction is either an imprisonment for a specific number of years not exceeding a maximum of 30 years or, if justified by the extreme gravity of the offence and the individual circumstances of the person so convicted, a life imprisonment.[105]

[104] Colombia and Costa Rica are parties to the 1981 Inter-American Convention on Extradition, but Article 33 of that Convention does not supersede any multilateral or bilateral treaty already in force unless expressly declared or agreed to by the parties, and no such declaration or agreement has been reported between those two States. Department of International Law, OAS, at http://www.oas.org/juridico/english/sigs/b-47.html.

[105] Rule 77(1)(a) and (b) of the ICC Rules.

If competing requests made by Parties to the Inter-American Convention on Extradition are made for crimes subject to the death penalty, since it is more severe than the ICC's statutory penalty, extradition to the State making such requests would take precedence according to Article 15 of the Convention. However, in the event that a request for extradition from a Party to the Convention, which abstractly provides that priority is given to extradition to "the State in which the most serious crime has been committed," conflicts with a request for surrender from the ICC, the requested State will compare the seriousness of the crimes for which extradition is requested and make a decision, and in this decision, the fact that the core crimes are said to be "the most serious crimes" will be taken into account.

5.2 *Gravity in Discretionary Provisions*

In discretionary provisions, the gravity of the offence is enumerated as an element for consideration. The discretionary provisions of many bilateral extradition treaties, including Article 16 of the Model Treaty, and regional treaties, such as Article 17 of the European Convention on Extradition and Article 23 of the ECOWAS Extradition Convention, list the (relative) gravity of the offence as a consideration, in addition to the time and place of commission of the offence, the date of the request, the nationality and residence of the extradition subject and whether the extradition is treaty-based. The ICC Statute also provides that the (relative) gravity of the offence is a matter for consideration. The coordination provisions of the ICC Statute also provide that where there is an international obligation to a requesting State that is not a State Party to the Statute, gravity is not a consideration in the case of competing requests for the same conduct, whereas in the case of competing requests for different conducts, Article 90(7)(b) of the Statute provides that the requested State "shall give special consideration to the relative nature and gravity of the conduct in question".

When gravity is not the only matter to be considered, other matters may be given more weight, and the seriousness of the offence may have no effect on the decision. For example, in the 1987 Swiss Federal Court case referred to above, a competing extradition request was filed against Switzerland, where the accused, an Italian national, was located, by Belgium, the place of execution of several armed attacks and hostage-taking acts against banks and post offices, and by Italy, the place of execution of a single armed attack against a jewellery shop. The Swiss Federal Court, approving an administrative decision that took into account the considerations under Article 17 of the European Convention on Extradition, namely, in addition to the gravity, the number of offences and the nationality, and in particular the improbability of subsequent extradition, decided to extradite the suspect to Belgium and rejected the extradition request from Italy.[106] In this case, the issue was also that the hostage acts committed in Belgium were crimes punishable by death, but what was decisive was that there was no possibility of a subsequent extradition from Italy to

[106] *C v. Federal Police Department*, 100 ILR 657, 661.

Belgium due to Italian law that prohibit extradition of its own nationals. The importance attached to the possibility of subsequent extradition as a measure to satisfy the prosecution interests of both States making extradition requests is a decision which consequently serves the interests of all the States concerned. If that is so, it can be assumed that the requested State may decide to give priority to extradition to a State that has the possibility of extradition later, even when, as in the present case, crimes of high gravity, such as hostage-taking and core crimes, were committed in a State that adopts non-extradition of its nationals.[107]

5.3 Two Meanings of "Gravity"

The question of what standard of gravity is to be determined in a coordination provision is an issue in the interpretation of a coordination provision regardless of whether it is a priority or discretionary provision. In the priority provision, the meaning of gravity as a criterion for its application will be questioned, while in the discretionary provision, the meaning of gravity as a question of the scope of discretion will be an issue.

The priority provisions can be categorized into the following three ways of stipulating gravity: (i) to provide priority for the request by a State that requests extradition for crimes that are "considered to be the most serious"—e.g. 1922 Extradition Treaty between Czechoslovakia and Italy, (ii) to provide priority for the State in which the offense considered to be the most serious was committed—e.g. 1919 Extradition Treaty between Brazil and Peru; 1928 Extradition Treaty between Costa Rica and Colombia, and (iii) to stipulate priority for the State making the claim for the offense punishable by the most severe penalty—Article 15 of the Inter-American Extradition Treaty. On the other hand, the gravity included in discretionary provisions is (iv) the relative seriousness/gravity of the offenses—e.g. 1956 Extradition Treaty between Israel and Italy; 1963 Extradition Treaty between the UK and Sweden[108]—and simply (v) the seriousness/gravity of the offenses—e.g. 1971 Extradition Treaty between Belgium and Yugoslavia[109], 1976 Extradition Treaty between Indonesia and the Philippines[110], 2002 Extradition Treaty between Japan and South Korea.

The provisions of (i) crimes *considered to be* the most serious and (ii) State in which the crimes *considered to be* the most serious were committed can be regarded as giving the requested State the discretion to determine the seriousness of the crimes. This is a standard that combines the principle of the territoriality and the seriousness of the crime. In many cases, the criterion for determining the gravity of the crime

[107] Extradition and Judicial Assistance in Criminal Matters (Israel–Italy), 316 UNTS 97, Article 13.

[108] Extradition Treaty (the United Kingdom-Sweden), 590 UNTS 117, Article 14.

[109] Convention concerning Extradition and Judicial Assistance in Criminal Matters Belgium-Yugoslavia (Socialist Federal Republic of), 590 UNTS 117, Article 15.

[110] Extradition Treaty (Indonesia-Philippines), 1031 UNTS 225, Article 18.

is not statutory. However, Article 14 of the 1946 Extradition Treaty between Iraq and Turkey explicitly stipulates that the gravity of the crime shall be determined in accordance with the law of the requested State. In addition, (iii) criteria of the Inter-American Convention on Extradition, which establishes priority for crimes punishable by the most severe sentences, are relatively clear. (iv) the parties to an extradition treaty compare the statutory penalties in their respective States for crimes subject to competing requests, and priority is given to the State requesting extradition for the most severe penalty. (v) In discretionary provisions stating that the relative seriousness of the crimes or (vi) gravity of the crimes will be taken into consideration, few explicitly state the criteria for determining the gravity of the crimes.

Thus, although the criteria for determining the gravity of a crime are not clear from the language in bilateral or regional extradition treaties, two meanings of gravity can be inferred by a consideration of the coordination provisions in the ICC Statute. One is the gravity of the conduct itself, such as the scale, nature, manner, and impact of the crime and the other is the gravity/seriousness of the nature of the crime.

Article 90(7)(b) of the ICC Statute provides that where competing requests for different conducts are made by non-State Parties to the Statute and there is an international obligation to extradite the State concerned, in addition to consideration of all relevant matters, such as the date of the request, the interests of the requesting State—such as the place of commission of the crime and the nationality of the victim and extradition subject, and the likelihood of subsequent extradition from the requesting State to the ICC, "special consideration" must be given to the "relative gravity and nature" of the conduct. However, it is not always clear how this "relative gravity or nature" should be considered in the context of competing extradition requests for core crimes and other international crimes. It is not clear how this language was inserted in the drafting process, but it has been commented that at the time of drafting there was probably an assumption that the crimes to be prosecuted by the ICC would always be the gravest.[111]

The relative gravity and nature of the crimes referred to in the ICC Statute can be discussed in the following manner based on the judicial practice regarding other provisions of the Statute. The ICC Statute states in its preamble that the ICC has jurisdiction over "the most serious crimes of concern to the international community as a whole". Thus, the preamble of the ICC Statute uses the word "the most serious", while Article 90(7)(b) of the Statute adopts the word "gravity". That is, the concept of "seriousness" is inherent in the criminal concept of the crimes under the jurisdiction of the ICC, while the concept of "gravity" is an additional property of what "serious" crimes are worthy of prosecution at the ICC.[112] "Gravity" is one of the criteria for reviewing the admissibility of a case, as set out in Article 17 of the ICC Statute, and is said to consist of four elements: the scale, nature, manner and impact of the specific

[111] However, recent trends suggest that this assumption is not always valid. Schabas [181], p. 1006.

[112] *Prosecutor v. Lubanga,* Decision concerning Pre-Trial Chamber I's Decision of 10 February 2006 and the Incorporation of Documents into the Record of the Case against Mr. Thomas Lubanga Dyilo (ICC-01/04-01/06-8-Corr) Pre-Trial Chamber I (24 February 2006), para. 42.

crime committed.[113] If "gravity" within the meaning of Article 90(7)(b) is "gravity" in this sense , then surrender or extradition for core crimes must be prioritized not because it is for one of the core crimes which are deemed to be the most "serious", but because the specific crime in question has a higher "gravity" in terms of the conduct in committing the offence, such as its scale, nature, manner and impact. Thus, the relative "gravity" specified in Article 90(7)(b) does not mean that, for example, in the case of genocide and terrorism, genocide is "more serious" than terrorism, but rather that when the scale, nature, manner and impact of the genocide is compared with the scale, nature, manner and impact of the terrorism, which act has the higher "gravity" must be determined.

On the other hand, as for the relative "nature", the expression seems to refer to the "seriousness" of the crime. In the ICC's decision to authorize the investigation of the Kenyan situation, the "nature" was discussed as one of the elements of "gravity". As the "nature" of the crimes in this situation, the brutality of the acts, such as mutilation of the human body by *matute*, poisoned arrows, broken glass, setting fire to the body alive, setting up checkpoints to select victims based on race, mutilation until death, gang rape and genital mutilation.[114] However, even core crimes are not necessarily more brutal than acts of terrorism. For example, in the ICC's 2016 *Al-Mahdi* case judgment, the accused were found guilty of war crimes involving the destruction of religious and historical buildings.[115] While the discriminatory intent against local indigenous beliefs aggravated the gravity of the act, the act itself was the destruction of a building, which is hardly more atrocious in comparison to atrocities against the human body. On the other hand, hostage-taking, bombings, and nuclear terrorism, for example, among the terrorist acts stipulated by the UN conventions on the prevention of terrorism, are assumed to result in cruelty to the human body. However, if this interpretation is taken, it means that only one of the criteria for relative seriousness has been extracted and given special treatment, and the reason for this is not clear.

Therefore, the "nature" referred to in Article 90(7)(b) of the ICC Statute should be considered as referring to "seriousness", which is different from the standard for determining gravity in Article 17. The nature of the core crimes and the nature of other international crimes should be judged comprehensively, considering the protected legal interests, the requirements of the crimes, the history of the concept, and so on. While the preamble of the ICC Statute describes the nature of crimes under ICC jurisdiction as "the most serious crimes of concern to the international community as a whole"—for example, the preamble of the Convention against the taking of hostages describes hostage-taking as "an offence of grave concern to the international community"—the preamble of the Convention against Terrorist Bombings and the preamble of the Convention against the Financing of Terrorism describe the subject

[113] ICC Prosecutor's Rule 29. See also, Ochi [143]. It is noted, however, that these four elements are an illustrative enumeration and there is an inherent discretionary element. Murai [132], pp. 493–494.

[114] *Situation in the Republic of Kenya*, Decision Pursuant to Article 15 of the Rome Statute on the Authorization of an Investigation into the Republic of Kenya (ICC-01/09-19-Corr) Pre-Trial Chamber II (31 March 2010), para. 192.

[115] *Prosecutor v. Al Mahdi*, Judgment and Sentence (ICC-01/12-01/15-171) Trial Chamber VIII (27 September 2016).

crimes as "a matter of grave concern to the international community as a whole". The preamble of the Convention on the Prevention of Nuclear Terrorism states that acts of nuclear terrorism "may result in the gravest consequences". If only the wording is taken, the crimes under the jurisdiction of the ICC are "most serious," terrorist acts other than nuclear terrorism are "grave," and nuclear terrorism is a crime that "may result in the gravest consequences".

In light of the above, the criterion of the gravity of the crime in the determination of extradition destination can generally have two meanings: the gravity of the criminal act and the gravity of the criminal concept. The fact that the core crimes have so-called contextual elements that distinguish them from ordinary crimes,[116] and the gravity of the nature of the core crimes from the perspective that their protected legal interests belong to the international community,[117] can be considered as the content of the gravity of the criminal concept in the criteria of seriousness specified as a matter of priority or consideration when determining the extradition destination. The criteria of gravity, however, include the gravity of the concept of the offence. But since the criteria of gravity include not only the gravity of the criminal concept but also the gravity of the criminal conduct, depending on the scale, manner, nature, and impact, in applying the criteria of gravity in the coordination provisions, extradition may be granted to the crime with the higher gravity of the act even if the gravity of the criminal concept is relatively low.

6 Conclusion

This chapter has examined the rules on the conflict and priority of extradition obligations in relation to international crimes and considered how the gravity criterion is applied in determining the destination of extradition/surrender. The international system based on the extradition treaties can be classified into four types of systems: bilateral, regional, universal, and vertical, from the viewpoint of the relationship with the other Party of the obligation. Since these extradition systems impose multilayered obligations, it can be assumed that States may receive extradition requests from several States under separate extradition systems. Conflicting extradition requests for the same offence have been disciplined mainly by placing provisions giving discretion to the requested State. On the other hand, conflicts between extradition requests for different offences are regulated by priority provisions, such as giving priority to earlier requests or extradition requests for more serious offences, and by discretionary provisions giving the requested State the discretion to decide. The criterion of the gravity of the offence contained in these coordination provisions is debatable in various situations and can have two meanings: the gravity of the criminal conduct in terms of the scale, nature, manner and impact, and the gravity of the nature of the concept of the crime.

[116] Jessberger and Werle [89], p. 35; Sakamoto [175], p. 30.

[117] Cassese [31], p. 11; Cassese and Gaeta [28], p. 20.

The issue of gravity—whether the core crimes are in fact considered more core and serious than other crimes—has been considered a key feature of core crimes. The implications of my examination of this issue for the premise of international criminal justice are as follows. First, among core crimes, only genocide is a crime for which extradition is obligated by the Genocide Convention and has no coordination provisions. Therefore, extradition with respect to genocide must basically be given priority, even if there are competing extradition requests for other crimes. Secondly, however, except for the Genocide Convention, there is no rule in any of the extradition regimes that gives priority by virtue of the fact that the subject offence is a core crime. The multilateral treaties concluded for each crime only ensure the "prosecution or extradition" of the respective target crimes, and none of them have provided for the relationship between the gravity of their subject crimes and the core crimes. Nor is the gravity of the offence a consideration in relation to competing extradition requests for the same offence between extradition to the ICC and mandatory extradition to a State not party to the Statute. Third, there are a number of provisions that take into account the gravity of the offence in the case of competing extradition requests for different offences. Although a more detailed examination of execution would be required to determine the criteria for this, the two meanings of gravity suggest that the gravity/seriousness of the core crime will be considered when assessing not only the gravity of the conduct, but also the gravity of the crime in the sense of the nature of the criminal concept itself.

The lack of prioritization for surrender/extradition for core crimes can be attributed to the fact that while core crimes are terminologically the "most serious crimes", the establishment of systems for their prosecution has taken a back seat, while various forms of crime of political importance and security necessity, such as transnational organized crime and terrorism, have arisen and responses to them have taken precedence. The ILC notes that there is a serious gap to be filled in the current treaty regime governing "prosecution or extradition" obligations.[118] It is the lack of an international treaty that places such obligations on some core crimes, namely many of the crimes against humanity, war crimes other than grave breaches, and war crimes in non-international armed conflicts.[119]

The fact that international responses to international crimes have been taken on an individual crime-by-crime basis has contributed to the complexity of the current extradition system. There are many challenges in building a system to prevent crimes that are harmful to the common interests of the international community through cooperation, but if we aim at an effective system, some systematization and coordination of customary law or general principles, including a hierarchy among crimes based on State implementation, will be necessary. There are some difficulties in attempting to systematize international crimes, such as the fact that the ICC Statute does not specify the degree of severity of punishment for each crime, the fact that the accumulation of precedents is still insufficient, and the fact that different States have different views on crimes. However, if this can be partially achieved, or at least

---

118 *The Obligation to Extradite or Prosecute*, para. 14.

119 *Ibid*.

some indicators can be established, consistency will be created among the procedural systems established for each treaty, and the relationship of application among treaties will become clearer. In order to achieve this, it is necessary to review the protected legal interests of crimes that have been the subject of international responses, and to identify indicators of the gravity of the crimes that can be derived from the various practices.

Chapter 4
Principles Prohibiting Trials *in Absentia*

Abstract This chapter considers the principle of prohibition of trials *in absentia* in international criminal justice and examines the impact of premises specific to international criminal justice on the scope of exceptions to the principle. It first confirms the two theoretical bases of the principle of prohibition of trials *in absentia*: accuracy of trial and the rights of the accused to be present. Through an analysis of the substantive impact of the identified legal principles on the particularities of the field of international criminal justice, it finds that the impact of the premises of international criminal justice on the current version of the principle is very limited. On the other hand, a one-sided trial that violates the rights of suspects and accused persons cannot be justified and cannot fulfil the purposes of the "punitive performance". A common understanding is that the ICC should not allow distortion of legal principles on the grounds of practical obstacles, such as the lack of cooperation from States and the inability to make arrests.

1 Introduction

The principle that the accused must appear in court in a criminal trial—the principle of no trial *in absentia* or the principle of the presence of the accused—seems at first glance to be a given in the modern criminal justice system, which uses a three-party system—prosecutor, accused and judge. However, as with many legal principles, the content of this principle differs greatly from one legal system to another. Moreover, being a principle, it usually has a number of exceptions, the scope of which is determined by a variety of factors. Furthermore, in international criminal trials for core crimes of international concern, such as genocide and crimes against humanity, there is a stronger demand for exceptions to the principle of prohibition of trials *in absentia* than in ordinary domestic trials.

The scale of core crimes causes a large number of victims and arouses strong international interest. At the same time, however, it is not easy to secure the cooperation for arrest and investigation from the State where the crime occurred or the State where the suspect is located, which is necessary for the apprehension of suspects.

M. Ochi, *The Premises of International Criminal Procedure*,
https://doi.org/10.1007/978-981-97-6786-1_4

Times have changed since the international trials against the Nazis, the earliest implementation of international criminal justice in which proceedings were also held in the absence of the accused, and today the principle of no trial *in absentia* is included in international human rights instruments as a human right of the accused. Nevertheless, in recent years, there has again been a certain rise in the acceptance of trials *in absentia* in international criminal justice.[1] Many of the objectives of international criminal justice, such as damage recognition, reparation, historical determination, and political messages, can be achieved in the absence of the accused. The debate over whether or not to allow trials *in absentia* raises fundamental questions about the purpose of international criminal justice and what it means to be effective.

This chapter considers the principle of prohibition of trials *in absentia* in international criminal justice and examines the impact of premises specific to international criminal justice on the scope of exceptions to the principle.[2] Note that "trial *in absentia*" in this chapter refers to a trial hearings *in absentia*—excluding preliminary hearing proceedings. The term "presence in court" conceptually means effective representation by the accused himself/herself[3] and includes not only physical appearances but also appearances by IT means yet does not include appearances by counsel only.

The following section confirms the theoretical basis of the principle of prohibition of trials *in absentia* through an overview of existing studies on comparative law, and then examines whether the principle can be regarded as a source of international law and international criminal procedure and its content through a comparative analysis of related laws and regulations to confirm their commonality. Then, through an analysis of the substantive impact of the identified legal principles on the particularities of the field of international criminal justice, it discusses what international criminal justice as an institution aims to achieve.

2 The Rationale for the Prohibition of Trial *in Absentia*: Effective Trial and the Right to be Present in Court

According to existing studies in comparative law, the scope of prohibition of trial *in absentia* differs between the Continental legal system and the Anglo–American legal system. In the discussions during the drafting process of the ICC Statute in which many of the member States of the UN participated, States mainly with Continental legal systems proposed a system that would allow more trials without the accused, while States with Anglo–American legal systems mainly argued that trials without the accused should be limited as much as possible.[4] These differences in opinion are influenced by the ideology on which each State's criminal justice system stands

[1] See Inazumi [79], p. 17.

[2] For more information on the premise concept, see Ochi [149].

[3] Zakerhossein and De Brouwer [255], p. 183.

[4] Friman [56], p. 256.

and its relationship to the system as a whole. The rationale for the necessity of the defendant's presence in a criminal trial may also differ between the Continental and Anglo–American legal systems. In the following, I will examine the basic rationale for the principle of prohibition of *in absentia* in criminal trials based on an overview of existing studies on this principle in each model of criminal procedure.

2.1 Accuracy of Trial

Generally, in Continental legal systems that adopt the inquisitorial method, the judges themselves take the initiative in discovering the truth, and the importance of the presence of the accused and defence counsel in court proceedings is relatively lower than that of the adversarial system. For example, German court proceedings are characterized by the distinction between the accused and the defence counsel, and the accused is guaranteed the opportunity to directly express his/her opinion in court.[5] In the first place, the ultimate purpose of inquisitorial criminal justice is to impose punishment on the perpetrator of the crime, not to bring the criminal to court to be judged in full view of the court, and therefore the very nature of a trial does not require the presence of the accused.[6] Rather, the accused is the object of the proceedings and is viewed as a method of evidence as the object of the investigation.[7] In other words, it is necessary for the judge to bring the accused to appear in court in order to fully hear and discover the truth about the case and to ascertain the accuracy of his or her testimony. For this reason, some States with Continental legal systems set the defendant's appearance in court as mandatory. Therefore, the so-called duty to appear at trial is essentially based on the State's interest in avoiding a mistrial.[8] On the other hand, the right of the accused to have his or her arguments heard before the court is guaranteed as the right to a hearing.[9]

In these respects, the principle of prohibition of trial *in absentia* in Continental law has as its main purpose the maintenance of the accuracy of the proceedings at trial, and the presence of the accused in court is not considered absolutely necessary, which is fundamental to the trial procedure. Therefore, cases in which a trial can be conducted *in absentia* can be widely recognized.

---

[5] Thus, in comparative studies of German criminal procedure from an American perspective, German court procedure has been described as 'delawyerized'; Langbein [112], p. 66.

[6] Miyamoto [127], p. 41.

[7] Roxin [169], p. 141.

[8] *Ibid.*, p. 438.

[9] E.g., Article 103 of the German Basic Law, Articles 201, 243, 258(2) of the Code of Criminal Procedure, etc.

2.2 *Presence as a Right*

In the Anglo–American legal system, the judge is, in principle, supposed to be an impartial referee between adversarial parties. Therefore, it is considered a fundamental and most important element of court proceedings to ensure that the parties to a lawsuit, the prosecutor and the accused, have a forum for fair discussion with their rights fully guaranteed.[10] Based on the adversarial concept, in addition to the traditional guarantees of the right to be heard[11] and in the UK the right to confrontation of witnesses, the accused must be guaranteed the right to be physically present in court during the testimony against him or her.[12] In this way, the accused is not viewed as the object of the lawsuit, but is placed in the status of a Party to the lawsuit, and presence in court is constituted as a right. Therefore, in Anglo–American law, since the presence of the accused in court proceedings is regarded as a matter that is fundamental to litigation, if the accused is absent when the trial commences, the trial basically does not proceed.

The presence of the accused is also considered necessary to ensure the accuracy of the trial, as the discovery of truth is believed to be secured by more active litigation taking place orally at trial.[13]

3 Comparison of Laws and Regulations on the Principle of no Trial *in Absentia*

In international law, "general principles of law" found by the court in principles common to various laws can be applied as a source of law [Article 38(1)(c) of the Statute of the ICJ].[14] In addition, the standards of human rights protection guaranteed in various international human rights instruments, various human rights courts, and national constitutions have recently been applied as "internationally recognized human rights" standards in various International Criminal Justice Institutions—e.g., Article 21(3) of the ICC Statute. In addition, "general principles" that take into account the premise of more specific areas of law, have also been widely applied in judicial precedents.[15] In order to ascertain how common the rationale for requiring the presence of the accused is in the relevant statutes, and what exceptions have been made, a comparative analysis of the existing statutes on the presence of the accused now follows.

---

[10] Jalloh [85], p. 137.

[11] *R v Preston* [1993] 2 AC 130.

[12] Del Carmen [41], pp. 380–381.

[13] Miyamoto [127], p. 42.

[14] On the difference between "general principles of law" in international law and "general principles of law" in international criminal law, see Ochi [149].

[15] *Ibid.*, see Chap. 3.

3.1 *Commonality of the Principle of Prohibition of Trial* in Absentia

A comparative study of the various laws and regulations on whether the accused must be present in court at trial can be summarized to point out the commonality of the principle of prohibition of trial *in absentia* and the exceptions to that principle, respectively. Although the scope is diverse in general, the principle is that the accused must be present at the trial, and the reasons for and scope of exceptions to the principle are set forth when the trial is held *in absentia.*

First, the first sentence of Article 14(3)(d) of the International Covenant on Civil and Political Rights ("ICCPR") stipulates that a person has the right to be guaranteed "To be tried in his presence, and to defend himself in person or through legal assistance of his own choosing". Article 6 of the European Convention on Human Rights also provides the right to a fair trial. However, Article 6(3)(c) did not directly stipulate the right to be present during the trial, stating that the accused has the right "to defend himself in person or through legal assistance of his own choosing". Nor is there any reference in the provisions of Article 8 of the Inter-American Convention on Human Rights, which establishes the right to a fair trial, that the accused must be present in court. However, paragraph 2(d) of the same article provides, as in the European Convention on Human Right, "the right of the accused to defend himself personally" must be guaranteed. The African Charter on the Rights of Persons and Peoples also provides for the right to defence in Article 7, which provides for the right to a trial.[16]

Article 75(4) of Additional Protocol I to the Geneva Conventions providing for the protection of victims of international armed conflict provides that the basic guarantees include "(e) anyone charged with an offence shall have the right to be tried in his presence" and "(g) anyone charged with an offence shall have the right to examine, or have examined, the witnesses against him and to obtain the attendance and examination of witnesses on his behalf under the same conditions as witnesses against him". In non-international armed conflicts, as one of the minimum guarantees, the imposition of sentences and the execution of sentences, without trial, is prohibited on persons who do not directly participate in the hostilities, in duly constituted courts, giving them all the guarantees which a civilized people find essential (Common Article 3, Geneva Conventions). Article 6(2)(e) of Additional Protocol II to the Geneva Conventions also prohibits, as an essential guarantee, the pronouncement of guilt and the imposition of sentence not by a court of independence and impartiality but provides in particular that anyone accused of a crime has the right to attend and be tried in person.[17]

---

[16] The African Commission on Human and Peoples' Rights has issued an opinion that the guarantee of the right to a retrial is a permissible condition for a trial in absentia. *Principles and Guidelines on the Right to a Fair Trial and Legal Assistance in Africa*, DOC/OS(XXX)247 (2003), 15.

[17] While the drafting process of the provision stated that "all persons" were entitled to the right, it was reported that, due to opposition from States that allow trials in absentia in their States, the adopted provision only understood that it was up to the accused to decide

Some conventions on international criminal justice cooperation provide grounds for mandatory refusal of extradition to prevent a conviction resulting from a trial *in absentia* being enforced if the suspect is extradited. Article 3(g) of the Model Treaty on Extradition states that extradition must be refused where (i) the judgment of the requesting State is delivered in the absence of the accused, (ii) the convicted person has not received adequate notice of the trial or the opportunity to coordinate his or her own defence, and (iii) there is or was no opportunity to have a retrial in person.[18] Commentaries confirm that interpretive issues remain regarding the conditions in (i), including whether to require mere physical presence, whether presence only at the beginning of the proceedings is acceptable, and whether cases where the defendant physically interferes with the trial by participating in another room through audiovisual equipment, or through counsel when he or she physically interferes with the trial, should be included. These vary from State to State.[19] On the other hand, a number of treaties provide for the refusal of extradition in response to a request for extradition based on a trial in the absence of the accused as optional rather than mandatory. For example, the European Convention on Extradition did not originally provide for a provision on trial in the absence of the accused, but Article 3 of Additional Protocol II of 1978 added a provision on refusal of extradition in the absence of the accused. The added provision provides that, unless adequate guarantees of rights are provided, the State against whom extradition is sought may refuse to extradite in the absence of the accused, if the extradition request is for the execution of a sentence imposed by a judgment in the accused's absence and for a restraining order made by such a decision (Article 3, first sentence of Additional Protocol II to the European Convention on Extradition of Offenders).

As seen above, in the national laws of various States, exceptions are made to the issue of the presence of the accused in court in many Continental law systems, such as Germany [Article 103(1) of the Basic Law, Articles 232 and 276 et seq. of the Code of Criminal Procedure] and France [Articles 410 to 416 et seq. of the Code of Criminal Procedure], whereas in Anglo–American law systems, for example in the US (the Sixth and Fourteenth Amendments to the Constitution), it is a matter of right. In recent years, however, human rights treaties have been adopted in many Continental law systems. On the other hand, the approximation between these two legal systems has been observed due to the requirements under human rights treaties and the necessity to allow trial *in absentia* as an exception, and the rules have become

whether to exercise the right. *Protocol Additional to the Geneva Conventions of 12 August 1949, and relating to the Protection of Victims of Non-International Armed Conflicts (Protocol II), 8 June 1977,* Commentary of 1987 Penal Prosecutions (International Committee of the Red Cross) at https://ihl-databases.icrc.org/applic/ihl/ihl.nsf/Comment.xsp?action=openDocument&documentId=C6692EB184B56F56C12563CD0043A476 (as of 29 March 2021).

[18] The commentary states that if all of these conditions (i) to (iii) are not met, it is not a ground for mandatory refusal of extradition. United Nations Office of Drugs and Crimes, *Revised Manuals on the Model Treaty on Extradition and on the Model Treaty on Mutual Assistance in Criminal Matters* (8 December 2002), at https://www.unodc.org/pdf/model_treaty_extradition_revised_manual.pdf (as of 27 December 2021), para. 60.

[19] *Ibid.*

more complex. There have been several cases where the European Court of Human Rights has found the system of trial *in absentia* in domestic criminal proceedings to be in breach of the European Convention on Human Rights and the defending State has amended domestic laws belonging to the Continental legal system.[20]

Thus, the principle of prohibition of trial *in absentia* is common to the various laws at an abstract level. Even in the drafting process of the ICC Statute, while international law did not provide a clear answer as to whether trial in the absence of the accused should be permissible, and there was diversity in the practice of the States, there was no dispute that the accused should be present during the trial in principle.[21] Such a principle may be seen as a "general principle of law", "internationally recognized human rights" standards, or a general principle for each area of law. The question is whether and to what extent there are exceptions to these principles, which will be identified below.

3.2 *Conditions of Exception*

The conditions for the exception that a trial in the absence of the accused is permissible are complex and vary from one statute to another. A comparative legal analysis suggests that, broadly, they can be organized as follows, depending on the combination of the three predicate circumstances under which a trial *in absentia* is required and the three requirements for allowing a trial *in absentia.*[22]

[20] Article 270 of the French Code of Criminal Procedure, prior to its amendment, provided for a trial *in absentia* if a defendant who is a fugitive fails to appear for trial. This procedure was called the "*procédure de contumace*" ("system of contempt of court") and covered defendants who had absconded or were at large ("*contumax*"). However, following the 2001 decision of the European Court of Human Rights in the case of *Krombach v.* France [*Krombach v. France*, Application No. 29731/96 (13 February 2001), paras. 9–91], the 9 March 2004 law (Perben II Act) was introduced and the system of trial in absentia was subject to various restrictions. For the revision of the law, see Suemichi [206], pp. 123–165. In Italy, too, when the accused fails to attend the trial despite being summoned or presumed so (*contumacia*), when the accused explicitly refuses to attend (*assenza al processo*), or when there are justifiable reasons why the accused cannot attend for reasons not of his/her own volition (*legittimo impedimento*), the court may order the accused to appear at the trial (*legittimo impedimento*), and trial *in absentia* is permitted [Articles 420-3, 420-4, 420-5, 484(2)(2) et seq. of the Italian Code of Criminal Procedure]. The European Court of Human Rights found a violation of the short time limit for filing an appeal against a judgment in absentia provided for by Article 175 of the Italian Code of Criminal Procedure and the fact that the burden of proof for not being aware of the summons was on the defendant was not in accordance with the principle of the burden of proof of the prosecutor under the European Convention on Human Rights; *Sejdovic v. Italy*, Application No. 56581/00 (1 March 2006); *Somogyi v. Italy*, Application No. 67972/01 (18 May 2004). In Italy, these judgments led to the amendment of Article 175 in 2005. See, Tracogna [229]. Article 420(2(1)) of the Italian Code of Criminal Procedure, as amended, provides that the court shall proceed in the absence of the accused if the accused expressly waives his or her appearance.

[21] Friman [56], p. 255.

[22] In addition, Inazumi, for example, lists the following as conditions for the legality of a trial in absentia: (1) the defendant's presence in court is a general rule and a trial in absentia is an exception,

There are three types of prerequisite circumstances that would require a trial *in absentia*: (i) when the judicial authorities have the defendant in custody; (ii) when the defendant is not in custody but is given proper notice of the criminal trial and indictment; or (iii) when the defendant has not been notified or the notice has not been received or its receipt cannot be verified. In addition, there are three requirements for the permissible conduct of a trial *in absentia*: (a) the accused himself/herself interferes with the proceedings ("obstruction of justice"), (b) the accused himself/herself waives the right to be present in court ("waiver"), or (c) there is a guarantee of a retrial ("retrial"). In the following, I will try to divide the cases into how the requirements (a)–(c) can be satisfied in the situations which are the preconditions for (i)–(iii).

3.2.1 If the Suspect is in Custody

First, I will lay out the three requirements for a permissible trial *in absentia* in a situation (i). First, (a) "obstruction of justice" by the accused is a justification for the continuation of the trial in the accused's absence after the initial proceedings have been completed—also called partial absence (*semel praesens*), as distinguished from total absence (*nunquam praesene*). In such a situation, trial *in absentia* is permissible under many statutes. In the UK, there is a tradition of guaranteeing the right to be in court, with the exception that misconduct of the accused has been a reason for the admissibility of trial *in absentia.*[23] Even in the US, where the right of the accused to be present in court is provided for in the Constitution, an explicit limitation on this right was established in the Federal Rules of Criminal Procedure 43 adopted in 1946. The rule cited cases in which a defendant interferes with the trial and justifies removal of the accused from the trial (para. (c)). In *Illinois v. Allen*, the court held that a defendant who interferes with the trial by improper speech or conduct in the courtroom, even in the absence of a waiver of rights, loses the right to be present and the judge may dismiss him/her.[24] However, in the 1993 *Crosby* case, the US Supreme Court held that a trial in which the defendant was not present at the start of the trial was not permissible.[25] In Japan, Article 341 of the Code of Criminal Procedure states that "if the accused does not make a statement, leaves the court without permission,

(2) the gravity of the trial procedure in absentia, (3) whether the defendant is notified of the fact of the trial and the disadvantages of not appearing, (4) whether the right to be in court is waived and the defendant's will is confirmed, (5) the availability of counsel who can represent the defendant, (6) whether a record of court appearances is kept, and (7) the right to a new trial in the event the defendant is detained after conviction. (7) If the defendant is detained in custody after conviction, the right to a new trial is guaranteed. Inazumi [79], p. 34. In this chapter, (2) is not considered because the discussion is limited to the procedures that would significantly affect the rights of the accused. In addition, since the focus of this chapter is on the presence in court of the accused himself/herself, (5) is also not considered.

23 *R v. Berry* (1897) 104 LT Jo 110; *R v. Browne* (1906) 70 JP 472.

24 *Illinois v. Allen*, 397 US 337 (1970). For a review of the case law, see Kojo [107].

25 *Crosby v. United States*, 506 US 255 (1993).

or is ordered to leave the court by the presiding judge for the purpose of maintaining order, the judge may pass sentence without hearing his statement."

Next, in the case of (b) "waiver", where the accused himself/herself waives his/her right to be present in court, it is possible to confirm his/her intention as long as he/she is in custody. Although it is difficult to find more commonality in this situation than in the case of obstruction by the accused, it is understood from the views of various human rights courts, which have examined the waiver in detail in particular, that the trial *in absentia* can be permitted on the ground of waiver of the right to be present "in the interest of the proper administration of justice".[26] In the US, for example, the right to be present is limited in cases where the accused waives his/her right or voluntarily leaves the courtroom after the trial has begun, or where the accused voluntarily absents himself/herself from the sentencing, except in a case equivalent to the death penalty [Rule 43(c) of the Federal Rules of Criminal Procedure]. In Japan, basically, if the accused fails to appear on the date of trial, the court may not open the case. However, Article 286(2) of the Code of Criminal Procedure, which was revised in 1952 in response to the confusion caused by the defendants' refusal to appear at the trial of the so-called *May Day* Case in 1952, provides that "When the court cannot be convened without the appearance of the accused, and the accused, who is under detention, has been summoned to the trial but refuses to appear without justifiable reason, and it is extremely difficult for the officials of the penal institution to bring the accused to the court, the court may commence the proceedings of the trial without the appearance of the accused."[27]

On the other hand, it is generally considered prohibited for public authorities to keep a person in custody and not allow him/her to appear for trial. The question is whether the "reemedy" in such a case can be granted by a (c) "retrial", which will be discussed in detail later.

3.2.2 Where Appropriate Notice is Given

Where a person is not in custody but has been given proper notice (situation (ii)), it is unlikely that (a) "obstruction of justice" is established. The situation that can be simulated is (b) "a case of waiver of the right to be present" by failure to appear.

Regarding (b) "waiver", the Human Rights Committee ("HRC") in *Mbenge v. Zaire*, for example, stated that Article 14 of the ICCPR cannot be understood as always making proceedings inadmissible in the absence of the accused without taking into account the reasons for the accused's absence.[28] It then explained that a trial in the

[26] E.g., *Mbenge v. Zaire*, Communication No. 16/1977, UN Doc. CCPR/C/OP/2 at 76 (1990), para. 14.1.

[27] For example, Articles 283, 284, 285, 286-2, 314, 390, 341, 451, etc. of the Japanese Code of Criminal Procedure. In addition, the cases in which the appearance of the accused is not required include cases in which the accused is a juridical person, cases on dates other than the pronouncement of judgment in relatively minor cases, cases of insanity, cases in which the accused has extreme difficulty in being brought to trial, and cases in which the accused is ordered to leave the court.

[28] *Mbenge v. Zaire*, para. 14.1.

absence of the accused can be tolerated in the interests of the proper administration of justice if the accused, having been properly informed of the proceedings in advance, waives his right to appear in court.[29] In the UK, in the 2003 *Jones* case, it was considered that a situation in which a defendant had absconded after arrest and was deliberately trying to gain an advantage by not appearing in court was unfair to a large number of traumatised witnesses.[30] In the US, which prohibits trial *in absentia* as a general rule, the Supreme Court decision in *Hopt v. Utah* in 1884 held that the right of the accused to be present in court could not be waived even by express declaration of intent,[31] but in the *Diaz* case in 1912 and other cases, the right to be present in court was waived by a declaration of will.[32] In Germany, Article 103(1) of the Basic Law provides that no person shall be convicted without a prior hearing. However, there is an exception to this rule: there is a procedure for "persons who fail to appear" (*Ausgebliebene*) (under Section 232 of the German Code of Criminal Procedure) in cases where the accused is located in the territory of the German jurisdiction and his/her place of residence is known and he/she fails to appear despite having been lawfully summoned to do so. Similarly, in France, there is a distinction between the "absence" (*défaut*) of a defendant subject to a failure motion (*l'oppositon*)[33] and a "failure to appear" (*absence*) (Articles 410–416 et seq. of the Code of Criminal Procedure of France).[34]

With regards to the waiver of the right to be present in court, the question arises as to when such a waiver can be presumed. From the case-law of the European Court of Human Rights, it is also a question of how it is proved whether the accused's absence on notice is of his/her own free will or whether there are legitimate or compelling reasons.[35] For example, in the case of an escape from custody, the accused

---

[29] *Ibid.*

[30] *R v. Jones* [2003] 1 AC 1. However, it has been pointed out that this decision could be an unreasonable restriction of the "right to be heard" and a possible violation of the European Convention on Human Rights. Willey [245].

[31] *Hopt v. Utah*, 110 US 574, 28 L Ed 262, 4 S Ct 202 (1884).

[32] *Diaz v. United States*, 223 US 442, 455–59 (1912).

[33] Under the system of failure petitions, the effect of the "absent" trial is extinguished by the petition, and the court that conducted this procedure accepts the case anew. Bouloc and Matsopoulou [19], pp. 435–436; Wagatsuma [240], p. 192, note 38.

[34] In France, a sentence rendered without the defendant's appearance is considered an "absent" sentence if the defendant has been lawfully summoned in person and has made a valid plea of non-appearance (Article 410-1 of the Code of Criminal Procedure), but otherwise it is considered a "no appearance" sentence. In addition, in the case of failure to appear in felony court, traditionally, if the defendant could not be taken into custody, or if the defendant fails to appear within ten days from the date the order to set the case for trial is served at his residence, or if he flees after being taken into custody or appearing, he is immediately considered "absent". Bouloc and Matsopoulou [19], pp. 436–437. However, the Law of 9 March 2004 of France (Perben II Law) introduced the felony absence procedure, replacing the previous procedure of sentencing a felony defendant *in absentia* (Article 379-2 of the Code of Criminal Procedure and following). The felony absence procedure is a procedure whereby if a felony defendant is absent without good cause at the opening of the court, it will conduct the trial without a jury present, unless the case is adjourned to a later term. Wagatsuma [240], p. 194, note 46.

[35] See, e.g., Bose [18], p. 500.

is considered to have been fully informed of the trial, which may be regarded as a waiver of the right to be present in court if the escape was of the accused's own free will.

3.2.3 In the Event that the Notice Has not Been Received or Its Arrival Cannot Be Confirmed

Finally, if notice has not been received or its arrival cannot be confirmed, the requirements of (a) "obstruction of justice" and (b) "waiver" are impossible, and thus the requirement of (c) securing a "retrial" must be satisfied, which creates a number of problems in this situation.

First of all, with regards to notice, various human rights norms take the view that it is not enough that reasonable steps have been taken for notice, but that the accused must in fact be aware of the criminal proceedings and that such knowledge must have come formally from the authorities, and therefore, in the circumstances described in (iii), a trial *in absentia* is not admissible in the first place. As the trial *in absentia* without adequate notice to the accused was a violation of Article 6 of the European Convention on Human Rights, the European Court of Human Rights in *Colozza v. Italy* held that the purpose of Article 6 as a whole is that a person charged with a criminal offence is entitled to a hearing.[36] In the case of *T v. Italy*, it also held, on the question of notification, that the important legal act of informing the subject person about the prosecution must be carried out in accordance with the procedural and substantive requirements that would enable the accused person to ensure the effective exercise of his rights, and that vague and informal knowledge is not sufficient.[37]

Furthermore, the guarantee of a (c) "retrial" is positioned as a remedy in the case of a trial *in absentia* in the situation described in (iii), but as it is a remedy, it does not change the fact that a trial *in absentia* itself is fundamentally illegal. In the case of *Maleki v. Italy*, the HRC held that Article 14 is remedied if it is violated by the lack of proper notice to the accused of the trial, provided that a retrial is secured if the accused is detained.[38] In the European Court of Human Rights' *Demebukov v. Bulgaria* case, where a retrial was at issue, the Court held that an accused convicted *in absentia* must be subjected to a new judgment on the issue of the facts of the indictment unless the accused expressly or implicitly waives his right to be present in court.[39] In France, if the defendant does not receive a summons to appear in person and is not alleged to have known of the summons (Article 412 of the Code of Criminal Procedure), a judgment made without the defendant's appearance is considered an "*absent*" judgment and is subject to a motion for failure.

---

[36] *Colozza v. Italy*, Application No. 9024/80 (12 February 1985), para. 27.

[37] *T v. Italy*, Application No. 14104/88 (12 October 1992), para. 28.

[38] *Maleki v. Italy*, Communication No. 699/2996 (27 July 1999), para. 9.5.

[39] *Demebukov v. Bulgaria*, Application No. 68020/01 (28 February 2008), para. 45.

4 Content of the Principle of Prohibition of Trial *in Absentia* in International Criminal Justice

From a comparative analysis of the various statutes, it can be summarized that certain commonalities can be found in the pattern of exceptions to the principle of no trial *in absentia*. First, when the defendant is in custody and there is an obstruction or waiver of the right to present, or second, when proper notice is given and there is a waiver of the right. As an exception to the rule, there is a position that a retrial may be secured even if it is unclear whether notice has been given, but the measure is a remedy for a right that has been violated, and the violation of the right itself occurs.[40]

So far, the content of the principle has been confirmed through a comparative study of the theoretical basis of the principle of no trials *in absentia* and various laws. In the following section, after reviewing the status of the provision about the principle in international criminal justice and judicial precedents, I will discuss how the basic rationale for the necessity of the accused's presence during the trial is considered in relation to the applicability of the principle of no trials *in absentia* to the international criminal justice field.

4.1 Rules of the International Criminal Justice Institution

4.1.1 IMT

Section 12 of the IMT Charter permitted trials *in absentia*, as the IMT had the power to proceed in the absence of the accused if the accused could not be found or if for any reason it was deemed necessary to proceed in his absence. Martin Bormann, a Nazi Party private secretary to Adolf Hitler, was the only accused at large at the commencement of the proceedings in the IMT, and Rule 2(b) of its Rules of Procedure established the duty of notice to accused persons at large and provided that notice must be given of the charges against the accused and the rights enjoyed by the accused. It said notice must be given in a form acceptable to the court. Notice to Bormann was given by radio broadcast once a week for four weeks and by newspaper.[41] However, at the trial, which was held in the absence of the accused because Bormann had not been found, Bormann's counsel argued that Article 12 should not apply because he was already dead.[42] However, because the evidence of the defendant's death was not

[40] Some of the exceptions adopted in the national laws of some States are specific. For example, some States allow a trial *in absentia* in cases where it is impossible or inappropriate for the accused to appear in person, for example, because he is abroad. In Germany, for example, there is a procedure for *Abwesenende* (under Article 276) in cases where the place of stay is not known, or the person is abroad and his/her appearance is deemed impossible or inappropriate.

[41] Schabas [181], p. 957.

[42] *Trial of the Major War Criminals before the International Military Tribunal Nuremberg*, Vol. 1 (1947), pp. 338–341.

confirmed, the trial was held in the defendant's absence pursuant to Article 12 and the death penalty was imposed.[43]

While it has been pointed out that the standard of fair trial was not met for the execution of the trial *in absentia* in the *Bormann* case, the clear provision in the IMT Charter itself allowing for trials *in absentia* suggests that trials *in absentia* were acceptable at the international level in the period immediately after World War II.[44]

4.1.2 *Ad hoc* Tribunals

The ICTY and ICTR which were established in the 1990s essentially recognize the right of the accused to be present in court. Article 21(4)(d) of the ICTY Statute and Article 20(4)(d) of the ICTR Statute provide that an accused person shall be entitled, on full equality, at least to attend and be tried in person, to have his guilt determined in accordance with the Statute, and to be guaranteed the right to defend himself or through a defence counsel of his own choice.[45]

However, case law confirms that this right is not absolute.[46] In the ICTR, boycotts by the accused were an issue. In the *Barayagwiza* case, the accused refused to attend the trial, questioning the independence and impartiality of the ICTR. The Trial Chamber therefore decided that a trial *in absentia* was permissible where the accused had expressly waived his right to appear.[47] The ICTR then inserted Rule 82(2) of the RPE in May 2003. The rule states that if the accused refuses to attend the trial, the Trial Chamber may order a trial in the accused's absence if the accused has completed the opening proceedings, the Registry has properly notified the accused that his/her presence is required at the trial, and the accused's interests are represented by a counsel. The ICTR has also held in the *Zigiranyirazo* case that the right to be present in court can also be limited by substantial obstruction of the trial.[48] However,

[43] However, it was later confirmed that Bormann was already dead at the time of the trial.

[44] Shaw [185], p. 119.

[45] In the ICTY, however, a hearing was held by a Continental law judge in accordance with Rule 61 of the ICTY RPE to examine, among other things, the sufficiency of the evidence *ex parte* with one Party (the Prosecutor) in a manner similar to proceedings in the absence of the accused. Schabas, *A Commentary on the Rome Statute*, 1192. The ICTR has also ruled that, with respect to appearance by video-link, presence in court means the physical presence of the accused. E.g., *Prosecutor v. Zigiranyirazo,* Decision on Interlocutory Appeal (ICTR-2001-73-AR73) Appeals Chamber (30 October 2006), para. 11; *Prosecutor v. Hategekimana,* Judgment (ICTR-00-55B-A) Appeals Chamber (8 May 2012), para. 37.

[46] E.g., *Prosecutor v. Blaškić*, Judgment on the Request of Croatia for Review of the Decision of Trial Chamber II of 18 July 1997 *(IT-95-14-AR108bis)* Appeals Chamber (29 October 1997), para. 59; *Prosecutor v. Nahimana* et al., Judgment (ICTR-99 52-A) Appeals Chamber (28 November 2007), para. 105.

[47] *Prosecutor v. Barayagwiza,* Decision on Defense Counsel Motion to Withdraw (ICTR-97-19-T) Trial Chamber I (2 November 2000), para. 6.

[48] E.g., *Prosecutor v. Zigiranyirazo*, para. 14.

this is limited to cases where the obstruction is intentional and prior notice of the restriction of the right to be present in court due to the obstruction is required.[49]

Article 17(4)(d) of the SCSL Statute and Article 21(4)(d) of the EAC Statute, as well as the ICTY and ICTR, guarantee the accused the right to be tried in his/her presence and to defend himself/herself or through his/her legal representative. On the other hand, Rule 60 of the SCSL RPE provides that an accused person may be tried *in absentia* if he/she has completed the opening proceedings and refuses to appear despite his/her own guaranteed right to appear, or if he/she flees after completing the opening proceedings and refuses to appear in court. The ECCC has a similar provision to the SCSL in Section 35(2)(d) of the ECCC Act. In addition, Internal Rule 81, which has more detailed provisions, firstly provides in paragraph 1 that the accused shall be tried in his/her presence, except as otherwise provided for in that Rule, but also provides in paragraph 4 of that Rule that the trial proceedings may continue even if he/she refuses to appear after the opening proceedings or is removed from the court in accordance with the Rules.

4.1.3 ICC

Article 63(1) of the ICC Statute provides that the accused shall basically remain in court for the duration of the trial. However, paragraph 2 of the same provision provides that only in exceptional circumstances, and only after other reasonable alternative measures have proved insufficient, and only for a period of time that is genuinely necessary, may an accused person present in court be removed from court if he/she continues to obstruct the trial. The same paragraph also allows the Trial Chamber to take measures to enable the accused to hear the trial from outside the courtroom and to instruct counsel, where necessary, by the use of communications technology. These measures are exceptions to the accused's right to be present in court as set out in Article 67(1)(d) of the ICC Statute, but were criticised by States, including the US, during the drafting process.[50]

In 2013, the issue arose as to whether the incumbent president and vice president, who were accused in the Kenyan situation, should be permitted to be absent in court when they are unable to do so due to their official duties.[51] In the *Ruto* case, in the case of the incumbent vice president, he himself filed a motion to be absent due to the performance of his official duties and the Trial Chamber granted his absence accepting substantially most of the motion.[52] The ICC Appeals Chamber was more restrictive and raised the conditions under which an exceptional absence trial would

[49] *Prosecutor v. Šešelj*, Decision on Assignment of Council (IT-03-67-PT) Trial Chamber I (21 August 2006), para. 23.

[50] See, e.g., Brown [22].

[51] See, Schwarz [184], pp. 100–101.

[52] *Prosecutor v. Ruto and Sang*, Decision on Mr. Ruto's Request for Excusal from Continuous Presence at Trial (ICC-01/09-01/11-777) Trial Chamber V(A) (18 June 2013).

be permitted.[53] On 27 November of the same year, the ICC Assembly of the States Parties adopted new rules on the use of video technology for court appearances (Rule 134 *bis* of the RPE), withdrawal from trial (Rule 134 *ter*) and withdrawal from trial due to special official business (Rule 134 *quater*), and added an exception rule allowing partial absences.[54]

On 28 May 2020, the Appeals Chamber decided the following in the *Gbagbo* case, on an appeal relating to a condition of release to sign that the proceedings would proceed in the absence of the accused if he did not appear in accordance with the Court's request to appear during the post-acquittal appeal period. First, the Trial Chamber distinguished the case from other cases in which the defendant did not appear because it was a case in which the threshold of Article 60 had already been crossedthe threshold for effective enforcement of the Court's jurisdiction—.[55] On that basis, the continuation of proceedings in the physical absence of the accused in cases of absence desired by the accused is not prohibited by the ICC Statute or by general principles of law.[56] However, it held that this is so long as the right to a fair trial, including securing representation by counsel, is respected.[57]

4.1.4 STL

The system adopted by the Special Tribunal for Lebanon ("STL"), a special tribunal based on UN Security Council resolutions, has attracted much attention in recent years with regards to proceedings in the absence of the accused.[58] The background to the introduction of the system of trial *in absentia* in the STL was the fact that the domestic law of the target State, Lebanon, was based on the Continental legal system and allowed for trial *in absentia*.[59] In addition, Article 22 of the STL Statute broadly permits proceedings in the absence of the accused, as the accused are seen to be dispersed throughout the world.

---

[53] *Prosecutor v. Ruto and Sang*, Judgment on the appeal of the Prosecutor against the decision of the Trial Chamber V(a) of 18 June 2013 entitled "Decision on Mr. Ruto's Request for Excusal from Continuous Presence at Trial" (ICC-01/09-01/11-1066) Appeals Chamber (25 October 2013). The sitting President of Kenya subsequently filed a motion to the same effect, but the trial in absentia was not granted. *Prosecutor v. Kenyatta,* Decision on Defence request for excusal from attendance at, or for adjournment of, the status conference scheduled for 8 October 2014 (ICC-01/09-02/11-960) Trial Chamber V(B) (30 September 2014).

[54] Resolution ICC-ASP/12/Res.7 (27 November 2013).

[55] *Prosecutor v. Gbagbo and Blé Goudé,* Decision on counsel for Mr. Gbabo's request for reconsideration of the 'Judgment on the Prosecutor's appeal against the oral decision of Trial Chamber I pursuant to article 81(3)(c)(1) of the Statute' and on the review of the conditions on the release of Mr. Gbagbo and Mr. Blé Goudé (ICC-02/11-01/15-1355-Red) Appeals Chamber (28 May 2020), para 68.

[56] *Ibid*., para. 70.

[57] *Ibid*. For a critique of the same judgment, see: Wheeler [243].

[58] For an overview of the STL, see Takemura [218].

[59] Aptel [5], p. 1121.

Article 22(1) of the STL Statute provides that a trial shall be conducted in the absence of the accused if the accused has expressly waived his/her right to be present in writing (STL Statute, Article 22(1)(a)); the accused is not surrendered by the State concerned ((b)); or the accused has fled or cannot be found and all reasonable steps are taken to bring the accused to court and inform him/her of the indictment as confirmed by the pre-trial judge ((c)). The conditions for a trial *in absentia* are that the accused has been notified of the indictment or that the indictment has been served on the accused or that the accused has been informed of the indictment through media advertisement or communication to his/her State of residence or nationality (para. 2(a)), that the accused has appointed his/her own counsel and that the counsel has been paid a remuneration or, if the accused is proved by the court to be indigent, remuneration has been paid by the court ((b)), and if the accused does not or is unable to appoint counsel, it must be ensured that counsel has been appointed by the Defence Office of the STL ((c)). If the defendant was convicted *in absentia* and the defendant did not appoint his/her own counsel, the defendant has the right to be present in court and be tried again in person, unless he/she accepts the sentence ((3)).[60]

In the case of Salim Jamil Ayyash et al. of the STL, a trial *in absentia* was decided and was started. In that case, after the arrest warrant was issued on 28 June 2011, information about the said arrest warrant was disseminated through newspaper advertisements in Arabic, French and English in Lebanon, and an International Criminal Police Organization international arrest warrant was also issued, but the four accused were not arrested, nor did they appear voluntarily or otherwise come under the jurisdiction.[61] The Trial Chamber's decision of 1 February 2012 granted a trial *in absentia* to the four accused in that case.[62]

4.1.5 Exceptions to the Rules of the International Criminal Justice Institution

The exceptions to the principle of no trial *in absentia* as a general principle include cases where there is an obstruction or waiver of proceedings where the accused is in custody, and cases where there is a waiver of rights or where proper notice is given. The statutes of the International Criminal Justice Institutions allow only these two exceptions, except in the cases of the IMT and the STL in which a retrial is guaranteed. Thus, it is considered that the same level of guarantees is maintained in international criminal justice as in ordinary criminal justice. So, is the principle of prohibition of trial *in absentia* in international criminal justice not affected by

[60] It has been pointed out that the guarantee of a retrial follows the precedent of the European Court of Human Rights, but that the scope of its application should follow within the scope of that precedent. Gaeta [63].

[61] *Prosecutor v. Ayyash* et al., Order to Seize the Trial Chamber Pursuant to Rule 105 Bis (A) of the Rules of Procedure and Evidence in Order to Determine Whether to Initiate Proceedings in Absentia (STL-11-01/I/TC) Pre-Trial Judge (17 October 2011), paras. 3–16.

[62] *Prosecutor v. Ayyash* et al., Decision to Hold Trial in Absentia (STL-11-01/I/TC) Trial Chamber (1 February 2012).

the special characteristics of international criminal justice? In the following, I will examine the impact of the demand to secure prosecution in international criminal justice on the theoretical basis of the principle of the prohibition of trial *in absentia.*

4.2 Balance Between Demand to Ensure Prosecution and Demand for Presence of the Accused in Court

4.2.1 Demand to Ensure Prosecution of Core Crimes

There is a strong premise in international criminal justice to admit trials *in absentia.* In the drafting process of the ICC Statute, a desire was expressed for an international criminal court to have the power to try an accused in his/her absence. The reason for this was that the jurisdiction of the Court would be subject to a substantial "veto" by the accused or the State where the accused is located if the accused refused to appear in court knowing that there is a trial or if the State where the accused is located refuses to extradite him/her.[63] Similarly, the ICC's Trial Chamber's decision in the *Ruto* case stated that prohibiting a trial *in absentia* in circumstances where the accused seems to have deliberately planned to obstruct the trial would act to hold the Trial Chamber "hostage to impunity" and that the outcome of such a scenario "plays into the hands of the very impunity that the Statute eschews so fundamentally".[64] It went on to note that the purpose of Article 63(1) of the ICC Statute, which establishes the principle of the accused's presence in court, is "to ensure that a Trial Chamber will maintain judicial control over the accused, from the perspective of making impositions on his time and whereabouts, for purposes of effective inquiry into his individual responsibility for the crimes as charged".[65]

It was also argued during the ICC drafting process that sentencing in the absence of the accused can constitute a kind of moral sanction that contributes to the isolation of the accused which ultimately leads to the capture of the accused.[66] Another observation was that in criminal cases, evidence that is likely to be lost during the period before the defendant appears in court can be effectively preserved by a speedy trial.[67] Some commentators have evaluated the innovation of the STL system, a criminal justice institution that has provided a wide range of conditions that permit trials in the absence of the accused.[68] Some commentators have also evaluated the effectiveness of the STL and encouraged the ICC to introduce a similar system.[69] This view appears to be based on the fact that even after the inception of the ICC, many

---

[63] UN Doc. A/48/10 (1993), p. 120. See also, Schabas and Caruana [180], p. 1567.

[64] *Prosecutor v. Ruto and Sang* (18 June 2013), para. 44.

[65] *Ibid.*, para. 53.

[66] UN Doc. A/48/10 (1993), p. 120.

[67] *Ibid.*

[68] Aptel [5], pp. 1107–1124.

[69] Shaw [185], pp. 107–140.

suspects remained at large or were unable to force surrender the States to surrender the suspects despite arrest warrants being issued.

4.2.2 Emphasis on the Request for the Presence of the Accused in Court

On the other hand, the need for the principle of trial in the presence of the accused has also been asserted in the international criminal justice domain. William Schabas and Veronique Curuana assess that although the theoretical basis for the prohibition of trial *in absentia* between the Continental and Anglo-American legal systems seemingly differs, the issue of the presence of the accused at trial is merely one of differences in practice and tradition rather than a matter of conflicting fundamental values between the legal systems.[70] This is reflected in the fact that even though the models of criminal procedure in the two legal systems remain different, the rationale for the accused's presence in court itself is shared between the legal systems. That is, there is no dispute that the presence of the accused is important for the guarantee of the accused's right to a hearing, in addition to the need to establish the accuracy of the accused's testimony and to compare it with that of victims and witnesses.[71] In addition, recent ICC case law suggests that presence in court is recognized by the ICC as both a right and an obligation.[72] Taken together, these observations suggest that the contemporary rationale for requiring the presence of the accused is both to ensure the accuracy of the trial and to guarantee the rights of the accused, and that exceptions to the principle of no trial *in absentia* are limited to cases where the grounds for the exception exceed these two demands.

(a) Accuracy of trial

The first demand of the principle of the presence of the accused before an International Criminal Justice Institution is related to the accuracy of the trial. For example, ICTY case law has held that core crime cases are so complex that it is very difficult or rather impossible for an International Criminal Justice Institution to determine a person's innocence or guilt in the absence of the accused.[73] It is also held that the absence of the accused significantly diminishes the truth-seeking function of the defence and the trial.[74]

These views are based on the large scale and complexity of the cases, which are characteristic of core crimes cases subject to international criminal justice. In pursuing individual criminal responsibility for criminal acts committed by a large number of perpetrators that result in a large number of victims, the prosecutor must

---

[70] Schabas [181], p. 1564.

[71] See, e.g., *Poitrimol v. France*, Application No. 14032/88 (23 November 1993), para. 35; *Lala and Pelladoah v. the Netherlands*, Application No. 16737/90 (22 September 1994), para. 40; *Van Geyseghem v. Belgium*, Application No. 26103/95 (21 January 1999), para. 29.

[72] *Prosecutor v. Ruto and Sang*, Dissenting Opinion of Judge Herrera Carbuccia (ICC-01/09-01/11-777-Anx2) Trial Chamber V(a) (18 June 2013), para. 4; Wheeler [242].

[73] *Prosecutor v. Blaškić*, para. 59.

[74] Jordash and Parker [92], pp. 501–506; Pons [160], p. 1319.

prove what criminal acts were actually committed by each of the individuals involved in the commission of the crimes, according to their respective forms of responsibility. Furthermore, witnesses to core crime cases are not limited to the victims. The outer limits of a defendant's responsibility for a core crime are determined by the interweaving of testimonies from people who were within the organization that committed the crime. Furthermore, in the case of internal witnesses, it is often assumed that there is a tendency to try to place their own responsibility on the accused.

Therefore, ensuring the presence of the accused in court is important to ensure the accuracy of the trial in core crime cases.

(b) Rights of the accused

From the perspective of a fair trial that respects the rights of the accused, trial *in absentia* in international criminal justice must be limited as much as possible.[75] Many international human rights documents were relied upon as the basis for the argument underlying the concept of fair trial in the drafting process of the ICC Statute. It has also been confirmed in various cases that the prohibition of trial *in absentia* under the ICC Statute establishes first and foremost the "right" of the accused to be present in court.[76] Furthermore, the Appeals Chamber decision in the *Ruto* case stated that the accused is not "a mere passive observer at trial" but "a subject of the criminal proceedings" and "an active participant"[77] and took a logical structure that seems to assume an Anglo-American litigation structure.

In addition, there are many commentators who take a critical view of the current situation in which trial *in absentia* is widely permitted in the STL as mentioned above. For example, some argue that Article 22 of the STL Statute is not consistent with Article 6 of the European Convention on Human Rights,[78] some argue that it constitutes a violation of the right to a fair trial,[79] and some further argue that such a violation of the right to a fair trial affects the legitimacy of the Court.[80]

4.2.3 Balance Between the Two Demands

The ICC Statute, adopted after a debate between those who attempted to broaden and those who wanted to narrow the exceptions to the principle of no trial *in absentia*,

[75] UN Doc. A/48/10 (1993), p. 120.

[76] *Prosecutor v. Ruto and Sang (18 June 2013)*, para. 35.

[77] *Prosecutor v. Ruto and Sang (25 October 2013)*, para. 49.

[78] Elberling [46].

[79] Jenks [87].

[80] Jordash and Parker [92]. On the other hand, some argue that the requirement of the presence of the accused in the international criminal justice domain is due to the protection of victims and witnesses and the effective administration of justice rather than a direct relation to the rights of the accused. Zappalá [257], p. 129. This argument is based on the fact that as the core criminal prosecution proceeds, many acts of interference (intimidation and bribery) with witnesses can occur. However, this seems to be a justification for the arrest and detention of the accused before the trial *in absentia*, and does not necessarily seem to be directly related to the trial *in absentia*.

allowed trial *in absentia* only in cases where the accused was in custody and there was interference by the accused. However, the subsequent amendments to the Statute and the decision in the *Gbagbo* case added a case in which the accused waives that right himself after the trial is over. Other institutions also basically provided for the possibility of trial *in absentia* when the accused is in custody, with two conditions: either there is obstruction by the accused, or the accused waives his/her right himself/herself.

On the other hand, in light of the arguments for the two demands, namely, the demand for the accused's presence in court and securing the prosecution, there are still difficulties to be overcome in adopting the principle of no trial *in absentia* in the field of international criminal justice. In addition to the low feasibility of securing the custody of the accused against the strong demand of securing prosecution in international criminal justice, the significant benefits that conducting a trial itself provide to the victims and society show that there is a strong and persistent demand to start the trial of core crime cases even without the accused present.

However, the seriousness and particularity of the target offence itself does not seem to have been a criterion for the admissibility of a trial *in absentia*. In some cases, the weight of the "procedure" of the trial *in absentia* was taken into consideration. For example, proceedings that do not involve the guilt/innocence of the accused on original charges or proceedings that are unlikely to prejudice human rights.[81] However, there were no cases in which the weight of the "crime" itself, which is the subject of the prosecution, was considered as a special consideration in comparison with other crimes and was used as a basis for allowing a trial *in absentia*.[82] The presence of the accused at trial is not considered to be affected by the fact that the subject offence is a core crime.

Two rationales for the principle of no trial *in absentia* also correspond to the universal values of international criminal justice.[83] First, ensuring the accuracy of the trial is an essential element in realizing a universal value of international criminal justice, the value of truth-seeking. If criminal proceedings are conducted without the accused, the accuracy of the evidentiary hearing at the trial may be questioned, and the reliability of the "truth" to be identified in the verdict may be reduced. In addition, in order to realize another universal value of international criminal justice, which is the guarantee of due process, it is necessary to guarantee the right of the accused to be present in court, which is regarded as part of the right to a fair trial. Therefore, the growing recognition of the right of the accused to be present in international human rights law is also a strong basis for the principle of the accused's presence in court. Therefore, it is considered that the recognition of the principle of no trial *in absentia*

---

[81] Inazumi [79], pp. 34–35.

[82] In *Jones v. United Kingdom*, Lord Bingham held that the "seriousness of the offence as it affects the defendant, victim and public" should not be considered in allowing a trial *in absentia* and that "the judge's overriding concern will be to ensure that the trial, if conducted in the absence of the defendant, will be as fair as circumstances permit and lead to a just result. These objects are equally important, whether the offence charged is serious or relatively minor"; *R v. Jones*, para. 14.

[83] See below on the various values of international criminal procedure; Turner [233], pp. 997–998.

in the area of international criminal justice is confirmed as an essential principle for achieving the universal value of international criminal justice as it is.

5 Conclusion

In this chapter, I have examined the principle of no trial *in absentia* in international criminal justice and found that the impact of the premises of international criminal justice on the current version of the principle is very limited.

The presence of the accused in international criminal justice is related to the issue of the significance of punishment in international criminal justice. International criminal justice has developed based on the principle of "prevention of impunity," but the question is whether "punishment" in this context refers to retribution or prevention through physical confinement, or "punitive performance" at the international level is more important. However, this "punitive performance" is significant in that it provides the international community with official recognition of the harm done to the victim community and is the beginning of a financial and substantive reparation mechanism. Furthermore, the meaning of trials *in absentia* includes that the historical recognition of the core crimes cases that affected the international community as a whole are established through that the facts are confirmed in jurisprudence[84] and this provides a basis for international reparations lawsuits. In this way, the trials of core crimes have a significance beyond the punishment of a single accused person.

On the other hand, a one-sided trial that violates the rights of suspects and accused persons cannot be justified and cannot fulfil the significance of the "punitive performance". A common understanding is that the ICC should not allow distortion of legal principles on the grounds of practical obstacles, such as the lack of cooperation from States and the inability to make arrests. However, in recent ICC precedents, exceptions to the principle of prohibition of trial *in absentia* have tended to expand, and it is necessary to keep a close watch on future trends.

[84] Such a request is also behind the 2012 amendment to the law allowing trials in absentia at the Bangladesh International Crimes Tribunal. Tapos K. Das, "Prosecuting Pakistani Perpetrators in absentia" (23 March 2021), at https://www.thedailystar.net/law-our-rights/news/prosecuting-pakistani-perpetrators-absentia-2065357 (as of 26 March 2021).

Chapter 5
Principles Concerning Redress for the Rights of Accused Persons in International Criminal Justice

Abstract This chapter examines the premises arising from the particularities of the ICC's vertical and complementary prosecution regime from the perspective of redress for violations of suspects' rights by State authorities. This topic includes two issues: (i) whether the ICC provides redress to suspects even when violations of their rights are committed by State authorities; and (ii) whether the ICC provides preventive and substantive redress by exercising its jurisdiction when violations by State authorities are actual or foreseeable. Regarding the first issue, the ICC has clarified that it takes an attribution-required and comparative balance approach in determining the provision of redress for violations of rights by State authorities. The ICC's current attribution and comparative balance approach is not only contrary to the recent development of the concept of the individual's right to compensation, but also cannot avoid criticism that the vertical system of the ICC itself has the aspect of promoting the violation of the rights of individuals. With regards to the second issue, the realization of the exercise of ICC jurisdiction as a preventive and substantive redress as claimed in the Libyan situation by the ICC is possible but limited as far as the ICC Pre-Trial Chamber's decision is concerned. As for institutional issues arising from the premise of the ICC's vertical and complementary prosecution system, it pointed out the need for a flexible comparative balance and a different way of understanding the responsibilities inherent in the vertical regime in order to provide effective redress. Moreover, the ICC's admissibility review is limited in its treatment of violations of the rights of individuals by State authorities in their prosecution efforts.

1 Introduction

Due to the structure of the ICC's prosecution regime, which is premised on the primary involvement of national authorities, the ICC has faced unique difficulties in relation to the guarantee of the rights of individuals subject to criminal proceedings. This is related to the original reason for the need for an international criminal court—the psychological and physical difficulties faced by local judicial authorities in investigating and prosecuting core crimes such as genocide and crimes against

M. Ochi, *The Premises of International Criminal Procedure*,
https://doi.org/10.1007/978-981-97-6786-1_5

humanity—. For example, it is assumed that the large-scale nature and brutality of core crimes may easily give rise to intense resentment and hatred towards the perpetrators, especially in the regions where the crimes were committed. In addition, core crimes are often committed against a backdrop of conflict and political turmoil, and the regions concerned often lack the infrastructure to ensure due process, such as well-developed courts and detention facilities and trained judicial officers.

In practice, the ICC has faced demands for redress for individuals who have suffered violations of their rights by State authorities in relation to ICC proceedings during its implementation. In other words, one of the key questions in the operation of the ICC system is whether the ICC has no obligations or must take any action when the rights of individuals subject to ICC prosecution are infringed by national authorities conducting investigations and prosecutions in response to requests for cooperation from the ICC.

This chapter examines some of the institutional challenges that have been identified through the actual operation of the ICC, particularly with regards to redress for violations of suspects' rights by State authorities, with the aim of clarifying one aspect of the institutional challenges arising from the characteristics of the ICC's prosecution regime. The following section will first provide a summary of the rights of suspects guaranteed by the ICC, the forms of redress that can be provided, and the characteristics of the ICC's prosecution regime, which consists of a vertical and complementary relationship with the State, and the relevant provisions. Next, I will analyse two issues from the perspective of the ICC's position in the jurisprudence—whether the ICC should provide redress for the violation of suspects' rights by State authorities, and the possibility of preventive and substantive redress through the exercise of ICC jurisdiction, based on the vertical cooperative relationship and complementary jurisdiction, which are features of the ICC's prosecution system—. It analyses these two issues from the perspective of ICC case law. Through these examinations, I will discuss the ICC's institutional challenges and suggestions regarding the inherent premise of international criminal justice.

2 Redress for the Rights of Accused Persons Under the ICC's Prosecution Regime

2.1 Remedies for the Rights of the Accused Under the ICC Statute

2.1.1 Rules on the Rights of the Accused

To ensure the legitimacy of criminal justice, it is essential that procedures are carried out properly in investigations and prosecutions.[1] The ICC, which began prosecuting core crimes in 2003, also has provisions to guarantee a high standard of rights to suspects and accused persons.

While the Statute of the IMT after World War II and the Statute of the *ad hoc* Tribunals did not include explicit human rights provisions on the rights of suspects, the ICC Statute contains human rights provisions at various stages of proceedings, from investigation, arrest, and extradition to detention. First, Article 21(3) of the Statute contains the general provision that "The application and interpretation of law pursuant to this article must be consistent with internationally recognized human rights", and international covenants, regional human rights treaties and judicial precedents have been widely referred to for the interpretation of the said provision.[2] Article 55(1) of the Statute, which stipulates the substantive rights of suspects, enumerates the rights to be free from self-incrimination or coerced confession, to be free from torture and other inhumane treatment, to have access to an interpreter, and to be free from arbitrary arrest and detention, in relation to investigations under the Statute. Paragraph 2 of the same article also stipulates the right to be informed of the alleged facts, the right to remain silent, the right to the appointment of counsel, the right to have counsel present, and other rights when being interrogated by State authorities based on an ICC arrest warrant.

At the stage of extradition from the detaining State, Article 59(2) states that "A person arrested shall be brought promptly before the competent judicial authority in the custodial State which shall determine, in accordance with the law of that State, that: (a) The warrant applies to that person; (b) The person has been arrested in accordance with the proper process; and (c) The person's rights have been respected." Paragraphs 3 and 4 of the same article also guarantee the right to request provisional release prior to extradition.

[1] For example, Robert Jackson, the US prosecutor at the Nuremberg Trials, said, "We must never forget that the record on which we judge these defendants today is the record on which history will judge us tomorrow." International Military Tribunal, *Trial of the Major War Criminals before the International Military Tribunal* 2, (International Military Tribunal, 1947), 101.

[2] See Sheppard [187], p. 52.

2.1.2 Available Forms of Redress

The term "remedy" includes two concepts: the procedural aspect, which refers to the process by which a claim of human rights violation is heard and decided by a court or other tribunal, and the substantive aspect, which refers to the relief granted to the claimant as a result of such proceedings.[3] Of these, the concept of "redress" is often used mainly in the sense of the latter, substantive relief, rather than the procedural aspect, such as the availability of courts to restore rights.[4] This is what is meant by "redress" in this chapter.

There are two types of violations that are subject to redress in international criminal justice. The violations of rights that have been an issue in international criminal justice can be categorized into (i) those that affect the outcome of the trial—such as non-disclosure of evidence and inadequate interpretation—and (ii) those that do not directly affect the outcome of the trial—including relatively minor violations such as delay of proceedings and non-disclosure of reasons for prosecution, and severe violations such as torture during interrogation and abuse during detention—.[5] Of these, the main redress for type (i) is the immediate removal of the illegal situation, while the violation of rights by State authorities is assumed to be of type (ii), where *ex post facto* redress is an issue, and this chapter will therefore mainly examine type (ii).

The main types of redress that have been used so far are monetary compensation, commutation of sentence, and stay of proceedings (release).[6] As for the implementation of International Criminal Justice Institutions, the courts have been deciding the method and degree of redress at their discretion.[7] It has been the practice to provide monetary compensation if the result of a trial is acquittal, and to reduce the sentence if the result is conviction.[8] Each form of redress is discussed below, examining the situation at the ICC through a comparison with the implementation of the *ad hoc* Tribunals.

(a) Compensation

The right to compensation for unlawful arrest and detention is a right recognized in various human rights treaties, including Article 9(5) of the ICCPR. In the *ad hoc* Tribunals, judges of the various tribunals appealed to the UN Security Council in 2000 for the need for a compensation provision,[9] but no provision on compensation

---

[3] Shelton [186], p. 7.

[4] *Ibid.*, p. 8.

[5] Starr [201], p. 761.

[6] Declaratory relief has been added where the damage is minimal; see *Prosecutor v. Bagosora* et al., Judgement and Sentence (ICTR-98-41-T) Trial Chamber I (18 December 2008), para. 97.

[7] Naymark [137], p. 13.

[8] E.g., *Prosecutor v. Karadžić,* Decision on the Accused's Motion for Remedy for Violation of Rights in Connection with Arrest (IT-95-5/18-PT) Trial Chamber (31 August 2009), para. 5.

[9] E.g., *Letter dated 26 September 2000 from the Secretary-General addressed to the President of the Security Council*, UN Doc. S/2000/904 [26 September S/2000/904 (26 September 2000)].

for violations of rights during proceedings was ever added.[10] Also, in the ICTY, there has been no case of compensation for violations during proceedings. On the other hand, ICTR precedents have recognized the right to compensation in several cases. For example, in the *Rwamakuba* case, which resulted in acquittal by the ICTR, the court ordered compensation of $2000 for violation of the right to legal assistance.[11] In making that decision, the court held that there is no doubt that the right to compensation forms part of customary law and it was appropriate to try to realise the right to compensation for violations of fundamental human rights under the ICTR.[12] The reason, it explained, is that the power to grant effective redress for violations of human rights arises from the combined effect of the court's inherent competence and its obligations to generally accepted international human rights norms.[13]

Article 85(1) of the ICC Statute, on the other hand, provides that "Anyone who has been the victim of unlawful arrest or detention shall have an enforceable right to compensation." The term "unlawful" has been interpreted concerning the drafting process to include not only violations of the ICC Statute but also violations of the RPE and other relevant applicable international law.[14] However, it is unclear whether the application of the provision is limited to violations by ICC officials or whether it also includes violations by national authorities.[15] The provision is very brief and, together with the related RPE (Rules 173–175), the subject matter of compensation, the criteria for the amount, and the source of funds are unclear, leaving a large part of the matter to the discretion of the court.

The question has also been raised as to whether Article 85(1) can even be interpreted to mean the obligation of each State to put in place a system of compensation for violations arising in the course of cooperation proceedings before the ICC.[16] A relevant case in this regard is the view of the HRC, which has ruled that even if unlawful detention is lawful under domestic law, it is subject to domestic compensation if it violates the ICCPR.[17] If this logic can be translated into the relationship between ICC States Parties and the ICC Statute, the following argument can be made. That is, States Parties to the ICC Statute have an obligation to guarantee the substantive rights of the accused as set out in Articles 55 and 59 of the Statute, and if their domestic conduct violates these provisions, the obligation of ICC States Parties to provide compensation to the subject individual based on a violation of the ICC Statute can be derived, even if the conduct is lawful under their domestic law.

---

[10] For criticisms on this point, see, for example, Michels [125], pp. 407–424. On the reasons for the lack of redress in *ad hoc* Tribunals, see Beresford [12], pp. 628–646.

[11] *Prosecutor v. Rwamakuba,* Decision on Appropriate Remedy (ICTR-98-44C-T) Trial Chamber (31 January 2007), para. 32.

[12] *Ibid.*, paras. 40, 44.

[13] *Ibid.*, para. 45.

[14] Staker and Nerlich [200], pp. 2000–2001.

[15] *Ibid.*

[16] *Ibid.*

[17] *A v. Australia,* Communication No. 560/1993, U.N. Doc. CCPR/C/59/D/560/1993 (30 April 1997), para. 9.5.

(b) Reduction of sentence

Several national and regional human rights courts have adopted sentence commutations as an appropriate redress.[18] Although the Statute of the *ad hoc* Tribunals does not provide for commutation of sentences as a redress, there are precedents that have held that sentences are reduced where there has been a violation of rights during the proceedings and the person has been found guilty. For example, in the case of *Semanza*, who was detained twice in Cameroon before being handed over to the ICTR, the ICTR Appeals Chamber found a violation at the initial stage of detention of the right to be informed of the grounds for prosecution and the right to make a complaint about the legality of his detention, but held that a reduction of sentence was appropriate in the event of conviction rather than release and granted a six month reduction.[19] Similarly, the Appeals Chamber in the ICTR *Kajelijeli* case reduced the sentence to 45 years' imprisonment where two life sentences and 15 years' imprisonment would have been appropriate, as a reduction of sentence rather than cancellation of the indictment was appropriate for the illegality of the arrest and the undue delay exceeding 200 days.[20]

On the other hand, Article 78(1) of the ICC Statute states that factors such as the gravity of the offence and the individual circumstances of the convicted person shall be considered in determining the sentence, and Rule 145 of the RPE provides a list of illustrative grounds for reduction of the sentence.[21] Paragraph 2 of the same article also provides that in imposing a sentence of imprisonment, the period of confinement ordered by the court or related to the acts constituting the basis of the offence may be counted towards the term of the sentence. In the *Lubanga* case, it was held that there were no factors other than the time spent by the accused in an ICC detention facility that could result in a reduction of the sentence.[22] The conclusion was similar in the decision to sentence in the *Katanga* case, but this decision explicitly states that it is appropriate to consider a fundamental violation of the accused's rights, if any, as a reason for reducing the sentence.[23]

The court has broad discretion in sentencing in criminal trials, although there may be various statutory factors to be considered. The human rights conventions do not explicitly stipulate the right to have one's sentence commuted upon conviction as a redress for the violation of rights committed during the criminal proceedings. In addition, commutations of sentences are sometimes viewed as problematic from

---

[18] Turner [234], p. 219.

[19] *Prosecutor v. Semanza,* Judgement and Sentence (ICTR-97-20-T) Trial Chamber (15 May 2003), para. 590.

[20] *Kajelijeli v. Prosecutor,* Judgment (ICTR-98-44A-A) Appeals Chamber (23 May 2005), paras. 255, 320–324.

[21] See, Jennings [88], p. 1437. However, Khan (a current ICC Prosecutor) said it must be remembered that "Sentencing is as much an art as it is a science." Khan [99], p. 1891.

[22] *Prosecutor v. Lubanga,* Decision on Sentence pursuant to Article 76 of the Statute (ICC-01/04-01/06-2901) Trial Chamber I (10 July 2012), para. 90.

[23] *Le Procureur c. Germain Katanga,* Jugement rendu en application de l'article 76 du Statut (ICC-01/04-01/07-3484) La Chambre De Première Instance II (23 mai 2014), para. 136.

the perspective of the objective of international criminal justice, which is the proper punishment of core crimes, and it is argued that compensation is a more appropriate redress even in cases of conviction.[24]

(c) Stay of proceedings

In relation to whether the court may continue to exercise jurisdiction over cases in international criminal courts where prosecution is possible based on illegal proceedings, the issue has been whether the abuse of process doctrine is a "general principle of law" as applicable law. The abuse of process doctrine holds that the violation of a suspect's rights in criminal proceedings is an abuse of process and that a trial based on such illegal proceedings should not be continued even if all other proceedings are in accordance with normal procedures. The application of this doctrine can be found in common law and the Roman Dutch legal system.[25] The application of this principle leads to a stay or suspension of proceedings. On the other hand, the principle that the illegality of an arrest does not impede a criminal trial is commonly referred to as the *Eichmann* principle.[26] The principle has its origins in the Roman law proverb *male captus bene detentus,* which states that arrest is illegal but detention is legal and is generally adopted in States with a Continental legal system and in the US.[27]

In the ICTR's Appeals Chamber decision in the *Barayagwiza* case, the *ad hoc* Tribunal found that pre-trial violations of human rights due to the prosecutor's dereliction of duty constituted an abuse of process and ordered the release of the accused, considering that the continuation of the trial would cause irreparable damage to the integrity of the judicial process and deterrence of serious future violations.[28] Similarly in the ICTY, in the *Nikolić* case, the Trial Chamber held that the three elements that prevent the exercise of jurisdiction are violation of State sovereignty by the act of abduction, violation of the international human rights of the accused, and abuse of process, and admitted that the court has discretion to withdraw the exercise of

---

[24] Shereshevsky [188], pp. 71–99.

[25] See, Nsereko [141]. See, for example, the English and Bennett cases (*R. v. Horseferry Road Magistrates' Court, Ex parte Bennett* [1994] 1 AC 42), the Australian case of *Levinge v. Director of Custodial Services* (1987), 9 NSWLR 546, the South African case of *State v. Ebrahim*, 1991 (2) SALR 553) etc.

[26] From the statement in the same case that "It is an established rule of law that a person being tried for an offence against the laws of a State may not oppose his trial by reason of the illegality of his arrest or of the means whereby he was brought within the jurisdiction of that State." *Eichmann*, in the District Court of Jerusalem, 36 ILR 5 (15 December 1961), para. 41. See also, Radosavljevic [161], p. 270, note 2.

[27] See, for example, the French case of *Re Argoud*, Cour de Cassation, 45 ILR 90 (4 June 1964); the *Berbie* case [*Berbie*, Cour de Cassation, 78 ILR 124, 148 (6 October 1983)]; the "German Infringement of Territorial Sovereignty" (BVerfG—Beschluß vom 17.07.1985 (2 BvR 1190/84)—DRsp Nr. 1994/2567), US—*Ker v. Illinois*, 119 US 436 (1886), *Frisbie v. Collins*, 342 US 519 (1952), *United States v. Toscanino*, 500 F 2d 267 (1974), *Alvarez-Machain*, 112 S.Ct. 2188 (1992), et al.

[28] *Prosecutor v. Barayagwiza*, Decision (ICTR-97-19-1) Appeals Chamber (3 November 1999), paras. 72–108.

jurisdiction when these elements are found, citing the ICTR's *Barayagwiza* Appeals Chamber decision.[29]

The ICC *Lubanga* case was suspended twice during the trial on the grounds that a fair trial was impossible. In the first decision, the ICC Trial Chamber, relying on the Appeals Chamber's decision in the *Lubanga* Jurisdiction case (discussed below), held that the disclosure of evidence in the prosecution's possession that was favourable to the accused was a fundamental aspect of the accused's right to a fair trial and that the trial proceedings were so subversive that a fair trial was impossible to conduct ("*Lubanga* Disclosure Case").[30] A subsequent appellate decision stated that a conditional stay of proceedings is an appropriate redress where it is impossible to preserve a fair trial but may later become possible due to a change in circumstances.[31] These decisions have been assessed as being a agonizing decision to ensure a fair trial in response to the prosecutor's actions in attempting to use the large amount of material obtained from the UN and non-governmental organisations through the use of confidentiality agreements.[32] The second decision to stay was based on the prosecutor's refusal to implement the court's order in relation to the disclosure of the intermediaries' identities. The Trial Chamber found an abuse of process and decided to unconditionally stay the proceedings on the grounds, among others, that the court could not guarantee that the accused would receive a fair trial ("*Lubanga* Refusal to Implement the Prosecutor's Order case").[33] However, in response to that decision, the Appeals Chamber reversed the decision to stay the proceedings on the grounds that it was not reasonable to find that stay of the proceedings was necessary without other sanctions or other measures for the prosecutor's failure to comply with the order.[34]

---

[29] *Prosecutor v. Nikolić,* Decision on Defence Motion Challenging the Exercise of Jurisdiction by the Tribunal (IT-94-2-PT) Trial Chamber II (9 October 2002), paras. 96, 111; Sloan [194], p. 548.

[30] *Prosecutor v. Lubanga,* Decision on the consequences of non-disclosure of exculpatory materials covered by Article 54(3)(e) agreements and the Prosecutor v. Lubanga, Decision on the consequences of non-disclosure of exculpatory materials covered by Article 54(3)(e) agreements and the application to stay the prosecution of the accused, together with certain other issues raised at the Status Conference on 10 June 2008 (ICC-01/04-01/06-1401) Trial Chamber I (13 June 2008), paras. 90–93.

[31] *Prosecutor v. Lubanga,* Judgment on the appeal of the Prosecutor against the decision of Trial Chamber I entitled "Decision on the consequences of the the ICC has not yet made a decision on the application of the Article 54(3)(e) agreements and the application to stay the prosecution of the accused, together with certain other issues raised at the Status Conference on 10 June 2008". (ICC-01/04-01/06-1486) Appeals Chamber (21 October 2008), para. 80.

[32] Higashizawa [74], p. 101.

[33] *Prosecutor v. Lubanga,* Redacted Decision on the Prosecution's Urgent Request for Variation of the Time-Limit to Disclose the Identity of the Intermediary 143 or Alternatively to Stay Proceedings Pending Further Consultations with the VWU (ICC-01/04-01/06-2517-Red) Trial Chamber I (8 July 2010), paras. 20–31.

[34] *Prosecutor v. Lubanga,* Judgment on the appeal of the Prosecutor against the decision of Trial Chamber I of 8 July 2010 entitled "Decision on the Prosecution's Urgent Request for Variation of the Time-Limit to Disclose the Identity of Intermediary 143 or Alternatively to Stay", (ICC-01/04-01/06-2582) Appeals Chamber (8 October 2010), paras. 59–61.

The above-mentioned ICC cases fall under the category of redress that affects the outcome of a trial [type (i)] and are different in character from those relating to the stay of proceedings as an *ex post facto* redress for infringement of rights [type (ii)], which is the subject of this chapter. Cases concerning stay of proceedings for the latter type of infringement are discussed below.

Several problems remain with the stay of proceedings itself as a redress for infringement by the State authorities. First, the procedural legal basis to stay the proceedings remains unclear.[35] Second, the measures to be taken after the suspension of the proceedings need to be discussed. If, after suspending the proceedings and releasing a person on the grounds of torture or other human rights violations that make a fair trial impossible, the person is handed over to the State that committed such violations, this will promote the continuation of the state of violation, which will not achieve the original purpose. Therefore, it is necessary to consider the release to a third State after the suspension of the proceedings. Thirdly, it is important to note that the suspension of proceedings has serious political consequences, as the above-mentioned decision to release Barayagwiza at the ICTR was strongly opposed by Rwanda, which refused to cooperate with the ICTR thereafter.[36]

2.2 Characteristics of the ICC's Prosecution System

The ICC criminal proceedings include provisions for the protection of the human rights of suspects and, in the event of a violation of such provisions, redress such as compensation, commutation of sentence, and suspension of proceedings are envisaged. However, the following structural features of the ICC's prosecution system affect the actual operation of the human rights protection provisions.

First, although the ICC has its own Office of the Prosecutor, it is not normally permissible for the ICC prosecutor to exercise coercive power, which is fundamentally the public authority of the State, within each State. In principle, the custody of suspects, which is the basis of criminal prosecution, cannot be achieved without the use of coercive force by national police and prosecutors, and thus cooperation by States is essential. For this reason, the ICC ensures vertical cooperation with States Parties, which is different from horizontal inter-State relations. Since the realization of prosecution at the ICC depends on the cooperation of States, it is the local judicial authorities who first come into contact with, arrest and detain suspects of core crimes.

Regarding the cooperation of States with the ICC, Article 99(4) of the Statute states that, in principle, ICC investigations may be conducted with the cooperation of the State. The arrest warrant is issued by the ICC Pre-Trial Chamber at the request of the ICC prosecutor and is executed by the State as long as the judicial system of the requested State is functioning. The ICC prosecutor may act directly only in

[35] On the other hand, with regards to release by the ICC Prosecutor in cases of unacceptable delay, see Rule 60(4) of the Statute.

[36] For more information, see Schabas [179], pp. 563–571.

exceptional cases where there is no national authority capable of fulfilling its mandate (Article 57(3)(d) of the Statute).

States Parties have a general obligation to cooperate fully with the ICC in investigations and prosecutions conducted by the ICC, except where their security interests may be threatened (Article 72), and to ensure that their national legal procedures are available for cooperation (Articles 86 and 88). In the event of difficulties in implementation, States Parties shall consult without delay with the ICC to resolve the situation (Article 97). If a State Party fails to comply with a request for cooperation and interferes with the exercise of the ICC's mandate and powers, it may refer the matter to the Assembly of States Parties, and the ICC may further refer it to the UN Security Council [Article 87(7)].

The drafting process for a system of cooperation between the ICC and States was divided between views that emphasized the similarities with horizontal inter-State cooperation and the need for a new vertical relationship that was quite different from inter-State relations.[37] Ultimately, unlike the vertical and coercive nature of the *ad hoc* Tribunals' cooperation,[38] it was developed as an institution that differed in many respects from inter-State cooperation, although it included provisions that took into account national sovereignty.[39] Vertical cooperation between the ICC and States differs from inter-State cooperation in that it imposes unilateral obligations of cooperation without reciprocity for States Parties to the ICC Statute, it excludes the possibility of reciprocity, and it involves the ICC in the extradition decision-making process.[40]

2.3 Complementary Jurisdictional Relationships

The ICC has adopted the "principle of complementarity", which makes State jurisdiction primary to the question of coordination between its own jurisdiction and that of the States. Because of the complementary jurisdictional relationship to the State, it is the local authorities that are encouraged to conduct primary prosecution and trial in the ICC's prosecution regime.

The relationship between the jurisdiction of the ICC and the States differs significantly from that of the *ad hoc* Tribunals regime. The ICTY/ICTR is considered superior to the States and the proceedings of the *ad hoc* Tribunals take precedence in certain cases, even if domestic criminal proceedings are pending or domestic cases are final (ICTY Statute, Articles 9 and 10; ICTR Statute Articles 8 and 9, etc.). The

---

[37] *Report of the Preparatory Committee on the Establishment of an International Criminal Court*, Vol. 1, UN Doc. A/51/22 (13 September 1996), para. 310.

[38] On the duty to cooperate at the ICTY, see, e.g., Furuya [62], pp. 189–209.

[39] Swart [210], p. 1594.

[40] The word "surrender" is used for extradition from a State to the ICC, rather than "extradition" as used between States; See e.g., Sluiter [196], p. 608. On the use of different words, see Ko [105], pp. 329–370.

ICC, on the other hand, has adopted the principle of complementarity regarding the relationship between its jurisdiction and that of the State. Therefore, the ICC supplements the criminal jurisdiction of the State and cannot accept a case when there is a genuine investigation, prosecution, trial, etc. by the State (ICC Statute, Preamble para. 10, Articles 1 and 17). A positive approach to complementarity, which emphasizes the primary jurisdiction of the State and the promotion of domestic proceedings, was emphasized by the first prosecutor immediately after the establishment of the ICC.[41] This has been noted as a move towards an alternative and more supportive nature of the ICC as opposed to the traditional exclusive and independent international criminal tribunals.[42]

Complementarity is embodied in the admissibility review of a case before the ICC, where the ICC decides not to accept a particular case if it is currently being investigated or prosecuted by a State having jurisdiction over it [Article 17(1)(a)], or if it has already been investigated and decided not to prosecute it [Article 17(1)(b)]. These two cases are generally regarded as the supplementary requirement in the admissibility review. The presumption of inadmissibility is triggered when there is an ongoing domestic investigation, prosecution or trial, or a decision not to prosecute.[43] However, Article 17(1)(a) and (b) are accompanied by the provision that this shall not apply where the State concerned is unwilling or unable genuinely to conduct the investigation or prosecution. The criteria for determining willingness and ability are set out in Article 17(2) and (3) respectively.

3 The Issue of Redress in Vertical Relationships

The first issue concerning the redress of the rights of the accused in the ICC's prosecution regime is whether, in the vertical cooperation between the ICC and the State, it is the State authorities who have the first contact with the accused and whether redress for violation of rights in domestic proceedings is transferred to the ICC when the accused is handed over to it. Various issues on this question have been addressed in the *Lubanga* Jurisdiction case[44] and the *Gbagbo* Jurisdiction case.

---

[41] E.g., International Criminal Court, *Statement of the Prosecutor Luis Moreno Ocampo to the Diplomatic Corps* (The Hague, Netherlands, 12 February 2004).

[42] See Ko [104], p. 241.

[43] *Prosecutor v. Germain Katanga and Mathieu Ngudjolo Chui,* Judgment on the Appeal of Mr. Germain Katanga against the Oral Decision of Trial Chamber II of 12 June 2009 on the Admissibility of the Case (ICC-01/04-01/07-1497) Appeals Chamber (25 September 2009), paras. 1, 75–79; Schabas [181], p. 345.

[44] For a precedent commentary, see Murai [131], p. 134.

3.1 Cases

3.1.1 The Lubanga Jurisdiction Case (2006)

Thomas Lubanga, a leader of an armed group, was detained for two years and seven months in the Democratic Republic of the Congo ("DRC") for different offences and later surrendered to the ICC based on a decision by the DRC Military Advocate General regarding an arrest and surrender request by the ICC. The defence filed a request for provisional release on the grounds that the arrest for unrelated charges in the State before his surrender was illegal and that the conditions of detention were inhumane, as well as a challenge to the jurisdiction of the ICC by invoking the abuse of process doctrine.

The Pre-Trial Chamber's decision ("*Lubanga* Pre-Trial decision")[45] held that violations by national authorities can be considered by the ICC if it is established that human rights violations prior to the execution of the ICC arrest warrant were committed by the "concerted action" of the ICC prosecutor and the State (p. 9), and that the abuse of process doctrine is applicable in cases of torture or gross ill-treatment by the authorities of the detaining State (p. 10).

However, the Appeals Chamber ("*Lubanga* Appeals judgment")[46] rejected the application of the abuse of process doctrine itself as having no basis in the Statute (para. 35), after constituting the said procedure as a unique (*sui generis*) procedure rather than a jurisdiction-related one. It then considered the existence of redress other than compensation as provided for in Article 85(1). The Appeals Chamber confirmed that the exercise of the ICC's jurisdiction must be conducted in accordance with internationally recognized human rights norms under Article 21(3) (para. 36) and held that where a violation of the fundamental rights of an accused person makes a fair trial impossible, it is inconsistent to submit that person to trial, and where the injustice of the treatment of the accused person is serious the need to stay the judicial process overrides the interest of the world community in bringing to trial suspects of the most serious crimes (paras 37–39), taking a comparative approach to the relief of suspects and the prosecution of core crimes.

3.1.2 The Gbagbo Jurisdiction Case (2012)

Following the *Lubanga* Appeals judgment, the Pre-Trial Chamber was again required to decide a similar case, the *Gbagbo* case. Laurent Gbagbo, the former president of Côte d'Ivoire, had been arrested in the State following a military operation by political

---

45 *Prosecutor v. Lubanga,* Decision on the Defence Challenge to the Jurisdiction of the Court pursuant to article 19 (2) (a) of the Statute (ICC-01/04-01/06-512) Pre-Trial Chamber I (3 October 2006).

46 *Prosecutor v. Lubanga,* Judgment on the Appeal of Mr. Thomas Lubanga Dyilo against the Decision on the Defence Challenge to the Jurisdiction of the Court Pursuant to article 19 (2) (a) of the Statute of 3 October 2006 (ICC-01/04-01/06-772) Appeals Chamber (14 December 2006).

adversary and current President Alassane Ouattara's forces, and later charged with economic crimes. He was subsequently held in detention under degrading conditions until the ICC issued a warrant for his arrest and handed him over to the ICC. The defence filed a challenge to the jurisdiction of the ICC, seeking a stay of proceedings on the basis of abuse of process doctrine.

The decision of the Pre-Trial Chamber ("*Gbagbo* Pre-Trial Chamber decision"),[47] in line with the discussion in the *Lubanga* Appeals judgment, refers to the possibility that the exercise of jurisdiction may exceptionally be suspended if the infringement makes it impossible for the proceedings to be conducted fairly. However, since a violation of a right will only stop proceedings if it makes fairness in the proceedings impossible, it follows logically that the violation of the right must be relevant to the process of bringing the accused to justice by the ICC, so that the violation of a fundamental right, regardless of its gravity, must be attributed to the ICC. The Court held that a violation of a fundamental right constitutes an abuse of process only when it can be attributed to the ICC, regardless of the gravity of the violation (para. 92). Attribution here refers to cases where the violation is directly committed by a person associated with the ICC or by a third party in collusion with the ICC (*Ibid.*). The Court then held that an abuse of process consists of a violation of Article 55 or 59 by itself or in combination with other circumstances (para. 93).

The decision also set out standards for the scope of application of individual provisions. First, as Article 55(1) provides "In respect of an investigation under this Statute", it clearly stated that the Article does not apply to criminal proceedings other than proceedings relating to crimes under the jurisdiction of the ICC (para. 96). As for Article 59, it also stated that the provisions of this Article do not apply prior to the timing when the detaining State receives an arrest and surrender request by the ICC, since its purpose is to ensure that ICC arrest warrants are executed in accordance with proper procedures and that the rights of the person subject to the arrest warrant are respected (para. 101). It further confirmed that other violations of rights require attribution to the ICC and clarified the criteria for attribution, stating that mere knowledge by the ICC prosecutor of an investigation by national authorities or communication with national authorities does not prove that the ICC prosecutor was involved in the proceedings by the national authorities (para. 107).[48]

The series of decisions of the Pre-Trial Chamber in the *Lubanga* case, the Appeals Chamber's judgment, and the Pre-Trial Chamber decision in the *Gbagbo* case suggest

---

[47] *Prosecutor v. Gbagbo,* Decision on the "Corrigendum of the challenge to the jurisdiction of the International Criminal Court on the basis of articles 12(3), 19(2), 21(3), 55 and 59 of the Rome Statute filed by the Defence for President Gbagbo (ICC-02/11-01/11-129)", (ICC-02/11-01/11-212) Pre-Trial Chamber I (15 August 2012).

[48] *Ibid.*, para. 107. An appeal was also filed against the same decision, but the Appeals Chamber dismissed the motion to stay proceedings on the ground that it did not constitute a challenge to jurisdiction and was not a valid ground of appeal and did not proceed to trial on the merits. It therefore did not rule on whether the Pre-Trial Chamber I decision in Gbagbo differed from the Lubanga Appeals Chamber decision. *Prosecutor v. Gbagbo,* Judgment on the appeal of Mr. Laurent Koudou Gbagbo against the decision of the Pre-Trial Chamber I on the jurisdiction and stay of the proceedings (ICC-02/11-01/11-321) Appeals Chamber (12 December 2012).

the criteria for attributing human rights violations in domestic proceedings to the ICC, the scope of application of various provisions in the ICC Statute that define the substantive rights of suspects, and the possibility of suspension of proceedings at the ICC on the grounds of human rights violations.[49]

3.2 ICC's Obligation to Redress Violations of Rights by State Authorities: Attribution of Acts and Balancing

The *Lubanga* and *Gbagbo* cases, in which illegality was alleged in domestic arrests and criminal proceedings that took place prior to surrender to the ICC, concerned whether the ICC should provide redress for violations of rights committed by State authorities. In these cases, the Court took a certain view on how the ICC should approach redress issues in cases of human rights violations committed by State authorities who are the first to encounter suspects, who face psychological and physical difficulties in the ICC's prosecution regime which is based on vertical cooperation.

These cases can be summarized as follows. The Pre-Trial Chamber focused on attribution, while the Appels Chamber did not require attribution but weighed the crime against the gravity of the infringement. There is no direct conflict between the approach that ICC redress requires attribution of conduct to the ICC and the approach that weighed the seriousness of the infringement against the crime. Rather, it is more accurate to view the ICC's approaches to redress as a combination of the first criterion of whether attribution is required or not ("attribution-required" or "attribution-not-required") and the second criterion of whether absolute redress or comparative balance is required ("absolute" or "comparative balance"). These two criteria of assessment allow us to sort out where the approach taken in each case stands in relative terms. While the *Lubanga* Pre-Trial Chamber decision expressed

[49] A subsequent case in which a commutation of sentence was sought for violations of rights by State authorities is the Katanga case, discussed above. The defence alleged violations of various rights during the period in which the accused was detained in the DRC from March 2005 until he was handed over to the ICC on 18 October 2007; the Trial Chamber's decision to sentence him on 23 May 2014 stated that it would not examine the period during which he was not detained in the name of the ICC (*pour la compte de la Cour*) that it would not examine the period during which he was not detained in the name of the ICC (para. 136). It also held that even if the accused was detained in the name of the ICC, the violation of his rights could not be attributed to the ICC unless it had a connection with the ICC proceedings (*ne pourraient être imputées à la Cour*) (para. 137). It then held that the accused in this case had been detained in the name of the ICC since 18 September 2007, when the notification of the issuance of the ICC arrest warrant was given to the DRC, and that the interrogation for extradition to the ICC after that date was subject to consideration, but no violation of rights was found (paras 131–140, 155). This sentencing decision in the Katanga case was the first case in which the ICC Trial Chamber referred to the possibility of domestic remedies for violations of rights. Although the decision expresses the criteria for determining whether to grant relief differently than the Gbagbo Pre-Trial Chamber decision, the substantive content of the decision appears to be largely the same. *Procureur c. Katanga*, Jugement rendu en application de l'article 74 du Statut (ICC-01/04-01/07-3484) La Chambre De Première Instance II (23 mai 2014).

an attribution-required approach (absolute approach only in cases of "torture or gross ill-treatment") and the *Lubanga* Appeals judgment expressed only a comparative balance approach, the Gbagbo Pre-Trial Chamber decision can be classified as clarifying that an attribution-required/comparative balance approach was adopted.

Below, I review the differences and significance of each approach with respect to these two criteria, and then evaluate the approach taken by the ICC and point out institutional issues.

3.2.1 First Criterion: Attribution-Required Approach and Attribution-Not-Required Approach

The difference between approaches that require attribution and those that do not require attribution for an international organization to grant redress for a violation of an individual's rights by a State may be related to the legitimacy of the redress.

On the one hand, the attribution-required approach focuses on the procedural legitimacy of the redress. The result seems to reflect the concern that, as the ICC is a treaty body, the legitimacy of the use of contributions by States Parties in the case of monetary compensation—and given that the original purpose of the ICC was to ensure the prohibition of impunity—may be undermined in cases of commutation of sentences or stay of proceedings by the actions of one State Party. Therefore, the position is that the ICC is justified in becoming the subject of redress only when the ICC itself can legally be constituted as the subject of infringement.

On the other hand, taking the attribution-not-required approach is considered to focus on the more substantive justification for redress. This position is one that broadly interprets the ICC's remedial responsibility to the individual referred to the ICC's proceedings, without taking issue with the alleged infringement of rights.

The approach that required attribution prevailed in the *ad hoc* Tribunals. In the ICTY *Nikolić* case, the accused was abducted by unknown persons inside the Federal Republic of Yugoslavia and secretly transported to Bosnia and Herzegovina before being arrested by Stabilisation Force ("SFOR") personnel. The perpetrators of the abductions were not related to SFOR or ICTY prosecutors. The attribution of the acts of the unidentified individuals to the ICTY was therefore in question. In this case, the Trial Chamber first held that there was no attribution to the SFOR for the acts of private individuals and, therefore it was not necessary to examine the attribution of the SFOR's acts to the ICTY.[50] On the other hand, early ICTR cases were evasive in their judgments. They held that it is the sovereign State that controls the authorities that execute requests for cooperation from the ICTR, and that the violation of the rights of the accused at the time of arrest by State authorities can be redressed by the State

[50] On the same part, the State Responsibility Article is referred to in *Nikolić*, "Decision on Defence", paras. 60–68.

under the law of that State.[51] In the Appeals Chamber decision in the *Barayagwiza* case, the ICTR was found liable and a stay of proceedings was handed down when human rights violations occurred due to the negligence of the ICTR prosecutor in the proceedings before the transfer to the ICTR.[52] However, in the review process in the following year on the basis of new evidence, including a report by the Supreme Court judge of Cameroon in which Jean-Bosco Barayagwiza was held in custody, the Appeals Chamber reversed its initial decision and continued the trial, as it found that the delay in the proceedings in detention was caused not by the ICTR prosecutor but by the Cameroonian authorities' negligence.[53]

In response to these *ad hoc* Tribunals precedents, the ICC precedents can be summarized as follows. The Pre-Trial Chamber decision in the *Lubanga* case held that attribution is not required in cases of "torture or gross ill-treatment", but held that in other cases, acts are attributed when there is "concerted action". The *Lubanga* Appeals Chamber judgment, on the other hand, did not specifically address the attribution of acts. Subsequently, the Pre-Trial Chamber decision in the *Gbagbo* case took the approach that a clear attribution of conduct is required, stating that the conduct of State authorities affects ICC proceedings only when that conduct can be attributed to the ICC.

3.2.2 The Second Criterion: The Absolute Approach and the Balancing Approach

Both in the framework of holding States accountable under international law and in the framework of remedies for violations of individual human rights by States, an absolutist approach to remedies is taken, which basically states that for every violation of a right, a redress must be provided to relieve the violation entirely. It is a principle of international law that full reparation should be available for violations of rights under international law.[54] In addition, in international human rights law, the "right to an effective remedy" may be set out in separate provisions in international human rights instruments, or it may be part of the right to a fair trial,[55] and

[51] *Prosecutor v. Ngirumpatse,* Decision on the Defence Motion Challenging the Lawfulness of the Arrest and Detention and Seeking the Return or Inspection of Seized Items (ICTR-97-44-I) Trial Chamber II (10 December 1999), para. 56.

[52] *Barayagwiza,* Decision (ICTR-97-19-1), (3 November 1999), paras. 60–68.

[53] *Barayagwiza v. Prosecutor,* Decision [Prosecutor's Request for Review or Reconsideration (ICC-97-19-AR72)] Appeals Chamber (31 March 2000).

[54] See *Affair relative* à *l'usine de Chorzow* [The Case Relating to the Chorzow Factory], CPJI Serie A, No. 9, 21; *Legal Consequenes of the Construction of a Wall in the Occupied Palestinian Territory,* Advisory Opinion, ICJ Reports 2004, 136.

[55] For example, Articles 2(3) and 14 of the ICCPR, Articles 13 and 41 of the European Convention on Human Rights, Articles 1 and 25 of the Inter-American Convention on Human Rights, and the Basic Principles and Guidelines on the Right of Victims of Gross Violations of International Human Rights Law and International Humanitarian Law to a Remedy and Reparation, adopted by the UN General Assembly in 2005, are relevant.

various human rights courts have held that the right to an effective remedy, such as monetary compensation or an order to amend domestic law, is an absolute right. In some cases, various human rights courts have issued substantive remedies, such as monetary compensation or orders to amend national laws.[56] The provision of such 'full' reparation, which considers only the extent of the violation, is also referred to as the 'rights maximizing' approach.[57]

In contrast, considering the wider societal benefits and the impact of granting redress on other entities is called the balancing approach.[58] Redress for violations of rights in criminal proceedings involve reflexive sanctions against the violator and the effect of deterring future illegal investigations. On the other hand, the fact remains that the infringed person is still a suspect or accused of a crime. Therefore, there are aspects in which monetary compensation to a fined person, commutation of sentence or release may impede the realization of the social interest of punishing the perpetrator of the crime, and it is the comparative balance approach to remedies that incorporates these considerations into the determination of the content of the redress.[59]

The *ad hoc* Tribunals are said to have taken a comparative balance approach in the past. In the *Barayagwiza* case, the ICTR Appeals Chamber ordered the release of the accused on the grounds that the violation of the accused's rights by the prosecutor was "a serious and egregious violation of the accused's rights that threatened the integrity of the Court".[60] However, the decision is regarded as forcing a reconsideration of the basic concepts of international criminal tribunals, such as the purpose of their establishment and the role of justice in establishing peace.[61] In the ICTR *Semanza* case, while finding that the rights of the accused had been violated in the course of the proceedings, the Court held that the appropriate remedy was not release but a reduction of the sentence in case of guilt, as it was necessary to be a proportionate redress and to bear in mind the task of the Court, particularly in terms of the maintenance of international public order.[62] The ICTY similarly held in the *Nikolić* case, citing the *Barayagwiza* appeal decision above, that the Court has the discretion to withdraw from exercising jurisdiction in cases of "serious and egregious violations of the rights of the accused which threaten the integrity of the Court", but that the rights of the accused must be weighed against the interests of the international community in the prosecution of international crimes and that the violation in the present case was not such a serious violation. The Court held that the violation in this case was not of such an egregious nature as to hamper the exercise of jurisdiction.[63]

---

56 See, Shelton [186], pp. 280–290.

57 Gewirtz [66], p. 588.

58 Turner [234], p. 194.

59 *Ibid.*, 204.

60 *Barayagwiza*, Decision (ICTR-97-19-1) Appeals Chamber (3 November 1999), paras. 72–108.

61 Inazumi [81].

62 *Semanza v. Prosecutor*, Decision (ICTR-97-20-A) Appeals Chamber (31 May 2000), paras. 125–126.

63 *Nikolić*, "Decision on Defence", paras. 112–115.

In the *Lubanga* Pre-Trial Chamber decision, the ICC held that release would be made under the abuse of process doctrine in cases of "torture or gross ill-treatment", a view that could be called a partial absolute approach. The *Lubanga* Appeals judgment, however, took a balancing approach, weighing the interests of staying proceedings against the interests of the international community as a whole in prosecuting the case, and held that if the violations were so serious as to render a fair trial impossible, the proceedings would be stayed. Although the Pre-Trial Chamber in the *Gbagbo* case did not apply the specific balancing approach because the imputation of acts of infringement was not found in the decision, it cited the *Lubanga* Appels judgment and similarly confirmed that the exceptional measure of stay of proceedings is only taken when the gravity of the infringement makes it impossible to hold a fair trial.

3.2.3 Evaluation of ICC's Approach and Institutional Challenges

The two main objectives of remedies for violations of individual rights in criminal cases are the direct restoration of rights and the deterrence of future illegal investigations.[64] First, the various approaches described above are evaluated in terms of these two remedial objectives, considering the particularities of international criminal justice.

Regarding the first objective—restoration of rights—, in relation to the first criterion ("attribution required" or "not required"), the way in which the responsibility of International Criminal Justice Institutions for substantive remedies is perceived will be affected. The vertical cooperation of the ICC requires States where conflict or genocide has occurred, regardless of the state of their domestic judicial systems, to provide obligatory cooperation with the ICC. For this reason, it has been argued that Article 85(1) of the ICC Statute, which succinctly provides for compensation to persons who have been unlawfully arrested or otherwise subjected to unlawful arrest, contains the intention that the ICC itself will secure remedies for all wrongful acts related to arrest.[65] In this sense, it seems necessary to take the meaning of the obligation to provide remedies in a broader sense, which here differs from "responsibility" for violations of international obligations and does not concern attribution. In relation to the second criterion ("absolute" or "comparative balance"), what is distinctive in international criminal justice is the question of the content of the balance with the prosecution of core crimes, which is its primary objective. The crimes under ICC jurisdiction are all "serious crimes of concern to the international community as a whole" and the gravity of prosecuting such crimes over and above the seriousness of prosecuting these crimes is likely to preclude most rights violations in practice.[66] However, the effectiveness and content of the comparison with the gravity of the crimes changes if the comparison is not limited to the most appropriate redress for

[64] Turner [234], p. 221.

[65] Currie [36], p. 374.

[66] The failure to elect to stay proceedings because the costs of granting relief outweigh the benefits is described as "remedial deterrence." Starr [201].

the violation, but downgraded to other redresses that are more restrictive and reflect the gravity of the crime, as was taken in the ICTR *Semanza* case ("a more flexible comparative balance approach"). In international criminal justice, however, the absolute approach—or at least "the more flexible comparative approach"—is preferable if only substantive relief is considered, since all the crimes to compare are serious and the remedies available under the comparative approach would have to be restrictive in any event. Therefore, the adoption of the attribution-not-required and absolute approach is preferable for the realization of the first objective.

Regarding the second objective—deterrence of illegal investigations—, what is distinctive for the prosecution regime of international criminal justice is that the target of deterrence is not only the prosecutors of International Criminal Justice Institutions but also the judicial authorities of States. Considering the first criterion ("attribution required" or "attribution not required") from this point of view, the redress secured by the ICC makes it less effective in deterring illegal investigations by States.[67] Therefore, a more direct deterrent effect can be expected if redress is provided by the ICC only when acts can be attributed to the ICC, and domestic compensation actions are brought against infringements by State authorities otherwise. However, when each State is exhausted by core crimes and faces physical difficulties, domestic use of the judicial system cannot be expected. It could be considered more effective if there is a system in which the ICC, an international organization, rather than a claim from an individual, provides redress on an intermediary basis and allows a claim to be made against a State after the fact. Regarding the second criterion ("absolute" or "comparative balancing"), there is room to incorporate the deterrence of illegal searches into comparative considerations. However, again, given that the ICC targets core crimes, it is unlikely that the element of deterrence, particularly in the case of minor violations of rights, would outweigh the seriousness of the offence in a comparative balance approach. Therefore, from the perspective of deterring illegal investigations, which is the second objective of the redress, the attribution-not-required and absolute approach is most desirable.

As discussed above, of the four combinations of approaches discussed in this chapter, the attribution-not-required and absolute approach is the one that seems to be preferred to maximize the realization of the remedial objective. The ICC, on the other hand, takes an attribution-required and balancing approach, under which the obligation to cooperate with the ICC is not discharged if, at the time of the review of the surrender to the ICC, it becomes clear that rights were violated during the previous arrest or detention. The ICC therefore takes over the proceedings even if the realization of surrender is due to violations of rights by State authorities. Therefore, it is considered that a contradiction arises where the ICC only takes over the proceedings but not the protection of rights. In addition, although the flexibility of the balancing approach in the ICC remains uncertain, it is inevitable to criticize the ICC as a regime in which relatively minor rights violations are ignored, with no possibility of exceeding the seriousness of the crimes under the ICC jurisdiction and their prosecution unless the rights violations are of a considerable degree of gravity.

67 *Ibid.*, 382–384.

The ICC's choice of approach naturally takes into account considerations other than the remedial objective itself, such as ensuring procedural legitimacy in relation to the State Party and ensuring the prosecution of core crimes, as well as other premises.

4 The Issue of Remedies for Rights in Complementary Relationships

The second issue regarding the ICC's prosecution regime is that the ICC's complementary relationship to States may give priority to the jurisdiction of States where violations of suspects' rights may be taking place. The question is whether the ICC should exercise jurisdiction and request that a suspect be handed over to the ICC when a violation of the suspect's rights by State authorities is present or foreseeable.

4.1 Judicial Precedents

4.1.1 The *Gaddafi* Admissibility Case (2013)

Saif, the son of Colonel Muammar Gaddafi, who was in power in Libya, was detained in a militia compound in Libya following the revolution in February 2011. After the ICC issued an arrest warrant for Saif, Libya initiated a domestic prosecution for acts similar to those charged by the ICC and filed an objection with the ICC challenging the admissibility of the case. Saif's counsel argued that Libya lacked the will or capacity to genuinely prosecute the case due to, among other things, the inadequate human rights protection under Libya's domestic judicial process.

The decision of the Pre-Trial Chamber ("*Gaddafi* Pre-Trial decision")[68] held that, as applicable law, the State's ability to genuinely investigate or prosecute as referred to in Article 17(3) of the ICC Statute must be examined in the context of the relevant national systems and procedures, and the Court held that it would examine the case based on an assessment of whether the Libyan authorities are capable of conducting an investigation or prosecution in line with Libya's substantive and procedural law (para. 200). In Libya, following the Italian model, a system of guarantees for the rights of suspects and witness protection during certain investigations was in place in the Libyan Constitution and Criminal Procedure Code, and Libya had ratified various human rights treaties, including the ICCPR and the Convention against Torture and Other Cruel Treatment (para. 201).

[68] *Prosecutor v. Gaddafi and Al-Senussi*, Public Redacted-Decision on the admissibility of the case against Saif Al-Islam Gaddafi (ICC-01/11-01/11-344-Red) Pre-Trial Chamber I (31 May 2013). On the case review, see Ochi [145].

However, it was clarified that prosecution efforts in Libya were being conducted under very difficult circumstances (para. 204). In particular, (i) the security situation made it difficult to transfer suspects from the militia compound in Zintan to Tripoli, where the trial would take place, (ii) the inability to obtain necessary testimony due to the lack of adequate witness protection measures, and (iii) the fact that suspects were unable to substantially exercise their right to appointed defence counsel (paras 206–214). In these circumstances, the Pre-Trial Chamber found that Libya was unable to investigate or prosecute in accordance with the law applicable in Libya and, therefore, that it was unnecessary to assess other requirements of Article 17, namely the question of willingness or the impossibility of a fair trial more generally (para. 216).[69]

4.1.2 The *Al-Senussi* Admissibility Case (2013)

A decision on a challenge to admissibility in the *Al-Senussi* case, issued after the *Gaddafi* Pre-Trial decision, denied admissibility at the ICC, despite the fact that it was a domestic Libyan case, like the *Gaddafi* case, and the appointment of counsel had not yet occurred. In that decision, the Court used the same criteria as in the *Gaddafi* case to hear the impact of domestic rights violations on the ICC's admissibility review. However, the *Al-Senussi* case differed crucially from the *Gaddafi* case in that the custody of the accused was under the control of the Libyan government. In the *Al-Senussi* case, it was held that the appointment of counsel was likely to be achieved in the future with the assistance of the Libyan government and that, at the time of the review, no conclusion could be drawn as to whether the proceedings in Libya would be impeded by the inability to overcome security problems or to obtain adequate counsel in the future (para. 308).[70]

The lack of willingness of the State to genuinely prosecute the case was also assessed. The defence challenged the "genuineness" of the Libyan domestic proceedings on four grounds: unjustified procedural delays, lack of counsel, violation of other fundamental human rights, and lack of independence and impartiality of the Libyan judicial system (paras 220–258). The Pre-Trial Chamber found that, although the violation of the accused's rights could be relevant to the examination under Article 17(2)(c), the determination of lack of genuineness under that paragraph has two cumulative requirements: lack of independence and impartiality and, in the circumstances, being conducted in a manner contrary to the intention to bring the accused to trial (para. 235). It then accepted the fact that, of the four arguments made by the defence, the lack of counsel was true, but held that there was no lack of willingness

---

[69] Ibid., paras 204–216. An appeal was filed against the decision, but in a judgment of 21 May 2014, the Appeals Chamber dismissed the appeal, finding no error in the original decision. *Prosecutor v. Gaddafi and Al-Senussi,* Judgment on the appeal of Libya against the decision of Pre-Trial Chamber I of 31 May 2013 entitled "Decision on the admissibility of the case against Saif Al-Islam Gaddafi" (ICC-01/11-01/11-547-Red) Appeals Chamber (21 May 2014).

[70] *Prosecutor v. Gaddafi and Al-Senussi,* Decision on the admissibility of the case against Abdullah Al-Senussi (ICC-01/11-01/11-466-Red) Pre-Trial Chamber I (11 October 2013), paras. 220–292, 308.

because of the absence of any suggestion that it was contrary to the intention to bring the accused to trial (para. 292).

The Appeals Chamber against the same decision essentially upheld the judgment of the original court but added that there may be circumstances where the violation of the accused's rights is so egregious that it may be regarded as "contrary to the intention to bring that person to trial".[71]

In the *Gaddafi* and *Al-Senussi* cases, attention was drawn to the judgment on the impact of ongoing or foreseeable human rights violations in the State on the ICC's complementarity. The decisions confirm that deficiencies in domestic criminal procedures affect the determination of the willingness and ability of States to investigate and prosecute, but only to a limited extent, both in terms of content and temporal scope.

4.2 Possible Exercise of Jurisdiction as a Preventive and Substantive Remedy

The phenomenon that the exercise of ICC jurisdiction can be a substantive guarantee of rights has been pointed out when there are problems with the guarantee of rights in domestic criminal proceedings.[72] This is because it is clear that suspects and accused persons are better treated when they are prosecuted by the ICC, which is well equipped and resourced and ensures a high standard of human rights, rather than by national authorities, which are exhausted by the conflict and face psychological and physical difficulties.

Considering the ICC's complementary relationship with the State from this perspective, the examination of the State's willingness and ability in the ICC's admissibility review can be seen as an examination of the existence of psychological and physical hardships faced by the State.

4.2.1 State's Willingness to Prosecute: Psychological Hardship

In reviewing the admissibility of an ICC case, a lack of willingness to genuinely prosecute and try the accused is found when any of the following three points are met, taking into account the principles of due process recognized by international law [Article 17(2)]: (a) the proceedings are intended to exonerate the suspect from criminal responsibility; (b) there is undue delay that is contrary to the intention to bring the suspect to trial in the circumstances of the case; or (c) the proceedings are

[71] *Prosecutor v. Gaddafi and Al-Senussi*, Judgment on the appeal of Mr. Abdullah Al-Senussi against the decision of Pre-Trial Chamber I of 11 October 2013 entitled "Decision on the admissibility of the case against Abdullah Al-Senussi", (ICC-01/11-01/11-565) Appeals Chamber (24 July 2014), para. 230.

[72] *E.g.* Heller [69].

not conducted independently or impartially and in a manner that is contrary to the intention to bring the suspect to trial in the circumstances of the case.

In the *Al-Senussi* case, which concerned the lack of genuine willingness of the State, the Court clarified that the determination of lack of willingness in Article 17(2)(c) has two cumulative requirements: lack of independence and impartiality, and that it is conducted in a manner contrary to the intent to bring the accused to trial in the circumstances of the case. In the same decision, the Pre-Trial Chamber found that the defence had not sufficiently proved either of its contentions as to whether it was contrary to the intention to bring the accused to trial. It remains ambiguous as to what evidence would prove a manner contrary to the intention to bring the accused to trial. However, when unjustified delays in proceedings or other violations of fundamental human rights are committed by a State with psychological difficulties in a manner contrary to its intention to bring a suspect to trial, there is room for the admissibility of the case by the ICC.

4.2.2 The State's Ability to Prosecute: Physical Hardship

On the other hand, the main problem in the *Gaddafi* case was the physical difficulties in the administration of the domestic criminal justice system, in other words, the examination of the ability to genuinely prosecute or try the case. With regards to the examination of ability, a State is found to lack ability if it is either (i) unable to secure a suspect, (ii) unable to obtain the necessary evidence and testimony, or (iii) unable to conduct proceedings for "other grounds" due to a complete or substantial breakdown or lack of a judicial system in the State. At the time the ICC Statute entered into force, "other grounds" were considered to encompass grounds other than securing a suspect or securing evidence, such as, for example, the lack of judicial officers to conduct a genuine prosecution.[73]

The *Gaddafi* case decision indicated that a State's genuine lack of capacity to prosecute or try a case is determined when it is physically unable to conduct domestic proceedings in accordance with domestic law, including human rights treaties ratified by the State concerned. However, even in the *Gaddafi* case, the issue concerned the State's capacity to genuinely investigate or prosecute, which was unlikely to be restored in the future, and not the fact that it had not been realized at the time of the hearing.

4.2.3 Evaluation of the ICC's Approach and Institutional Challenges

From the interpretation of the ICC Statute, even if an investigation, prosecution or trial is ongoing in a State, if the lack of willingness—psychological hardship—or lack of ability—physical hardship—of a State as referred to in Article 17(2) and (3) is found, the ICC may find the case admissible and exercise ICC jurisdiction.

[73] Holmes [78], p. 678.

However, the decisions of the ICC Trial Chamber in the *Gaddafi* and *Al-Senussi* cases demonstrated the limits of the possibility of preventive and substantive remedies for the rights of the accused through the exercise of ICC jurisdiction.

First, the lack of intention by the State to bring an accused person to trial does not necessarily derive from the delay in the proceedings or the lack of independence or impartiality of the trial. In other words, the violation of the rights of the suspect or the accused does not alone prove that the domestic trial was motivated by a grudge or vengeance and that the State concerned did not genuinely intend to bring the accused to trial. Second, the examination of competence only examines whether domestic proceedings are conducted in accordance with domestic law and does not conduct a substantive examination as to whether substantive rights under the ICC Statute are guaranteed. Third, potential domestic violations of human rights are only considered in the examination of competence within the scope of Article 17(3), and no other grounds are considered. In other words, procedural fairness in the determination of ability is only relevant if it constitutes a factual or legal "obstacle".[74] Fourth, the problem is that the situation of rights violations in the State is unlikely to improve. Thus, for example, even if torture has taken place at some point in domestic criminal proceedings, the fact of past torture is not at issue if there is a prospect that these circumstances will improve in the future. Fifth, although the theoretical consequences of the various provisions of the Statute and the logical development of the above-mentioned *Lubanga* Appeals judgment do not exclude the possibility that Article 21(3) may affect the admissibility review, the applicability of that paragraph was not considered in either the *Gaddafi* or *Al-Senussi* cases. This may not exclude the possibility that Article 17(2) and (3) may be interpreted in combination with the provisions of Article 21(3) in the future as well, but the question is how these precedents will be dealt with in the future.

This approach to the ICC's complementarity review induces harm to the protection of individual rights by the complementarity regime itself. In practice, some States rush to prosecute before they are ready domestically to be inadmissible at the ICC. In other words, the (positive) complementarity regime potentially promotes arbitrary domestic detention. While (positive) complementarity facilitates prosecution by States that are not yet psychologically and physically prepared to prosecute in the first place, the examination of willingness and ability will only examine violations of suspects' rights to a limited extent. Therefore, another institutional challenge is that the ICC's prosecution regime can be criticized as a regime that promotes arbitrary detention in the State while also providing no preventive and substantive remedy.[75]

---

[74] Kleffner [102], p. 158.

[75] On the other hand, the ICC's system of admissibility review is said to be neither a forum for redressing general human rights violations in domestic criminal proceedings nor an appellate court. Stahn [197], p. 344.

5 Conclusion

This chapter has dealt with the institutional challenges arising from the particularities of the ICC's prosecution regime from the perspective of remedies for violations of suspects' rights by State authorities under the ICC's vertical and complementary prosecution regimes, including: (i) whether the ICC provides redress to suspects even when violations of their rights are committed by State authorities, which analysis of ICC case law has shown to be the case; and (ii) whether the ICC provides preventive and substantive redress by exercising its jurisdiction when violations by State authorities are actual or foreseeable.

Regarding the first issue, the ICC has clarified that it takes an attribution- required and comparative balance approach in determining the provision of redress for violations of rights by State authorities, which requires attribution of the infringing acts to the ICC and that redress are selected on the basis of comparative balance with other interests. The ICC's current attribution-required and comparative balance approach is not only contrary to the recent development of the concept of the individual's right to compensation, but also cannot avoid criticism that the vertical system of the ICC itself has the aspect of promoting the violation of rights. As for institutional issues, it pointed out the need for a flexible comparative balance and a way of understanding the responsibilities inherent in the vertical regime in order to provide effective remedies.

With regards to the second issue, the realization of the exercise of ICC jurisdiction as a preventive and substantive redress as claimed in the Libyan situation by the ICC is possible but limited as far as the ICC Pre-Trial Chamber's decision is concerned. The ICC's admissibility review is limited in its treatment of violations of rights by State authorities in their prosecution efforts.

In this chapter, I re-examined the ICC's prosecution system in relation to the redress for the rights of the accused, and through this work, one aspect of the institutional challenges arising from the premise of the ICC's vertical and complementary prosecution system has become clear. The ICC's practical difficulties lie precisely in the fact that the various actors must cooperate to address the ICC's institutional challenges within its unique vertical and complementary structure. The precedents discussed here have only examined one aspect of the problem, and in the absence of rules applicable to the practical aspects of investigation, arrest, and surrender, it will be necessary to wait for specific rules to become customary through accumulated practice, or to create detailed procedural rules, such as a Status of Forces Agreement, for dealing with cases in which the rights of suspects are violated during the proceedings when cooperating with national authorities. Although the vertical and complementary regime is a compromise between States and international courts, for the institutional challenges identified in this chapter to be overcome, it is considered important for each actor dealing with core crimes to face their own psychological and physical difficulties and to work on mutual cooperation in their operations.

Chapter 6
Principles on Admissibility of Evidence in International Criminal Justice

Abstract This chapter considers the evidentiary principles applied in core crimes trials before international courts, particularly the ICC, and examines the impact of the premises specific to international criminal justice on the content of these principles. It finds that, firstly, video-link is made available whenever necessary as a facilitator of live testimony rather than an exception to the orality principle, considering the ICC's premise that crime scene is remote. The use of previously recorded statements has been greatly expanded, as there are many cases where witnesses are not available or are subject to interference. Secondly, with regards to the exclusionary rule, it requires balancing while emphasizing compliance with internationally recognized human rights standards, in which the gravity of the core crime itself does not affect the consideration. Since the application of the exclusionary rule does not take violations of or compliance with national laws into account, the issue is how to deal with domestic rules on investigative that differs from State to State. This chapter highlights that exceptions have been devised with regards to the orality principle and the exclusionary rule, considering the wide variety of special circumstances in international criminal justice, but the direction of the impact of these special circumstances on these principles is different.

1 Introduction

Core crimes, such as genocide and crimes against humanity, are committed on a large scale, sometimes systematically, involving large numbers of victims and perpetrators. In many cases, core crimes are tried years after their actual occurrence. Furthermore, when international courts are used, trials may be held in States far from the State where the crimes occurred. These circumstances have led to a variety of features in the law of evidence used in core crimes trials.

Considerations relevant to the law of evidence as applied in core crimes trials include, for example, the need for special considerations for witnesses and ensuring testimonies. Even if in-person public trials are required as a principle, the burden on extremely vulnerable witnesses, such as former child soldiers or victims of sexual

M. Ochi, *The Premises of International Criminal Procedure*,
https://doi.org/10.1007/978-981-97-6786-1_6

slavery in remote trials, to travel to foreign courts, and the high degree of personal risk involved in giving testimony in person, such as threatened internal witnesses in organized core crimes cases, should be considered. Special rules on the way evidence is to be presented are required. In addition, since it is the national investigating authorities that conduct the primary investigation, and therefore the evidence used in international courts is essentially provided by the State, except for oral statements, there is an issue of how an international court should treat such evidence if it was obtained domestically through a violation of human rights. The issue is how an international court should treat such evidence if it was obtained through a domestic violation of human rights. The principles relating to evidence to fairly reveal the truth in a public trial in a manner that complies with internationally recognized human rights standards have required appropriate consideration of the particularities of such core criminal trials.

This chapter considers the evidentiary principles associated with core criminal trials before international courts, particularly the ICC, and examines the impact of the premises specific to international criminal justice on the relevance and content of these principles. It will therefore examine the principle of orality, which is characteristic of ICC proceedings and is problematic in relation to the protection of witnesses. The following section discusses the two issues of the exclusion of illegally collected evidence ("exclusionary rule") in relation to the collection of evidence by actors other than the ICC, such as States. It first provides an overview of the ICC's evidentiary law system and its characteristics, and then, for each of the orality principles and the exclusionary rule applicable at the ICC, confirms the theoretical basis of the principles in the national laws of several States. Then, through an analysis of various rules, regulations, and precedents in the ICC, it will discuss how the premise of international criminal justice is reflected in the application of these principles in the ICC.

2 The ICC's Legal System of Evidence

2.1 Mixing the Inquisitorial and Adversarial Models

Designed as a world criminal court, the ICC was also conceived as a mixture of the world's major legal systems, rather than embodying a specific national law, in terms of its applicable law. This is particularly emphasized in the RPE, which expressly provides a specific rule that national laws governing evidence shall not be applied at the ICC except in accordance with Article 21 (general principles of law) (ICC RPE Rule 63(5)). However, the ICC rules cannot be completely original, although theoretical models such as the inquisitorial model found in Continental law and the adversarial model that is mainstream in Anglo-American law are not directly applicable to the ICC, as has been pointed out.[1] The models of criminal procedure

[1] Kress [108], p. 605, Ambos [3], p. 2–5. See also, Findlay [52], p. 38, 40–41.

may differ fundamentally between these two legal systems, and as a result, the rules of either legal system may have similarities. The result is the ICC's adoption of rules similar to those of either legal system.

It is said that there is a general difference in that the principle of the inquisitorial system focuses on the discovery of the truth as the primary objective of criminal justice, whereas the principle of the adversarial system focuses on the fair resolution of disputes between the parties. Furthermore, the most significant difference in the law of evidence stems from the different understanding of the role of the judge.[2] In Continental law, rules on the admissibility of evidence are said to be less important because much is left to the discretion of the judge, assuming that the trial is conducted by a trained professional judge. As a result, the approach has been taken that the admissibility of evidence is determined by the judge's expertise on its relevance, while the reasons for this are given in detail in the judgment.[3] On the other hand, in Anglo-American law, citizens, rather than professional judges, may examine evidence as jurors, and detailed rules on the admissibility of evidence are required to exclude evidence that may prejudice the jury.

Trial proceedings and other proceedings at the ICC are structured exclusively on the premise of the adversarial model, but there are many important exceptions from the typical features of that model, influenced by the fact that the trial is held without a jury.[4] In addition, the purpose of the ICC's evidentiary rules can be read from the wording of the Statute as being from a Continental legal perspective. Article 69(3) of the ICC Statute provides that "... The Court shall have the authority to request the submission of all evidence that it considers necessary for the determination of the truth." This general attitude contrasts with the exclusively Anglo-American structure of the ICTY's RPE Rule 89(B) which provide that evidence is required for "a fair determination of the matter".

Early ICC cases confirmed the adversarial trial structure at the ICC.[5] On the other hand, due to the circumstances inherent in proceedings before the ICC, various exceptions to the principles of adversarial doctrine were recognized in the precedents, as will be seen below, as well as amendments to the rules.

2.2 *Role of the Trial Division and Outline of Proceedings*

The ICC's judicial divisions consists of three chambers: the Pre-Trial Chamber, the Trial Chamber, and the Appeals Chamber. Of these, the Trial Chamber plays the primary role in the law of evidence. The role of the Trial Chamber is stipulated in

---

[2] See, Keen [98].

[3] See, Buisman et al. [25], pp. 7–20.

[4] Takayama [211], p. 230, Caianiello [26], p. 288.

[5] See, *Prosecutor v. Katanga and Ngudjolo*, Directions for the conduct of the proceedings and testimony in accordance with Rule 140 (ICC-01/04-01/07-1665) Trial Chamber II (20 November 2009).

Article 64 of the ICC Statute, which states that it is responsible for the submission of evidence and the examination of the admissibility or relevance of evidence. The admissibility or relevance of evidence may be determined on the motion of a Party or *ex officio* by the judge.

In practice, parties may submit evidence either in writing by filing a "bar table" application, by email, or orally at the hearing. A distinction is made between prior recorded testimony and other documentary evidence.[6] Prior recorded testimony refers to recorded media of out-of-court statements made by a prospective witness, or written statements or transcripts of such statements, while other documentary evidence refers to such things as trial transcripts, reports, books, photographs, etc.[7] Evidence is examined if there is a motion regarding relevance or admissibility, but with rare exceptions a *prima facie* examination of the criteria—relevance, probative force, potential prejudice—regarding the evidence is not made at the time of submission. These considerations are often deferred until the time of sentencing.[8] These judgments are made at the time of submission when there are procedural obstacles—Article 69(7) or Rule 68, which we will see later—in relation to them.[9] Once the procedural obstacles are cleared, the submission is "recognized", which is also a confirmation that relevance, probative force and prejudice will be considered at the time of final judgment.[10]

The issue at the submission stage is the question of exceptions to the orality principle, such as statements made remotely by video-link or prior recorded statements, and at the admissibility stage it is the question of admissibility of evidence and the exclusion of illegally collected evidence.

3 Necessity of Witness Protection and Orality Principles

3.1 Necessity of Witness Protection

Witnesses at the ICC generally require much greater caution than in ordinary trials. The ICC aims to try core crimes, which tend to be committed on a large scale and in an organized manner.[11] When core crimes are committed by an organized group of perpetrators, the ICC has the important task of prosecuting those who are most responsible, in particular those in leadership positions. For this reason, the testimony of not only the victims of the crimes, but also witnesses from inside the organizations of the perpetrators of the crimes is important evidence. However, the anonymity

---

[6] Naruse [136], p. 16.

[7] *Ibid.*

[8] See, *Prosecutor v. Bemba* et al., Judgment pursuant to Article 74 of the Statute (ICC-01/05-01/13-1989-Red) Trial Chamber VII (19 October 2016).

[9] *Ibid.*

[10] *Ibid.*

[11] See Yamaguchi [246].

and physical safety of insider witnesses may be at risk when the organization—and sometimes the political regime—involved in the crime remains powerful. How to handle the testimony of witnesses who have been subjected to some form of interference has been an issue in cases where they have been denied testimony in court due to threats—*e.g.*, the *Ruto* case—or have been found to have changed their testimony due to bribes—*e.g.*, the *Bemba* case—.[12]

In general, the ICC must take appropriate measures to protect the safety, physical and mental health, dignity and privacy of victims and witnesses (Article 68(1), Rule 87). For the purpose of protecting witnesses, the submission of evidence by electronic or other special means may be permitted (Article 68(2)). In addition, if the disclosure of evidence or information could pose a serious risk to the safety of the witness or his/her family, the prosecutor may withhold such evidence or information and submit a summary of it instead of these (Article 68(5)). Furthermore, it provides for measures to be taken in cases of testimony by victims of sexual violence or children (Article 68(2), Rules 70 and 71) and for in-camera proceedings of relevance and admissibility (Rule 72).

3.2 Rationale for the Orality Principle

The orality is the basic principle that requires a balance with the need for witness protection—the first feature concerning the law of evidence in international criminal justice—in trials at the ICC. Article 69(2) of the ICC Statute states that, in principle, testimony at the ICC shall be given in person at trial. Case law has clarified that the primacy of orality is the principle ("orality principle") and that other methods of evidence are permissible only in exceptional cases.[13]

Three exceptions are envisaged. First, where witness protection measures are provided. Second, when direct testimony by video/audio means is desired. Thirdly, if Parties wish to provide pre-existing testimony by video-audio means, documents, or transcribed documents ("prior recorded statements"). These exceptions, however, may not be granted if they are prejudicial to or incompatible with the rights of the accused.

The orality principle, as well as the principle of immediacy and the principle of publicity, was introduced in the formative period of the modern criminal trial to criticize and supersede the inquisitorially proceedings in private by legal experts

[12] On the operation of Rule 70 as a sanction for such violations, see: Richardson [166].

[13] *Prosecutor v. Bemba*, Dissenting Opinion of Judge Kuniko Ozaki on the Decision on the admission into evidence of materials contained in the prosecution's list of evidence (ICC-01/05–01/08–1028) Trial Chamber III (23 November 2010), paras. 6–12; *Prosecutor v. Bemba*, Judgment on the appeals of Mr. Trial Chamber III (23 November 2010), paras. 6–12; *Prosecutor v. Bemba*, Judgment on the appeals of Mr. Jean-Pierre Bemba Gombo and the Prosecutor against the decision of the Trial Chamber III entitled "Decision on the admission into evidence of the materials contained in the prosecution's list of evidence" (ICC-01/05–01/08–1386) Appeals Chamber (3 May 2011), paras. 76–77.

based on written documents, which were conducted in the old French system.[14] The orality principle as a way of trial hearing requires that the proceedings on the trial date be conducted orally, while the rule of evidence requires fact-finding and judgment to be made only by the case materials provided orally.[15] Although the oral method is in some respects inferior to the written method in terms of accuracy and logicality, it is superior in that it allows all litigants to participate simultaneously and directly in the trial, which is important in relation to the principle of publicity.[16] The advantages also include the possibility of making a strong impression on the judges and enabling judges to take impressions directly from the evidence presented orally at the trial, which is open to the public in court.[17]

In States with a jury system, orality principles become indispensable, but even for professional judges, orality principles are considered important to ensure accurate fact-finding.[18] In Japan, too, the importance of orality principles has been reaffirmed with the introduction of the lay judge system.[19]

One of the discussions on exception to the orality principle is the question of whether testimony given outside the courtroom during trial by means of telecommunications technology that involves the intercommunication of video and audio, principally web conferencing systems (the term in the ICC Rules is "video-link"), is considered to be given "orally" in the courtroom. There is also the issue of whether pre-trial statements recorded in the form of video, audio or written statements are admissible as "testimony". The following sections examine the state of the applicable law of the ICC on these two issues.

3.3 Examination of Witnesses by Video-Link

At the ICC, the need for rules permitting the provision of evidence by video-link has been recognized in order to protect witnesses. In many cases, the crime scene is far from the ICC in The Hague, and the use of video-link can be more cost-effective than making travel arrangements for witnesses and can reduce the burden on witnesses, particularly in the case of vulnerable witnesses who may be elderly, ill, or extremely poor. Particularly in ICC cases, where there is a period of recovery following large-scale violence, the vulnerability of witnesses and the risks involved

[14] On the other hand, in Germany, the "direct principle" (*Unmittelbarkeitsgrundsatz*), which criticizes the indirectness of written proceedings, was advocated. Sakamaki [173], pp. 326–327.

[15] Shiratori [191], p. 310.

[16] Uto et al. [235], p. 265.

[17] Shiratori [191], p. 311.

[18] *Ibid*.

[19] Okubo [152]. In Japan, too, although the documentary principle is applied with regards to procedural acts that require strict formality, such as the filing of a public prosecution (Article 356(1) of the Code of Criminal Procedure), in principle a judgment must be based on oral argument [Article 43(1)], and the main text and reasons for the documentary evidence and judgment are also read out (Articles 305 and 307).

in testifying must be considered. Also, where the accused is a leadership figure, the cost of measures that must be taken to protect witnesses can be significant if the accused has a large number of supporters. In addition, the relationship between video-links and protective measures can be problematic, particularly where there is a special need for witness protection, such as in the case of sexual offences.

The following rules apply to the use of video-link. First, if cross-examination would be difficult to conduct via video-link, it should not be permitted (ICC RPE Rule 67(1)). Moreover, the question arises as to how to ensure the environment in which the video-link is to be carried out (Rule 67(3)). In other words, moving a witness who lives in a rural area without an internet environment to an urban area where there is a securer connection with The Hague may entail the risks described above.

Under the ICC Statute, in addition to the general provision, Article 69(2), Rule 67(1) permits oral testimony to be given by means of audio or video technology, provided that such technology enables cross-examination by the prosecution, the defence and the Trial Chamber itself at the same time that the witness is giving testimony. Rule 67(3) also provides that the Trial Chamber must ensure that truthful and open testimony is provided and that the location where audio or video-link testimony will be given is convenient to safety, physical and psychological health, dignity, and privacy.

However, in the case law, the Trial Chamber has exercised its broad discretion and has basically clarified that video-linking can be permitted whenever necessary.[20] It has also been held that the discretion to allow video-linking should be exercised broadly, as there is no difference in meaning between video-linking and testifying in court oneself.[21] There have also been cases in which the attitude has been expressed that video-linking should be allowed because of the duty to protect the psychological health and dignity of the witness.[22]

However, there are a number of matters that were raised as matters to be taken into account when allowing the use of video-links. For example, in relation to preparation by the registry, the logistical burden and the obligation to ensure a fair and speedy trial must be considered.[23] The relationship to the rights of the accused is also mentioned, basically taking the position that any conflict with the rights of the accused in testifying by video technology will not be considered unless it is claimed.[24]

---

[20] *Prosecutor v. Lubanga*, Decision on various issues related to witnesses' testimony during trial (ICC-01/04-01/06-1140) Trial Chamber I (29 January 2008), para. 41; *Prosecutor v. Bemba*, Redacted Decision on the "Request for the conduct of the testimony of witness CAR-OTP-WWWW-0108 by video-link" (ICC-01/05-01/08-947-Red) Trial Chamber III (12 October 2010), para. 10.

[21] *Prosecutor v. Bemba* et al., Decision on Video-Link Testimony for Defence Witnesses (ICC-01/05-01/13–1697) Trial Chamber VII (4 March 2016), para. 14.

[22] *Prosecutor v. Lubanga*, Redacted Decision on the defence request for a witness to give evidence via video-link (ICC-01/04-01/06-2285-Red) Trial Chamber I (9 February 2010), para. 15.

[23] *Prosecutor v. Bemba* et al. (4 March 2016), para. 16.

[24] *Prosecutor v. Bemba* (12 October 2010), para. 12.

With regards to the examination of the need for video-links, providing general criteria has been avoided as they are fact-specific to each case.[25] Examples of where necessity has been found include the personal circumstances of the witness—age, vulnerability, health and psychological health of the witness—[26] and procedural and logistical considerations—logistical difficulties relating to the movement of witnesses—.[27] However, there are cases where the opinion was attached that it should be specified what special facts were considered and adopted.[28]

Examples of where the need has been found are manifold. There are cases, for example, of traumatised and vulnerable witnesses, in particular former child soldiers,[29] extreme vulnerability—living in an inaccessible suburb, living in extreme poverty and having never used modern equipment, testifying abroad was considered potentially traumatic—,[30] health issues,[31] and lack of valid passports—video-link is the only way to secure a court appearance on the hearing day—.[32]

With regards to the issue of the place where the testimony would be given, the following decisions have been made in the following cases. In the *Lubanga* case, in response to an application to move the testimony to Bunia, where internet access was available, rather than the witness's place of residence, there was concern that Bunia, where the testimony would be given, had a large number of supporters of the accused. In this case, the Trial Chamber asked the registry to reaffirm its commitment to appropriate measures to ensure conditions that promote truthful and open testimony.[33]

Thus, the use of video-links is not an exception to the orality principle but is used as a tool to facilitate live testimony by the person in question. In addition, especially in recent years, there has been awareness and practice of the usefulness of widely accepted online provision of evidence using internet technology as a measure against

---

[25] *Prosecutor v. Ntaganda*, Decision on Prosecution's request to hear P-0039's testimony by way of video-link (ICC-01/04-02/06-897-Red2) Trial Chamber VI (12 October 2015), para. 12.

[26] *Prosecutor v. Bemba* (12 October 2010), para. 13.

[27] *Prosecutor v. Bemba*, Public redacted version of "Decision on 'Defence Motion for authorization to hear the testimony of Witness D-45 via video-link'" of 6 March 2013 (ICC-01/05-01/08-2525-Red) Trial Chamber III (7 March 2013), para. 7; *Prosecutor v. Bemba*, Decision on the "Second Further Revised Defence Submissions on the Order of Witnesses" (ICC-01/05-01/08-2644) and on the appearance of Witnesses D04-02, D04-09, D04-03, D04-04 and D04-06 via video-link (ICC-01/05-01/08-2646) Trial Chamber III (31 May 2013), para. 9.

[28] *Prosecutor v. Gbagbo and Blé Goudé*, Decision on the mode of testimony of Rule 68(3) witnesses, Partially Dissenting Opinion of Judge Henderson (ICC-02/11-01/15-721-Anx) Trial Chamber I (18 October 2016), para. 6; see also, *Prosecutor v. Gbagbo and Ble Goude*, Decision on the "Prosecution's application to conditionally admit the prior recorded statements and related documents of Witnesses P-0108, P-0433, P-0436, P-0402, P-0438, P-0459 and P-0109 under rule 68(3) and for testimony by means of video-link technology for Witnesses P-0436, P-0402, P-0438, P-0459 and P-0109 under rule 67(1)" (ICC-02/11-01/15-870) Trial Chamber I (4 April 2017), note 37.

[29] See, *Prosecutor v. Lubanga* (29 January 2008).

[30] See, *Prosecutor v. Lubanga* (9 February 2010).

[31] See, *Prosecutor v. Ntaganda* (12 October 2015).

[32] See, *Prosecutor v. Bemba et. al.*, (4 March 2016).

[33] *Prosecutor v. Lubanga* (9 February 2010), para. 17.

new COVID-19 infections.[34] The relationship between video-links and protective measures has also been organized as follows. Firstly, it has been stated that video-linking as a protective measure can be applied for by victims (Victims and Witness Unit ("VWU")).[35] However, it has also been confirmed that video-linking should not be seen as a safeguard. That is, the use of video-links should essentially be seen as facilitating live testimony made possible by technological advances and should be understood as a means of giving live oral testimony, rather than as an exception to live testimony.[36]

3.4 Handling of Prior Recorded Statements

3.4.1 Necessity of Prior Recorded Statements

While the principle of the submission of evidence at ICC trials is oral, it allows for the admissibility of statements that have been recorded in some form prior to the trial. The need for such a rule is to save time by making statements made during investigative interrogations in States other than the ICC's host State, in which the crimes have been committed, to deal with cases where the statements are unavailable because of death, disappearance, threats, bribery, etc., after the statements have been made, and to allow for the use of recorded statements in cases where the witness is in a remote location and a video-link is unavailable. The reason for allowing previously recorded statements to be made at the ICC for reasons other than inability to make a statement is that the Trial Chamber of the ICC does not have the power to coerce the appearance of witnesses and it is inherently difficult to secure their appearance.[37] One problem, however, is that there is no opportunity to confirm the content and probative value of the previously recorded statements, i.e., no opportunity for cross-examination.

The need for the use of written evidence in international criminal courts was recognized by the pre-ICC tribunals and a number of procedural evidence rules have been amended to allow the use of written evidence in place of evidence given orally.[38] One of the reasons for being able to adopt written evidence is that because trial hearings are conducted by trained professional judges rather than a jury system, there is no need for strict hearsay rules to exclude evidence of low probative value.[39]

---

[34] Abtahi [1], pp. 1069–1076.

[35] *Prosecutor v. Gbagbo and Ble Goude*, Decision on the mode of testimony of Rule 68(3) witnesses (ICC-02/11-01/15-721) Trial Chamber I (11 October 2016), para. 15.

[36] *Ibid.*, para. 16.

[37] Naruse [136], p. 22.

[38] Boas [15], p. 171.

[39] However, there is much criticism of such an explanation; e.g., Caianiello [26], p. 304.

3.4.2 Before Amendment of Rule 68

The current provision in the ICC is a new provision that was amended in 2013. Originally, as a general provision in the Statute, Article 69(2) stated that the Trial Chamber "may also permit … the introduction of documents or written transcripts". Under the former Rule 68, the conditions under which the Trial Chamber may adopt a previously recorded statement were either (a) if the witness does not appear at trial and the prosecution and defence have an opportunity to examine him or her at the time of the recording, or (b) if the witness does appear at trial but does not object to the recorded testimony and the parties and the Trial Chamber.

The case law up to the amendment has held on to the exceptional nature of prior recorded statements and the considerations in reviewing them. For example, in the *Lubanga* case the Trial Chamber held that it had discretion to order the replacement of written statements with "live" evidence in accordance with Rule 68.[40] In the *Bemba* case, the Trial Chamber also held that it must consider the need for exceptional circumstances to justify a departure from the general principle of orality, such as whether there are in fact any advantages, such as the expeditiousness of adopting previously recorded statements.[41] Such decisions are fact-specific decisions[42] and when relying on Rule 68(b) to depart from the orality principle, the Court will consider, among other things, the following.[43] First, whether the issue is substantially uncontested; second, whether it is not central to the core issues in the case; and third, whether it is complementary to other evidence ("three criteria of *Bamba* OA5, OA6").[44]

The *Bemba* case further held that written statements of witnesses who had already testified at trial were admissible as relevant to assist the Trial Chamber in examining, contextualising, and weighing the significance of their testimony.[45] However, Judge Kuniko Ozaki's individual opinion was given in response to this, stating that the admissibility of written statements to supplement oral testimony is contrary to the principle of the primacy of orality.[46]

---

[40] *Prosecutor v. Lubanga*, Decision on the prosecution's application for admission of the prior recorded statements of two witnesses (ICC-01/04-01/06-1603) Trial Chamber I (15 January 2009), para. 19.

[41] *Prosecutor v. Bemba*, Decision on the "Prosecution Application for Leave to Submit in Writing Prior- Recorded Testimonies by CAR-OTP-WWWW-0032, CAR-OTP-WWWW-0080, and CAR-OTP-WWW-0108" (ICC-01/05-01/08-886) Trial Chamber III (16 September 2010), paras. 7–8.

[42] *Prosecutor v. Lubanga* (15 January 2009), para. 21.

[43] *Prosecutor v. Bemba* (3 May 2011), para. 78.

[44] *Ibid.*

[45] *Prosecutor v. Bemba*, Decision on the admission into evidence of items deferred in the Chamber's "First decision on the prosecution and defence requests for the admission of evidence" (ICC-01/05-01/08-2012) (ICC-01/05-01/08-2793) Trial Chamber III (3 September 2013), para. 142.

[46] *Prosecutor v. Bemba*, Partly Dissenting Opinion of Judge Ozaki on the Decision on the admission into evidence of items deferred in the Chamber's "First decision on the prosecution and defence requests for the admission of evidence" (ICC-01/05-01/08-2012) (ICC-01/05-01/08-2793-Anx) Trial Chamber III (3 September 2013), para. 4.

3.4.3 After Amendment of Rule 68

Rule 68 was amended by the Assembly of States Parties on 27 November 2013. The reasons given were the need to increase the efficiency and effectiveness of the courts and to reduce the length of trial proceedings. Rule 68(1) of the new RPE provides that the submission of a previously recorded statement may be permitted if—in principle—it is compatible with and does not prejudice the rights of the accused and if the following conditions are met. First, where the Parties had an opportunity to examine the accused at the time of recording (new Rule 68(2)(a)); second, where the evidence establishes an act other than that of the accused (new Rule 68(b)); third, where the witness is not available (new Rule 68(c)); and fourth, where the witness is interfered with (new Rule 68(d)). Further, the new Rule 68(3) (old Rule 68(b)) provided that a previously recorded statement is admissible if the deponent is present and there is no objection and there is an opportunity for cross-examination.

In subsequent cases, there have been the following developments, first with respect to the general issue. With respect to the scope of a "prior record statement," in the *Ruto* case, it was confirmed that Rule 68 applies to recorded statements under Rules 111 and 112 (written interrogatory statements during an investigation) and generally does not require an oath.[47] It was also indicated that with respect to other exhibits accompanying a prior recorded statement, both are permissible when used or explained by that witness in testimony and when necessary to read and understand the prior recorded statement being submitted.[48]

The second, the previously recorded statements concerning matters other than the defendant's conduct, are subject to certain conditions under the rules, including the following. First, particular consideration is given to whether the statement relates to a matter that is not in substantial dispute, is cumulative or reinforcing in nature, provides background information, serves the interests of the trial, and bears a sufficiently reliable testimony (Rule 68(2)(b)(1)). There must also be a declaration of the truthfulness of the deponent (Rules 68(2)(b)(2) and (3)). Case law has confirmed, for example, in the *Gbagbo* case, that it is not necessary to prove that the reason for the unavailability of the witness is a legitimate one,[49] that Rule 68(2)(b)(1) is an illustration of the elements[50] and that factors other than formal considerations can also be considered.[51] It was also held that testimony about disputed facts about

---

[47] *Prosecutor v. Ruto and Sang*, Public Redacted Version of Corrigendum: Decision on Prosecution Request for Admission of Prior Recorded Testimony (ICC-01/09-01/11-1938-Corr-RED 2) Trial Chamber V(a) (19 August 2015), para .28.

[48] *Ibid.*, para. 33.

[49] *Prosecutor v. Gbagbo and Ble Goude*, Decision on the Prosecutor's application to introduce prior recorded testimony under Rules 68(2)(b) and 68(3) (ICC-02/11-01/15-573-Red) Trial Chamber I (9 June 2016), para .11.

[50] *Ibid.*, para. 10.

[51] *Prosecutor v. Gbagbo and Ble Goude*, Judgment on the appeals of Mr. Laurent Gbagbo and Mr. Charles Blé Goudé against the decision of Trial Chamber I of 9 June 2016 entitled "Decision on the Prosecutor's application to introduce prior recorded testimony under Rules 68(2)(b) and 68(3)", (ICC-02/11-01/15-744) the Appeals Chamber (1 November 2016), para. 104.

the offence, even if not the conduct of the accused, is properly subject to cross-examination (Rule 68(3)).[52] Further, in relation to the requirement of benefit of the trial, it has been confirmed that it is in the interest of the trial to provide written statements on evidence that is immaterial and can be bolstered by other evidence, as it helps to reduce the time and burden on the witness.[53]

On the other hand, the third, "unavailable witness" refers to a person who is unable to appear in court due to death or a disability which cannot be overcome by reasonable efforts, but where it is accepted that the person is unavailable and the need for measures to preserve evidence (Article 56) is unforeseeable and there is evidence of reliability (Rule 68 (2)(c)(1)) and the fact that the testimony will be used to prove the conduct of the accused is taken into account (*ibid.* (2)). As examples of "unavailability", in case law, it has been held that Rule 68(2)(c) can be applied in cases where all attempts to contact and trace the witness have failed, where the witness's sudden disappearance could not be anticipated[54] and where the witness is dead.[55] Here, the phrase "not available" is to be interpreted broadly to include cases where a witness cannot be protected or contacted, but can be traced with reasonable efforts.[56] It has also been confirmed that the provision is inconsistent with Rule 68(1) of the Statute on the Protection of Witnesses where the attendance of a witness would cause unnecessary hardship in comparison with the seriousness of the evidence.[57] As for the requirement that the necessity of measures under Article 56 could not be anticipated, the *Bemba* case confirmed that cases involving the failure to take steps to apply for such measures also include those where such measures were anticipated but could not be implemented.[58] It further confirmed that the exercise of discretion in a decision on Rule 68(2)(c)(ii) will take into account the three criteria confirmed in the *Bemba* case.[59] The test in this regard was formulated in the *Ntaganda* case by considering Rule 69(2)(c)(ii) in addition to: (i) that the examination of the evidence in question would not be prejudicial to or inconsistent with the rights of the accused, (ii) that the need for measures under Article 56 was unforeseeable, and (iii) that the pre-recorded statements bear sufficient evidence of reliability.[60]

Regarding the fourth case of "witnesses who have been interfered with", the rules allow a pre-recorded statement to be used where a witness has not appeared

---

[52] *Prosecutor v. Gbagbo and Ble Goude* (9 June 2016), paras. 38–41.

[53] *Ibid.*, para. 21.

[54] *Prosecutor v. Ruto and Sang* (19 August 2015), para. 140.

[55] *Prosecutor v. Ntaganda*, Decision on Prosecution application under Rule 68(2)(c) of the Rules for the admission of prior recorded testimony of P-0022, P-0041 and P-0103 (ICC-01/04-02/06-1029) Trial Chamber VI (20 November 2015), para. 12.

[56] *Prosecutor v. Bemba et, al.*, Corrected public redacted version of Decision on 'Prosecution Submission of Evidence Pursuant to Rule 68(2)(c) of the Rules of Procedure and Evidence' (ICC-01/05-01/13-1481-Red-Corr) Trial Chamber VII (12 November 2015), para. 16.

[57] *Ibid.*, para. 18.

[58] *Ibid.*, para. 19.

[59] *Ibid.*, para. 21.

[60] *Prosecutor v. Ntaganda* (20 November 2015), para. 12.

or has appeared but has not testified on a material aspect of the pre-recorded statement, a witness has been affected by improper interference, reasonable efforts have been made, the interests of justice would be best served by their inclusion or there is evidence of credibility (Rule 68(2)(d)(i)), and the interference is against the person's physical, psychological, economic or other interests (Rule 68(2)(d)(ii)). It also provides that in cases relating to offences against the administration of justice (Article 70), facts already tried can be considered (Rule 68(2)(d)(3)) and the fact of that testimony will be used to establish the conduct of the accused (*Ibid.* (4)). Although case law has raised the issue of witnesses who have been interfered with giving testimony in court that differs from their prior recorded statements, it has been confirmed that there is no need to distinguish between not testifying and changing testimony.[61] Moreover, with respect to whether the interference must be attributed to the defendant, it has been held to be a relevant consideration in reviewing whether the provision of a prior recorded statement is in the interest of the trial, although not a requirement under the rules.[62] Further, examples of "credibility testimony" include oaths, signatures and declarations, quality interpretation, absence of contradictions, cross-examination, and corroborating evidence.[63]

Finally, with regards to when a witness does not object and has an opportunity to appear and be cross-examined (Rule 68(3)), case law has recognized the standard of good trial management, i.e., taking into account the importance, volume and detail of the evidence on a case-by-case basis, with due regard to expeditiousness and efficiency in its presentation.[64] The *Gbagbo* case also confirmed that Rule 68(3) provides for wider discretion than the three criteria confirmed in the *Bemba* case.[65]

Thus, with respect to the amended Rule 68, it is understood that "certain conditions" and the like in the Rule are enumerated as mere factors of consideration rather than as requirements. In case law, most previously recorded statements are permitted to be submitted in the exercise of broad discretion by the Trial Chamber. However, it is regarded important to guarantee the opportunity to cross-examine in court those statements that should be cross-examined.

---

[61] *Prosecutor v. Ruto and Sang* (19 August 2015), paras. 40–41.

[62] *Ibid.*, para. 44.

[63] *Ibid.*, para. 65.

[64] *Prosecutor v. Gbagbo and Ble Goude* (9 June 2016), para. 25.

[65] *Prosecutor v. Gbagbo and Ble Goude* (1 November 2016), paras. 17–19.

4 Provision of Evidence and Exclusion of Illegally Collected Evidence by Actors Other Than the ICC

4.1 Provision of Evidence by Actors Other Than the ICC

The second factor unique to the ICC is that evidence is obtained primarily through the cooperation of States and other actors; the ICC prosecutor is not expected to conduct investigative activities directly on the territory of a particular State alone. Therefore, the investigative authorities of the State where the offence was committed are the primary investigators, particularly with regards to physical evidence, and the ICC receives its evidence through judicial cooperation.

However, it is not always realistic to expect to secure judicial staff with sufficient investigative capacity and to collect evidence in a manner that complies with the law, particularly in regions that have experienced core crime that have created tens of thousands of victims. There have been States and regions that have been the subject of United Nations transitional administrations or European Union special missions following internal wars that have been the setting for many core crime incidents, and in some cases, core crime evidence has been collected by these staff, multinational force mission personnel and non-governmental organizations ("NGOs").[66]

In addition, the national criminal procedural laws of States differ, as do the various rules governing investigations and evidence. In light of this, the ICC expressly states that in determining the admissibility and relevance of evidence collected by a State, it will not make a decision on the application of that State's domestic law (Article 69(8)). However, if the way the evidence was obtained violates the ICC Statute or infringes "internationally recognized human rights", the evidence is inadmissible if the violation or infringement raises serious doubts about its reliability. Furthermore, if its admission could seriously prejudice the integrity of the trial proceedings, the evidence is inadmissible (Article 69(7)). In the *Al Hassan* case, it was found that severe torture and inhuman treatment had been committed in Mali by Operation *Barkhane*, a French-led counterinsurgency operation, which had taken Al Hassan into custody during the period of his interrogation by the ICC prior to his transfer to The Hague, and the ICC prosecutor himself proposed the exclusion of evidence obtained during this period.[67]

---

[66] For example, East Timor and Kosovo, which were subjected to UN Transitional Administration. In the case of the former Yugoslavia, SFOR contributed to the arrest of suspects. Other organizations often used by the ICC include international organizations such as the Fact-Finding Commission, international human rights NGOs such as Human Rights Watch and Amnesty International, the Commission for International Justice and Accountability ("CIJA"), which is dedicated to the collection of evidence, and other evidence-gathering NGOs.

[67] *Prosecutor v. Al Hassan*, Public redacted version of "Article 69(7) Application" (ICC-01/12-01/18-1346-Red2) Trial Chamber X (8 March 2021).

4.2 Theoretical Basis of the Exclusionary Rule

4.2.1 Outline of the Exclusionary Rule in National Laws

The exclusionary rule is said to have originated with its adoption in the US federal courts in the early twentieth century[68] and is today established as case law in the US.[69] On the other hand, Article 78(1) of the UK's Police and Criminal Procedure Act provides, in relation to the admissibility of illegally collected evidence, that the court may refuse to admit such evidence if it would prejudice the fairness of the proceedings.

Continental law systems have used the nullity theory (*théorie des nullités*), a system of sanctioning evidence by nullifying it if there is illegality in the evidence collection process, as the standard for admissibility.[70] One of the nullity theories is prejudicial nullity, which is based on the existence of prejudice (*grief*) of a Party.[71] In Germany, the Code of Criminal Procedure 136a provides for the exclusion of statement evidence obtained by certain illegal interrogation techniques, and several other provisions specifically provide for the exclusion of evidence obtained by certain techniques.[72] It has been noted that national legal provisions in European States have been influenced by recent decisions by the European Court of Human Rights.[73] For example, Article 32 of the Belgian Code of Criminal Procedure, adopted by the Law of 24 October 2013, states that the judge may declare illegally obtained evidence inadmissible only if: statute law explicitly mentions nullity as the sanction for neglecting the formality; the irregularity affects the reliability of the evidence; or the use of the illegally obtained evidence would violate the right to a fair trial.

In Japan, the rule of exclusion was adopted by the Supreme Court in 1978[74] and is said to be still valid. Although there is no explicit basis in actual law, Articles 1 and 317 of the Code of Criminal Procedure and Articles 31 and 35 of the Constitution are considered to be the basis for the rule.[75] The criteria for excluding evidence in Japanese judicial precedents are: (i) when there is a serious illegality in the procedures for seizing evidence, that subverts the spirit of the principle of warrant stipulated in Article 35 of the Constitution and the Code of Criminal Procedure, and (ii) when it is not reasonable from the perspective of suppressing illegal investigation to admit the said evidence.[76]

---

[68] Inoue [63], p. 63.

[69] Shiratori [191], pp. 377–378.

[70] Sato [178], p. 85.

[71] *Ibid.*

[72] Viebig [239], p. 66.

[73] Sato [178], p. 79.

[74] The Supreme Court, September 7, 1978, Penal Code, Vol. 32, No. 6, p. 1672.

[75] Uto et al. [235], p. 386.

[76] Shiratori [191], p. 378; Morita [130], p. 11.

4.2.2 Various Rationales for the Rule of Exclusion

The rationale for excluding illegally collected evidence today generally falls into four main categories: (i) maintaining judicial integrity and fairness, (ii) deterring illegal investigations, (iii) ensuring due process (human rights), and (iv) maintaining the reliability of evidence.[77]

In the US, which is believed to be the first to adopt the exclusionary rule, it originally arose as a rule that functions to regulate law enforcement agents not to violate the privacy of individuals under the constitutional norms.[78] The rationale for the exclusionary rule in the US today is the demand for judicial integrity, which is to exempt courts from complicity in illegal activities by investigative agencies and to ensure public trust in the judiciary (category (i)), the deterrent effect against illegal investigations by making police illegal activities less beneficial (category (ii)), and the rights of those who have suffered illegal infringement of their rights or the remedy of their rights (category (iii)).[79]

On the other hand, British precedents have denied that the theoretical basis for excluding illegally collected evidence is to deter future illegal investigations (category (ii)), and have taken the position that fairness at trial is the basis for exclusion (category (iii)).[80] In Germany, scholars take the position that it is to prove the truth (category (iv)) and to deter illegal investigations (category (iii)), but there is also a theory that is based on the protection and relief of individuals who are illegally infringed (category (iii)).[81] In this way, which of these grounds should be set as the theoretical basis for the exclusionary rule differs from one legal system to another, and even within a particular legal system, it is possible for exclusion of evidence to be conducted by relying on different grounds depending on the case.

On the other hand, the way in which the protection of human rights is used as a ground for exclusion of evidence is found in human rights treaties. For example, Article 15 of the Convention against Torture and Other Cruel, Inhuman or Degrading Treatment or Punishment provides that any statement found to be the result of torture shall not be taken as evidence in proceedings, except as evidence as to the fact that such a statement was made and against the accused of the crime of torture. The precedents of the international or regional human rights courts, which held that the admission of illegally collected domestic evidence was a violation of human rights treaties, can be based on the protection of human rights (category (iii)). The European Court of Human Rights has held that if there is a violation of Article 3, which prohibits torture and other acts in the collection of evidence, rather than a violation of Article 8 of the European Convention on Human Rights, such as mere intervention in private life, the use of such evidence may be a violation of Article 6, which provides for the

77 See Uto et al. [235], pp. 385–386.

78 Mizuno [128], p. 101.

79 Inoue [83], p. 98.

80 Sasayama [177], p. 1351.

81 Viebig [239], pp. 68–69.

right to a fair trial.[82] On the other hand, in cases other than torture, if any illegally collected evidence has already been used for a finding of guilt, the right to a fair trial is not deemed to be have been violated.[83]

4.3 Exclusionary Laws in the ICC

4.3.1 Article 69(7)

With regards to the exclusion of evidence, Article 69(7) of the ICC Statute provides that "evidence obtained by means of a violation of this Statute or internationally recognized human rights shall not be admissible if (a) The violation casts substantial doubt on the reliability of the evidence; or (b) The admission of the evidence would be antithetical to and would seriously damage the integrity of the proceedings." In other words, evidence obtained by methods that violate internationally recognized human rights is admissible unless the evidence itself is reliable and the "integrity" of the trial proceedings is not significantly affected.[84] In the *Lubanga* case, arguments arose in relation to evidence suspected of having been obtained illegally from the

[82] E.g., *Jalloh v Germany*, Application no. 54810/00 (11 July 2006), paras. 99–105.

[83] Sato [178], pp. 61–86.

[84] Rule 69(4) of the ICC Statute states that "The Court may rule on the relevance or admissibility of any evidence, taking into account, *inter alia*, the probative value of the evidence and any prejudice that such evidence may cause to a fair trial or to a fair evaluation of the testimony of a witness, in accordance with the Rules of Procedure and Evidence." Thus, at the ICC, the admissibility and relevance of evidence is reviewed by the Trial Chamber, which considers the "probative force" and "prejudice" of the evidence. The timing for raising an issue as to the admissibility of evidence is "at the time when the evidence is presented to a Chamber" (ICC RPE 64(1)). In response, "A Chamber shall give reasons for any rulings it makes on evidentiary matters" (Rule 64(2)) and, of course, "Evidence rules irrelevant or inadmissible shall not be considered by the Chamber" (Rule 64(3)). In *Bemba*, the Trial Chamber held that all of the evidence on the list of evidence was apparently admissible. *Prosecutor v. Bemba*, Decision on the admission into evidence of materials contained in the prosecution's list of evidence (ICC-01/05-01/08-1022) Trial Chamber III (19 November 2010). In contrast, that appeal confirmed that Rule 69(4) is a mandatory provision requiring the Trial Chamber to make a decision on the admissibility of each item of evidence presented at some stage in the proceedings. *Prosecutor vs. Bemba* (3 May 2011), ICC-01/05-01/08-1386. See also, Schuon [183], pp. 511–520. Thus, at the ICC, the admissibility of evidence is reviewed on an item-by-item basis. The standard of review for the admissibility of bar table material, which refers to evidence other than that provided by or through a witness, is set out in the following case law: "three-step approach" (or "three-part test"). That is, we examine the evidence for (1) its apparent relevance, (2) its apparent probative force, and (3) a weighing of the probative force of the evidence against its prejudicial effect, *Prosecutor v. Lubanga*, Decision on the Admissibility of Four Documents (ICC-01/04-01/06-1399) Trial Chamber I (13 June 2008). A later case declared that the three-part test is to be used for affidavit evidence as well as for court sitting documents. *Prosecutor v. Ngudjolo*, Judgment pursuant to article 74 of the Statute (ICC-01/04-02/12-3-tENG) Trial Chamber II (26 December 2012); *Prosecutor v. Katanga*, Judgment pursuant to article 74 of the Statute (ICC-01/04-01/07-3436-tENG) Trial Chamber II (7 March 2014); *Prosecutor v. Bemba*, Judgment pursuant to Article 74 of the Statute (ICC-01/05-01/08-3343) Trial Chamber III (21 March 2016).

private home in question in the presence of investigators from the ICC Prosecutor's Office while the resident was detained on the orders of the domestic authorities.[85] The Trial Chamber noted, in general terms, that in cases where reliability (Article 69(7)(a)) is at issue, such as those involving coerced confessions[86] and, on the other hand, with regards to the impact on integrity (Article 69(7)(b)), there is a need to strike an appropriate balance between the rights of the accused in the fight against impunity and a need to meet the expectations of the victim and the international community.[87]

With regards to the Trial Chamber's discretion and balancing in reviewing the impact of violations of human rights on the soundness of the Court, the two appropriate approaches to review are the relative exclusion theory ("comparative assessment") and the normative theory ("absolute assessment"). The Trial Chamber declared that it has been given discretion to balance between the fundamental values of the Statute because the Statute does not state that evidence obtained due to a violation of an internationally recognized human right should automatically be excluded.[88] It went on to confirm that Article 69(7) adopts a "dual test" and that a violation of the Statute or human rights alone does not exclude evidence.[89] From this, the ICC seems to has fundamentally taken the theory of relative exclusion.

4.3.2 Rationale for Article 69(7)

The rationale for excluding illegally collected evidence can be broadly classified into four categories as described above: Article 69(7)(a) is based on category (iv) ensuring the reliability of evidence, while (b) is based on the notion of judicial integrity (category (i)).

However, in the *Lubanga* case, it was held that a possible purpose of the exclusionary rule is to discipline and deter unusual or illegal behaviour by law enforcement officers (category (iii)).[90] However, its effect must be directed to those who discipline and deter individuals who have the authority to control proceedings or prevent improper or illegal behaviour, which in this case was the authorities of the DRC who were leading the investigation, and the ICC agents were merely "authorised to assist". Therefore, the Court held that the purpose of such exclusionary rule did not apply to the ICC agents in this case.[91]

---

[85] *Prosecutor v. Lubanga*, Decision on the confirmation of charges (ICC-01/04-01/06-803-tEN) Pre-Trial Chamber I (7 February 2007), para. 62; *Prosecutor v. Lubanga,* Decision on the Admission of Material from the "Bar Table" (ICC-01/04-01/06-1981) Trial Chamber I (24 June 2009).

[86] *Prosecutor v. Lubanga* (29 January 2007), ICC-01/04-01/06, para. 85.

[87] *Ibid*., para. 86.

[88] *Prosecutor v. Lubanga* (29 January 2007), para. 84.

[89] *Prosecutor v. Lubanga* (24 June 2009), para. 39.

[90] *Ibid*., para. 45.

[91] *Ibid*., para. 46.

4.3.3 Manner of Violation

With regards to what degree of violation should be the basis for exclusion of evidence, the majority opinion in traditional international tribunals has been that only serious violations of human rights lead to the exclusion of evidence.[92] On the other hand, Article 69(7) of the ICC does not quantify "seriousness" by reference to the degree of seriousness, and it has been held that evidence may be inadmissible even for violations of human rights that are not themselves serious.[93]

It has been confirmed that it does not matter whose human rights are violated in the process of evidence collection and it does not have to be the accused.[94]

In addition, domestic law and domestic precedent are generally irrelevant to the application of the exclusionary rule. Regarding the domestic appellate court ruling that evidence should not be examined because it was searched and seized in a manner that violated the domestic criminal procedure code, the Court ruled that although the domestic law has meaning as a general principle of law (Article 21 (1) (c) of the Statute), domestic precedents cannot be directly applied.[95] Moreover, evidence obtained through a violation of domestic procedural law does not automatically trigger the application of Article 69(7).[96] In the *Bemba* et al. case, the ICC prosecutor's receipt of Western Union remittance records without a warrant in Australia raised the issue of a violation of the internationally recognized human right to privacy.[97] In this case, the Trial Chamber held that domestic legality is reviewed only to the extent of determining whether there has been a violation under Article 69(7) of the Statute, and only to determine whether something so "manifestly" illegal has occurred as to constitute a violation of the Statute or an internationally recognized human right.[98] It then did not order the exclusion of the relevant evidence on the basis that the obtaining of the information in advance of the warrant was not "manifestly" unlawful.[99]

---

[92] *Prosecutor v. Lubanga* (29 January 2007), paras. 87–88.

[93] *Prosecutor v. Lubanga* (24 June 2009), para. 35.

[94] *Ibid.*, para. 37.

[95] *Prosecutor v. Lubanga* (29 January 2007), ICC-01/04-01/06, para. 69.

[96] *Prosecutor v. Lubanga* (24 June 2009), ICC-01/04-01/06-1981, para. 36.

[97] *Prosecutor v. Bemba et. al.*, Decision on Requests to Exclude Western Union Documents and other Evidence Pursuant to Article 69(7) (ICC-01/05-01/13-1854) Trial Chamber VII (29 April 2016).

[98] *Ibid.*, para. 34.

[99] *Ibid.*, paras. 59–60.

5 Conclusion

The following are some of the premises of international criminal justice as incorporated in the ICC's evidentiary rules that have been identified in this study. Firstly, video-links are made available whenever necessary as a facilitator of live testimony rather than an exception to the orality principle, considering the ICC's premise that the place of the crime is remote. The use of previously recorded statements has also been greatly expanded, as there are many cases where witnesses are not available or are subject to interference. Secondly, with regards to the exclusionary rule, it requires balancing while emphasizing compliance with internationally recognized human rights standards, in which the gravity of the core crime itself does not affect the consideration. Since the application of the exclusionary rule does not take violations of or compliance with national laws into account, the issue is how to deal with investigative discipline that differs from State to State.

As described above, exceptions have been devised with regards to the orality principle and the exclusionary rule, considering the wide variety of special circumstances of international criminal justice, but the direction of the impact of these special circumstances on these principles is different. With regards to the orality principle, importance is placed on ensuring the protection of witnesses and speed by allowing many exceptions to the orality principle while maintaining its application. On the other hand, with regards to the exclusionary rule, a relatively high threshold of a double test is first used as a criterion for the application of the principle, and a wide range of exceptions are allowed so that even evidence illegally collected through actors other than the ICC can be used. It is also clear that the rationale for the exclusionary rule at the ICC is that it is given only a limited role in deterring illegal searches. This is because the exclusion of evidence at the ICC does not have any deterrent effect on other actors cooperating with the ICC. Furthermore, the lack of discussion on the use of the system as a redress for violations that occur in the course of investigations is also characteristic of the ICC, which has long been concerned with how to deal with problems that arise during investigations. Since the ICC itself leaves investigations to other actors, procedural safeguards with respect to the actors involved must be improved.

Chapter 7
Principles on Reparation for Victims in International Criminal Justice

Abstract This chapter analyses the structure of the victim reparation procedure adopted by the Appeals Chamber's decision in the first case in the ICC and considers whether more weight was given to the demand for restorative justice or the demand for redress of victims' rights, seeking implications on what premises of international criminal justice were taken into account. It finds that, first, the reparation procedure in this case ensured the participation of both the victim and the accused in the reparation process. Second, emphasis was placed on clearly indicating the harm suffered by the victim and the extent of the responsibility of the accused. Third, the structure of the reparation procedure has adopted a restitution order type. In addition, the structure of the reparation procedure in the present case was designed mainly to meet the demands of restorative justice. In turn, it became clear that the reparation procedure in the case would not operate as an ancillary private action in which the victims themselves would be able to bring civil claims to the international organization, the ICC.

1 Introduction

In the aftermath of criminal acts of mass violence that have become the focus of international attention, the importance of restorative justice, which cares about healing and reconciliation of offenders, victims and communities, as well as retributive justice, which focuses on sanctioning offenders, has been acknowledged.[1] The ICC has also developed various forms of reparative justice, including victim participation aimed at healing and reconciliation, in addition to prosecuting core crimes. In particular, the ICC's victim reparation system has attracted attention as providing victims with a new way to be remedied under international law. However, it was not clear what kind of reparation procedures would be used in ICC cases which are characterized

[1] *E. g.*, Minow [126]. The concept of "Syuuhukutekishihou" is a new way of looking at criminal justice in contrast to traditional retributive justice, but it is translated as "Shuuhukutekiseigi" when referring to a concept that is not limited to the area of crime and delinquency but also has a broad view of peacebuilding and other issues. Shukuya and An [192], p. 17.

M. Ochi, *The Premises of International Criminal Procedure*,
https://doi.org/10.1007/978-981-97-6786-1_7

by the large number of victims expected to be involved. In particular, there has been a search for an appropriate reparation procedure between the demand for restorative justice, which focuses on the restoration of the relationship between the perpetrator and the victims and the community, and the demand for an effective remedy for the rights of the victims. In this context, on 7 August 2012, the Trial Chamber issued its first decision on victim reparations in the *Lubanga* case, which was substantially modified by the Appeals Chamber in its decision of 3 March 2015.[2]

This chapter analyses the structure of the victim reparation procedure ultimately adopted by the Appeals Chamber's decision in the *Lubanga* case and considers whether more weight was given to the demand for restorative justice or the demand for providing remedy for the victims' rights in this case, seeking for implications on what international criminal justice premise was taken into account.[3] To this end, first, I will examine the background and content of the demand for restorative justice and the demand for remedying victims' rights after a criminal act involving large-scale violence. Second, I will present an overview of the various systems for the restoration of criminal damage in domestic criminal justice. Third, I will conduct an analysis of case law, focusing on the modification of the Trial Chamber decision in the *Lubanga* case by the Appeals Chamber decision. Finally, I will analyse the precedents with a focus on the point that the Appeals Chamber's decision was modified in the *Lubanga* case, and examine the procedural structure of the case and which of the two demands was given more weight.

The use of terms related to means of restoration of damage varies according to legal systems and academic disciplines, but in this chapter, "reparation" refers to general measures for restoration of damage that do not refer to a specific system.[4] In addition, "compensation" refers to restoration for harm inflicted by the State, "restitution" refers to the reparation made by the perpetrator to the victim which is criminal in nature and "damage compensation (indemnity)" is compensation given by a perpetrator to a victim, and is used as a civil sanction, but it is not necessarily limited to money but may include return and apology.

[2] *Prosecutor v. Lubanga*, Decision establishing the principles and procedures to be applied to reparations (ICC-01/04-01/06-2904) Trial Chamber I (7 August 2012); Prosecutor *v. Lubanga*, Judgment on the appeals against the "Decision establishing the principles and procedures to be applied to reparations" of 7 August 2012 with AMENDED order for reparations (Annex A) and public annexes 1 and 2 (ICC-01/04-01/06-3129) Appeals Chamber (3 March 2015).

[3] For an analysis of subsequent developments, see Mansfield [116].

[4] Used interchangeably with relief or redress; Shelton [186], pp. 7–8.

2 Calls for Restorative Justice and the Redress of Victims' Rights

2.1 The Importance of Restoring Relationships Between Offenders, Victims, and Communities in Transition

In times of transition, when people are recovering from situations involving large-scale violence, the restoration of relationships between perpetrators and victims of criminal acts and communities is a critical issue for subsequent recovery.[5] A fundamental perspective of restorative justice is one that sees crime as destroying relationships between people and creating an obligation to repair those relationships, and sees justice as engaging perpetrators, victims and communities in solutions that promote restoration, reconciliation and security.[6] The restorative approach is said to have originated in the US in the 1970s.[7] In recent years, there have been attempts to conceptualize restorative justice internationally.[8] In 2002, the United Nations adopted "Basic Principles on the Use of Restorative Justice Programmes in Criminal Matters", the document adopted in the 11th session of the Commission on Crime Prevention and Criminal Justice and a resolution of the Economic and Social Council.[9] According to Daniel Van Ness and Karen H. Strong, restorative justice programmes consist of four stages: "inclusion", "encounter", "amends" and "reintegration", of which reparations can be part of "amends", although agreed reparations are the most effective mending measure.[10] Thus, in restorative justice, victim reparations can be part of that program,[11] and public recognition of the extent of harm through the award of reparations is particularly important,[12] although caution against

---

[5] See e.g., Clamp [33].

[6] Zehr [259], p. 183.

[7] Nishimura [139], p. 15.

[8] Economic and Social Council resolution (1999/26) "Development and implementation of mediation and restorative justice measures in criminal justice" of 1999, the Vienna Declaration on Crime and Justice of the Tenth United Nations Congress on Crime Prevention and the UN Commission on Crime Prevention and Criminal Justice, Ninth Session, "Basic principles on the use of restorative justice programmes in the criminal Basic Principles on the Use of Restorative Justice Programmes in Criminal Matters" resolution and preliminary draft (later Economic and Social Council resolution 2000/14), and other resolutions, etc.

[9] In addition, there have been discussions on how to implement the Bangkok Declaration on Synergies and Responses in 2005 and the United Nations Office on Drugs and Crime's Guide on Restorative Justice Programmes in 2006, among others, in various States.

[10] Van Ness and Strong [238], p. 58.

[11] There are two positions that view restorative programs as solely programs of restoration of the relationship between victim and offender, limiting the role of coercive and formal criminal justice (the Pure Approach), and that include all actions (including punishment) that repair the harm caused by the crime, which is the goal of restorative justice (the Maximalist). Walgrave [241].

[12] E.g., Barnett [8].

placing excessive emphasis on monetary reparations has been called for,[13] and the importance of victim participation in the reparation process itself has been argued.[14]

Restorative justice, which allows for effects on relationships between individuals, is used in a modified form in the context of transitional justice for large-scale crimes such as ethnic conflicts and persecution by dictatorships.[15] For example, restorative justice on a national or regional basis is distinctive in that its aim is primarily collective healing and reconciliation, and in the use of customary local procedures and truth commissions, such as Gacaca in Rwanda.[16] The role of reparations in core crime cases goes beyond the recovery of individual economic damages and contributes to healing through rehabilitation and reintegration of victims into society. In the case of reparations by perpetrators, not only monetary compensation but also more symbolic forms of reparations such as apologies and expressions of remorse are important for reconciliation; for example, in Rwanda, activities in the form of reconstruction of houses destroyed during the conflict by perpetrators have been effective.[17] In addition, due to the dysfunction of the domestic judicial system, it is often difficult for victims to seek compensation themselves, and compensation is often provided through administrative payments rather than through litigation.[18] Recent discussions at the United Nations have also argued that reparations through the courts cannot be the primary means of amends in core crime cases involving a complex totality of victims, but rather large-scale administrative programs is useful.[19]

Regarding the role that victim reparations through international criminal courts can play, some have suggested that it is unrealistic to expect the ICC's reparation system to realize the ideals of restorative justice,[20] while others have argued that the ICC can have a dramatic impact on the local human rights situation by incorporating a restorative justice approach.[21] The importance of the value of healing and reconciliation through some form of reparation itself is shared, and it is necessary for international criminal tribunals to seek procedures of reparation that are optimal for the healing and reconciliation of perpetrators, victims and communities.

[13] Johnstone [90], pp. 62–63.

[14] E.g., Braithwaite [20].

[15] Antkowiak [4], p. 286.

[16] Menkel-Meadow [124], pp. 160–170.

[17] Ishihara [84].

[18] Roht-Arriaza [167], pp. 121, 122, 127.

[19] *Report of the Special Rapporteur on the Promotion of Truth, Justice, Reparation and Guarantees of Non-Recurrence,* UN Doc. A/69/518 (14 October 2014), para. 3.

[20] McCarthy [121], pp. 56–59.

[21] Sarkin [176].

2.2 *Demands for the Redress of Victims' Rights: Limitations of the Reparation System in Various Areas of International Law*

That reparations must be made for violations caused by internationally wrongful acts has already been confirmed as a principle of law in various fields of international law. However, the concept of reparation to victims of core crimes committed by individuals against individuals has a legal structure that cannot be fully encompassed by the conventional framework of international law.

First, the law of State responsibility has the following limitations. Where the perpetrator of the infringement is an individual, the law of State responsibility is applicable where the act is attributable to the State and can be simulated as if it were the State's own act, and where the act is a breach of the international obligation of the State concerned (Article 2 of the Articles on State Responsibility), or where the State is found to have breached its obligation of due diligence. The obligation of due diligence of a State is limited to a breach of duty based on an act of omission where it is found that "all necessary measures" should have been taken in accordance with "general and well-accepted principles" (ICJ, *Corfu Channel* case, pp. 22–23), or where there has been a breach of a treaty obligation to prevent (e.g. Article 1 of the Genocide Convention). The law of State responsibility in cases where the subject of the violation is an individual is scheduled only in cases where the State of the victim's nationality seeks to receive reparationto the State allegedly responsible by exercising its right to diplomatic protection, and where the violation suffered by the individual can be simulated as a violation against the State of his/her nationality.[22] The draft article on State responsibility also failed to place a clear statement on direct reparation to individuals who have actually suffered harm as a result of an internationally wrongful act.[23] Thus, the law on State responsibility has been described as failing to incorporate individuals as direct beneficiaries of reparations.[24]

In the field of international humanitarian law and international human rights law, we see the development of legal norms concerning the granting of effective remedies by a State concerned to individuals who have been violated due to a breach by

[22] Therefore, the infringement suffered by the individual is only considered as a convenient measure for calculating the compensation to be made to the State under the law of State responsibility, or as a factor for establishing the validity of the cause of claim. See Banzai [7], p. 182.

[23] The Commentary to Article 33 states that "When an obligation of reparation exists towards a State, reparation does not necessarily accrue to that State's benefit. For instance, a State's responsibility for the breach of an obligation under a treaty concerning the protection of human rights may exist towards all the other parties to the treaty, but the individuals concerned should be regarded as the ultimate beneficiaries and in that sense as the holders of the relevant rights." International Law Commission, *Draft articles on Responsibility of States for Internationally Wrongful Acts, with commentaries*, Article 33, para. 3.

[24] Evans [47], p. 31. However, some argue that the traditional system of State responsibility should not be replaced by one in which individuals enjoy new rights arising from internationally wrongful acts. Tomuschat [226], p. 25.

the State of an international legal obligation owed by the State.[25] We also see the implementation of the establishment of various compensation commissions to deal with claims for reparation for harm during armed conflict, such as the United Nations Compensation Commission established in connection with the Iraqi invasion and occupation of Kuwait.[26] In human rights treaties, sharing the principles of Article 8 of the Universal Declaration of Human Rights, Article 2(3), 9(5) and 14(6) of the ICCPR, Article 41 of the European Convention on Human Rights, Articles 25 and 63 of the Inter-American Convention on Human Rights, Article 14 of the Convention against Torture, Article 6 of the Convention on the Elimination of All Forms of Racial Discrimination, Article 39 of the Convention on the Rights of the Child, Article 24(4) of the Convention on Enforced Disappearances, and others, provides for the right of individuals whose rights have been violated to obtain an effective remedy from the State. Following these developments in the law, the advisory opinion on the *Palestinian Wall* case before the ICJ of 9 July 2004 confirmed Israel's obligation to restore the original state and to provide monetary compensation to all natural and legal persons who have suffered material damage following the construction of the separation wall.

There has also been a movement towards the generation of norms with regards to the responsibility of States for humanitarian or human rights violations between individuals. With regards to victims of ordinary crimes involving violations of the rights of others, the 1985 Declaration of Basic Principles of Justice for Victims of Crime and Abuse of Power provides that, with regards to restitution, "Offenders or third parties responsible for their behaviour should, where appropriate, make fair restitution to victims, their families, or dependants. Such restitution should include the return of property or payment for the harm or loss suffered, reimbursement of expenses incurred as a result of the victimization, the provision of services and the restoration of rights" (para. 8), and that "Governments should review their practices, regulations and laws to consider restitution as an available sentencing option in criminal cases, in addition to other criminal sanctions" (para. 9). With regards to compensation, it was also confirmed that "... When compensation is not fully available from the offender or other sources, States should endeavour to provide financial compensation..." (para. 12). In addition, with regards to particularly grave violations, the 2005 Basic Principles and Guidelines on the Right to a Remedy and Reparation for Victims of Gross Violations of International Human Rights Law and Serious Violations of International Humanitarian Law state that "...In cases where a person, a legal person, or other entity is found liable for reparation to a victim, such

---

[25] While Article 3 of Hague Convention IV and Article 91 of Additional Protocol I to the Geneva Conventions, which provide for reparation for damage during armed conflict, were structured in a similar way to the law of State responsibility, in that reparations could be sought through inter-State mechanisms, the fact that these articles were also aimed at redress for individuals who had suffered damage has been reinterpreted by Kalshoven [95], pp. 827, 830, Henckaerts and Doswald-Beck [71].

[26] See Furuya [60].

party should provide reparation to the victim or compensate the State if the State has already provided reparation to the victim" (para. 15).[27]

However, no amount of emphasis on the international obligations of States can be effective in situations where human rights violations serious enough to constitute core crimes that lead to criminal punishment of the perpetrators are not expected to be addressed domestically, particularly because they take place under conditions of conflict or oppression. This concern has led to expectations of the role of international criminal tribunals in pursuing international responsibility against individuals, ensuring reparation procedures, and providing a forum for redressing the rights of victims.

3 Various Systems for the Restoration of Crime Victims in Domestic Criminal Justice

Due to the limitations of the conventional framework in international law, the function of redressing the rights of victims has come to be expected from international criminal courts. However, how to link the relationship between public authority and private individuals—criminal matters—, with compensation as an individual right, is a complex issue that has been debated for many years in the context of building a domestic criminal justice system.

The reparation procedures in domestic criminal justice are diverse depending on the legal system. In traditional criminal justice, the concern for crime victims was secondary. However, with the development of the concept of human rights of crime victims and the spread of the concept of restorative justice in recent years, various systems of reparation for victims have been introduced in domestic criminal justice. There are three main types of victim reparation systems. Firstly, the administrative system, in which compensation is paid to victims of crime by the State, is a measure that developed in various States following lobbying by S. Margery Fry in the UK in 1957, in view of the situation of victims of crime who were unable to access civil reparation systems.[28] Secondly, the civil system of making offensers pay indemnities is usually operated through civil lawsuits brought by victims to pursue the civil liability of the infringer. Finally, the system as a criminal sanction includes, apart from fines, restitution orders that directly order the convict to recover damages.

In terms of the actual claim procedures, the victim compensation system is mainly a system in which benefits are paid by the public treasury through applications from

[27] Furthermore, the General Comment No. 3 by the Committee against Torture in 2012 pointed out that "Notwithstanding the evidentiary benefits to victims afforded by a criminal investigation, a civil proceeding and the victim's claim for reparation should not be dependent on the conclusion of a criminal proceeding" and that "Disciplinary action alone shall not be regarded as an effective remedy within the meaning of article 14" (para. 26).

[28] For a history of the system, see Oya [156]. The British-like understanding that Japan takes regarding the theoretical basis is based on the spirit of social solidarity and mutual aid, while Germany seeks the basis in the State's failure in its duty to prevent crime. Okumura [153], p. 133.

victims to administrative agencies, while indemnity for damages is paid through civil lawsuits. On the other hand, as for the restitution system within the criminal procedure, there are two systems, one is the system in which civil lawsuits are unified in relation to criminal trials, such as ancillary private action (*Entschädigung des Verletzten/action civile*), which is said to have its origin in the Continental legal system, and the other is the system of the order for restitution, which is mainly adopted in the Anglo-American legal system.[29] An ancillary private action is one in which a civil claim arising from a crime is realized in the criminal proceedings against the accused, and the criminal court tries to realize the civil claim in parallel with fact finding.[30] A restitution order is an order made directly against the convicted person, awarding the amount of restitution to the victim at the sentencing stage.

Among the reparations that can be realized through a criminal trial, there are advantages and disadvantages in ancillary private action and the restitution ordered as a penalty, respectively. First, in the case of ancillary private action, reparation is based on the victim's request, which provides an opportunity for the victim to clearly state what they want, and reparation will not be paid if the victim does not want it. However, there are also disadvantages to this, such as the imbalance that arises between victims who do not apply, the rejection of cases by criminal judges due to their aversion to civil procedures, and the lack of interest of lawyers due to the low feasibility of the case.[31] Next, the advantage of a restitution order is that there is no burden on the victim and no imbalance arises depending on whether or not an application is filed. In addition, since the magnitude of the criminal damage can be indicated and expressed in monetary units, it has the function of public recognition of the damage, and since the aspect of compulsory deprivation of legal interests is taken into consideration, it is constrained from the perspective of substantive due process[32] and can take the accused into consideration. However, it has some drawbacks, such as the fact that it is indistinguishable from a fine in cases other than the violation of personal legal interests, the lack of opportunity for agreement between the offender and the victim, and possible confusion regarding the calculation of damages due to the difference between criminal and civil proceedings.

In recent years, New Zealand's system of reparation orders has been attracting attention as a new system that supplements for the shortcomings of restitution orders and strengthens their significance in restorative justice, while taking advantage of their merits. The State's reparation order system was enacted in the same vein as the world's pioneering introduction of a crime victims' compensation system in the

[29] Takahashi calls the restitution type the "sanction model" and the incidental private prosecution type the "combination model". There is also a "circumvention model" (e.g. Switzerland) in which a fine is paid to the victim, and a "sentencing model" (e.g. Germany) in which a fine is considered as a reason for sentencing. The "criminal procedure-related model" is an aspect that preserves the offender's property, confiscates it, or collects it to recover damages, and the "civil procedure support model" such as a deposition order to promote victims' claim for recovery based on the distinction between civil and criminal cases, can be used in an overlapping manner. Takahashi [210], pp. 12–18.

[30] Takizawa [219], p. 149.

[31] *Ibid.*, p. 154.

[32] Nagata [134], p. 54.

1980s, and has been understood as a form of restorative justice.[33] Although the system of reparatrion orders has undergone various amendments, the current system under the Sentencing Act 2002, which requires the court to take into account the results of restorative discussions between the victim and the accused when awarding the amount of reparation, is regarded as a reflection and evaluation of restorative justice.[34]

4 The ICC's Reparation Framework for Victims and the *Lubanga* Case

4.1 Breadth of Interpretation in the ICC's Reparation-Related Provisions

In the sections above, after confirming the demand for restorative justice in the transitional context and the demand for redress of victims' rights under international law, I have examined the system of reparations for victims of crimes in domestic criminal justice systems and summarized the relevant issues regarding the expected role and procedural options for the reparation system in international criminal tribunals. Based on these considerations, I will now examine the ICC's reparations-related provisions and the position taken by the Court in the *Lubanga* case with regards to what kind of reparations procedures the ICC has actually adopted.

The ICTY and ICTR, the predecessors of the ICC, only had provisions for ordering restitution of property and proceeds obtained through criminal acts, and despite various attempts in practice, no actual reparations were made to the victims. However, the ICC Statute, after discussions during the drafting process, included an explicit provision on reparation to victims; the 1993 Preliminary Draft had a provision for the distribution of fines to victims (Article 47), but this provision was removed based on the claim that the criminal courts were not the appropriate forum for reparation to victims.[35] However, at the 1997 Preparatory Committee, France proposed Article 45(2), which would determine the scope and reach of damages through the ICC judgment and allow victims to obtain civil remedies in the State based on this judgment.[36] While asserting the responsibility of States to compensate, it also added a proposal that the ICC would "directly" enforce reparations in cases where national judicial authorities lack competence.[37] However, this proposal for "direct" enforcement received a lot of opposition, and the UK proposed the possibility of limiting

[33] Fujimoto and Senzu [57], p. 48.

[34] Okumura [154], p. 6.

[35] Donat-Cattin [42], p. 1855.

[36] Muttukumaru [133], pp. 265, 266.

[37] *Ibid.*

the award to that of issuing an order against a convicted person "as a penalty".[38] As a result, a final proposal was submitted in the form of a joint French-British proposal, which was coordinated between States with different models of criminal procedure.[39] At the 1998 Rome Conference, opposition to the reparation system itself arose from States that did not have domestic reparation systems for criminal damage. In particular, the responsibility of States for reparations became controversial, but the concept of restorative justice and the importance of reconciliation in transitional justice gradually became more widely understood, and the debate eventually shifted to the creation of an effective reparation framework.[40]

Article 75(1) of the adopted ICC Statute states that the Court shall establish principles for reparation and provides that the Court may determine the extent and degree of damages on the basis of an individual victim's claim for reparation and, in exceptional circumstances, *ex officio*. However, as a practical matter, it was expected that the Court would be able to examine individual claims in cases where the number of victims was small but would otherwise make an award of reparation *ex officio* without examining individual claims.[41] It was seen as necessary to specify the details in the RPE. However, in drafting the RPE, it was only recommended that they should be in line with international instruments, as it is for the Court itself to set up the appeal procedure and other procedures in the absence of individual review.[42] In addition, Rule 94 of the RPE provided only for formalities such as matters to be included in the request from the victim, and Rule 95 provided for notification in cases of *ex officio* review. The representative of a State that sees reparations at the ICC as a civil sanction stated that collective reparations cannot meet the demands of individuals, while the representative of a State that sees it as a criminal sanction took the view that reparations would be a symbolic gesture and that forms such as the construction of hospitals and monuments that would benefit many residents for a small amount would be available.[43] Rule 97, adopted from a compromise proposal, provided that the Court may award reparations to an individual, to a group where appropriate, or to both. Furthermore, Rule 75(2) of the ICC Statute provided that an order for reparations could be made against a convicted person, but Rule 98(1) of the RPE specified that "Individual awards for reparations shall be made directly against a convicted person."

In addition, Article 79 of the ICC Statute established the Trust Fund for Victims ("TFV") for the benefit of victims of crime and their families. While individual payments of awards of reparation in accordance with Rule 98 of the RPE are made directly by convicted persons, awards may be deposited in the TFV or paid

---

[38] *Ibid.*

[39] UN Doc. A/CONF.183/C.1/WGPM/L.28, in *Official Records of the United Nations Diplomatic Conference of Plenipotentiaries on the Establishment of an International Criminal Court*, Rome, 15 June-17 July 1998, Vol. 3 (2002), p. 307.

[40] Muttukumaru [133], p. 264.

[41] A/CONF.183/C.1/WGPM/L.2/Add.7 (13 July 1998), footnote 6.

[42] Friman and Lewis [54], p. 478.

[43] *Ibid.*, p. 483.

through the TFV, for example, when it is appropriate to pay to a group ("reparation mandate"). The TFV may also use other resources, such as voluntary contributions and "other assets" allocated by the Assembly of States Parties, to provide a wide range of victims and their families, not limited to victims participating in criminal trials, with respect to situations over which the ICC exercises jurisdiction, including physical and psychological rehabilitation and material assistance ("general assistance mandate").[44] A general assistance mandate can be understood as providing administrative compensation to victims of crime and those affected.

The distinctive feature of the ICC's reparation system is that it can operate in the following three ways, depending on the range of interpretation of the reparations-related provisions.[45] The first is the administrative compensation type, which is structured in such a way that the victims are directly rehabilitated by the International Criminal Justice Institution through benefits as compensation. For example, Claude Jorda and Jerome Hemptinne have suggested that in cases where the convicted person does not have sufficient assets, the ICC should provide the victim with compensation funds, in the spirit of fairness and solidarity, and as the international community is responsible for the consequences of its failure to prevent those crime.[46] The framework envisaged was based on the traditional rationale of State reparations, which are to be compensated for using the assets of the TFV. Administrative compensation-type reparations are seen as an administrative decision by an international organization to provide compensation in respect of the victims' right to reparation, which is not synonymous with the victims' exercise of their civil claims to such reparation.

The second is the ancillary private action type, where a civil action involving an individual's claims for damage is attached to a criminal procedure in the international criminal adjudication. Many commentators have understood that the ancillary private action type based on individual claims is also acceptable because the wording of Article 75(2) of the ICC Statute states that a judgment can be made based on the claim "except in exceptional circumstances." This understanding seems to have been the prevailing view.[47] For example, Furuya commented that "the right to claim compensation, which had been concentrated in the State, is now granted to individuals, and furthermore, the procedural standings to specifically file such a claim has been recognized in an international forum."[48] The ancillary private action type reparation procedure can be evaluated as a procedural innovation for individual reparations under international law, as it recognizes a new function of international criminal tribunals, where the victims themselves realize their civil claims under international law against the individual violators of their substantive rights under

[44] For more information, see Noguchi [140], pp. 339–354.

[45] This is said to be an example of the "constructive ambiguity" contained in the ICC Statute. Van den Wyngaert [237], p. 488.

[46] Jorda and Hemptinne [91], p. 1416.

[47] E.g., Henzelin et al. [72], Inazumi [82], Zegveld [258], pp. 88, 100–103. Tatsuta evaluates the ICC's attempt to shift the conception of "restitution of damages" from being a form of punishment to one that focuses primarily on the restoration and recognition of victims' dignity as groundbreaking. Tatsuda [223], p. 323.

[48] Furuya [61], p. 157.

international law through international tribunals. On the other hand, Birte Timm and Eva Dwertmann, who also argue that reparations at the ICC are essentially civil in nature, state that the ICC's provisions do not provide victims with classical "claims" because reparation orders are discretionary and cannot be understood as entitling individuals to compensation under certain conditions.[49]

The third is the restitution order type, which is structured in such a way that restitution is ordered as a punishment for an individual's criminal responsibility. Although reparation as punishment was raised as an option in the drafting process and was left open to interpretation, there is little reference to this structure in previous studies. Although the substantive criminal law is based on international law and the forum is an international organization, it is not recognized as a structure in which the victim realizes his/her rights through an international criminal trial, and it is understood as only a reflexive enjoyment of reparation as punishment.

Thus, due to the wide range of interpretations of the ICC's reparations provisions, there were three possible structures of reparations procedure, and it was not clear which structure would be adopted in a specific case, but the first reparations judgment in the *Lubanga* case provided an example of a reparation procedure at the ICC. The following section will examine which of the three possible types of reparation procedure was used in the *Lubanga* case, and whether it was more focused on the demands for restorative justice or the redress of the rights of the victims.

4.2 The Lubanga *Reparation Case*

4.2.1 Trial Chamber Decisions—Full Entrustment to the TFV

In the *Lubanga* case, the accused was found guilty of conscripting and using directly in hostilities children under the age of 15 as soldiers from the Hema ethnic group, from which Thomas Lubanga himself originate. The number of child soldiers was said to be in the thousands. However, the impact of the case did not stop there, as it was found that the child soldiers had victimized the neighbouring Lendu people through murder, extortion and looting, and furthermore that some of the child soldiers had been victims of sexual violence by members of the same armed groups.[50] However, the number of individual applications actually submitted to the ICC in accordance with Rule 94 of the RPE stopped at 85.[51] In addition to the prosecutor, defence counsel, victims and the TFV, various NGOs and the United Nations Children's Fund ("UNICEF") also submitted views in the reparations decision. The main issues

---

[49] Timm [225], p. 303, Dwertmann [44], p. 295.

[50] *Prosecutor v. Lubanga*, Judgment pursuant to Article 74 of the Statute (ICC-01/04-01/06-2842) Trial Chamber I (14 March 2012).

[51] Of these, 77 were under the age of 15 at the time, seven were parents and one was a school principal; 19 requested individual reparations, five requested collective reparations and 59 requested both. *Prosecutor v. Lubanga*, First Report to the Trial Chamber on applications for reparations (ICC-01/04-01/06-2847) Trial Chamber I (28 March 2012).

in the case can be broadly divided into two categories: first, the manner in which reparations were to be made, and second, the determination of eligibility to receive reparations.

With regards to the manner of reparation, the Trial Chamber sought to limit the Court's involvement to the role of resolving and finally approving any disputes between the parties and to entrust the reparation procedure entirely to the TFV. The Trial Chamber considered it unnecessary for judges to be bound throughout the reparation process (para. 261), and while confirming that the reparation stage was an integral part of the trial, it was primarily dealing with the victim, as opposed to the conviction and sentencing, and left the appropriate form of victim participation in the reparation process to the Registry (para. 268). It also held that, in view of Lubanga's impoverished condition, he could only make non-pecuniary reparations, while symbolic reparations, such as public or private apologies, were only appropriate with the consent of the convicted person, and therefore it would not take this approach (para. 269). It therefore held that reparations were to be made through the TFV in the present case, but interpreted the words "through" in Article 75(2) of the Statute as "by means of", citing an English dictionary for the ordinary meaning of the term, and held that other resources of the TFV could also be used for reparations (paras 270–273). It then gave the TFV the dual task of "determining the appropriate forms of reparation and carrying them out" (paras 281–288). It also upheld the "community-based approach" which was clearly compatible with prompt collective reparations through the TFV, without deciding on individual applications as a result.

Several appeals were filed against this decision by the defence and the victims. Particular issues raised were that the criteria and procedures for the identification of victims were vague and could violate the fundamental rights of convicted persons,[52] that the decision did not take into account individual claims for compensation, that it was an error in the application of the law for the Trial Chamber to delegate the responsibility for compensation to another department, that the responsibility for reparation of convicted persons was limited.[53] The question of whether the decision of the Trial Chamber remains a principle as referred to in Article 75(1) of the Statute or an order as referred to in Article 75(2) of the Statute was raised in relation to the admissibility of these appeals.[54]

[52] *Procureur c. Lubanga, Requête de la Défense sollicitant l'autorisation d'interjeter appel de la* « Decision Establishing the principles and procedures to be applied to reparation» *rendue le 7 août 2012* (ICC-01/04-01/06-2905) *La Chambre de Première Instance I* (13 août 2012); *Procureur c. Lubanga, Acte d'appel de la Défense de M. Thomas Lubanga à l'encontre de la* « Decision establishing the principles and procedures to be applied to reparation» *rendue par la Chambre de première instance I le 7 août 2012* (ICC-01/04-01/06-2917) *La Chambre D'appel* (*6 septembre 2012*).

[53] *Procureur c. Lubanga, Acte d'appel à l'encontre de la "Decision establishing the principles and procedures to be applied to reparation" délivrée par la Chambre de première instance I le 7 août 2012* (ICC-01/04-01/06-2909) *La Chambre D'appel* (*24 août 2012*); *Procureur c. Lubanga, Acte d'appel contre la* "Decision establishing the principles and procedures to be applied to reparation" *du 7 août 2012 de la Chambre de première instance I* (ICC-01/04-01/06-2914) *La Chambre D'appel* (*3 Septembre 2012*).

[54] For details, see Higashizawa [75], pp. 161–162.

4.2.2 Appeals Chamber's Judgment—Emphasis on the Role of the Trial Chamber and the Responsibility of the Convict

In relation to the acceptance of the appeal, the Appeals Chamber, which was first required to determine the nature of the Trial Chamber's decision, arranged the contents of the Trial Chamber's decision into a principle part and an order part (paras 49–56). It also clarified the requirements for a reparation order and adopted a formula whereby the Trial Chamber's decision, as modified in accordance with Rule 153(1) of the RPE, was attached as Appendix A ("Amended Reparation Order") so as to satisfy those requirements.

Next, in respect of the main appeal, the matter was divided into five essential elements to be included in the reparation order. The three relating to the manner of compensation are as follows.

The first element is that an order for reparations must always be made directly against the convicted person. In other words, the Appeals Chamber found that it is clearly compatible from the French codification to issue an order for reparations against the convicted person and to make reparations "through the Trust Fund (*par l'intermédiaire du Fonds*)" (paras 57–76). Furthermore, the Trial Chamber's abstract standard of causation of "proximate cause" was modified to the principle that the circumstances of an individual case require sufficient evidence to prove causation (para. 81). With regards to the standard of proof, whereas the Trial Chamber's decision stated that the "balance of probabilities" standard would be used for compensation orders and the "wholly flexible approach" for compensation through the TFV, the Court held that it was legally incorrect to set different standards for the two procedures and adopted only the "balance of probabilities" standard for compensation orders against convicted persons (para. 83).

The second factor was that the liability of the convicted person must be established, and the convicted person must be notified. The Trial Chamber based its decision on the assumption that the Trial Chamber had the power to decide on the TFV's "other assets". In response, the Appeals Chamber, applying TFV Regulations 50 and 56 with reference to Rule 98 of the RPE and the arguments made in the drafting process, held that the allocation of "other assets" for the purpose of supplementing the resources collected through an award of reparation was solely a matter of discretion for the TFV's board and that the Trial Chamber had no power to decide (paras 106–116). It then declared that the TFV may lend "other assets" in circumstances where the convicted person is incapable of fulfilling the reparation order due to his impoverished condition, but that despite such intervention the responsibility for reparations still remained with the convict, Lubanga (paras 115–117).

The third element was that the form of reparations ordered had to be specified and reasons attached. The Appeals Chamber held that there are two types of ICC reparation awards: individual applications under Rules 94 and 95 of the RPE, and collective reparation awards under Rules 97(1) and 98(1), and that, as to the latter, reparation is inherently linked to the criminal responsibility for the offence committed by the convicted person and the eligible persons are therefore not limited to the applicants (paras 149–152). Rather, it noted that there are cases where collective reparations are appropriate, such as when the number of applicants is too small compared to the number of victims, and that the context of the ICC is different from the context of international human rights cases, where there is an obligation to assess all applications (paras 152–154).

On the basis of these judgments, the Appeals Chamber decided that, exceptionally in the present case, it would be appropriate to enlist the assistance of the TFV already active in the field in calculating the amount it considered necessary to remedy the harm caused by what Lubanga was found guilty of, and requested the TFV to submit to the new Trial Chamber a draft implementation plan for collective reparations, including an estimated amount (paras 240–242).

5 Structure and Evaluation of the Reparation Proceedings in the *Lubanga* Case

In the decision, the Trial Chamber stated that "The Statute and Rules introduce a system of reparations that reflects a growing recognition in international criminal law that there is a need to go beyond the notion of punitive justice, towards a solution which is more inclusive, encourages participation and recognises the need to provide effective remedies for victims" (Trial Chamber Decision, para. 177; Amended Reparation Order, para. 1). It also states that reparations must alleviate the suffering caused by the commission of serious crimes, bring justice to victims by mitigating the consequences of unlawful acts, deter future violations, and effectively contribute to the reintegration of former child soldiers into society, while also providing a means for convicted persons, crime victims, and affected communities to promote reconciliation among them (para. 179 of the Trial Chamber's Decision). In the Amended Reparation Order, this point was also stated in a new section entitled "Objectives of reparation" (para. 71 of the Amended Reparation Order). These statements indicate that the Trial Chamber is seeking to meet both the demands of restorative justice, which is to ensure that victims participate and that perpetrators are aware of their own conduct and consciously fulfil their responsibilities, and the substantial remedy of victims' rights, which is to help them recover from their harm and alleviate their suffering.

However, the reparation procedure actually adopted in this case, for the following reasons, seems to have been more concerned with meeting the demands of restorative justice than with victims' remedies *per se*.

The first is that it ensures that both the victim and the accused are given the opportunity to participate in the reparation calculation process. It also ensures that both the victim and the accused submit their views when the Trial Chamber makes a reparation order based on the proposed reparation plan submitted by the TFV (paras 241–243).

Second, the effect of the public display of harm and responsibility through reparation awards was emphasized. In the words of Carsten Stahn, the Appeals Chamber "provides greater weight to expressivist features, such as the direct recognition of harm in the Reparation Order and the judicial acknowledgement of the link between the convicted person and victims." (Footnote omitted)[55] The representation/expression of harm is an important effect that contributes to the healing of the victim, the reflection of the perpetrator, and the reconciliation of both sides and the community in the context of restorative justice.

Third, the structure of the reparation procedure in this case can be evaluated as a reparation order type procedure. As mentioned above, in domestic criminal justice system, there have been attempts to incorporate the concept of restorative justice into reparation procedures requiring compensation orders. The reparation procedures in this case also showed an attempt to reflect the perspective of restorative justice. There are two reasons why the reparation procedure in this case can be said to be of the restitution order type.

The first is that it was emphasized that liability for reparations is limited to the crime for which the person was convicted, and it was confirmed that regulations analogous to substantive due process are at stake, with due consideration given to ensuring fairness for the accused. The point, emphatically confirmed by the Appeals Chamber, that liability for reparations is based exclusively on the criminal responsibility of the convicted individual, was also repeatedly confirmed in the four resolutions of the Assembly of the States Parties since 2011.[56] The Appeals Chamber also confirmed that the need for the award of reparations to be made by the newly constituted Trial Chamber was to ensure the accused had an opportunity to appeal (paras 237–239).

The second reason was that the victims who had not made individual applications were also eligible for reparations. The Appeals Chamber found it necessary to distinguish between the context of international human rights law, which holds that all individual applications for reparation must be heard, and the context of international criminal trials. In other words, it was clearly stated that in the criminal justice system, instead of placing the burden of proceedings on the victim, the amount and scope of reparations should be determined solely on the basis of the acts for which the court found him or her guilty. From this point of view, compensation based on the conviction is based on the understanding that it is different in character from both administrative measures and civil suits. This point is also linked to the clear distinction made between the general support duties of the TFV, which are administrative in nature, and the nature of the reparation duties based on a conviction. While the Trial Chamber's decision envisaged a framework in which the TFV would be used as if it were a compensation commission for individual claims, the Appeals Chamber's decision that individual applications for reparation by victims were merely material for determining the scope of reparation and that the existence of such applications was

[55] Stahn [197], p. 811.

[56] Rather, the term "exclusive" in the resolutions of the Conference of the States Parties is mentioned in the context of confirming that under no circumstances can a State be ordered to use its property for compensation, ICC-ASP/10/Res.3 (20 December 2011), para. 2; ICC-ASP/11/Res.7 (21 November 2012), para. 3; ICC-ASP/12/Res.5 (27 November 2013), para. 4; ICC-ASP/13/Res.4 (27 November 2013), para. 5; ICC-ASP/11/Res.7 (21 November 2012), para. 8; ICC-ASP/12/Res.5 (27 November 2013), para. 9; ICC-ASP/13/Res.4 (17 December 2014), para. 9.

not decisive for the award of reparation suggests the punitive nature of the reparation procedure in the *Lubanga* case.

From these points of view, the reparation procedure in this case can be evaluated as adopted a framework that was neither an administrative compensation nor a system to which damages are attached, but a punitive restitution order system modified to a restorative one, which focuses on the relationship between the perpetrator, the victim and the community, rather than the concept of victim-centeredness that is traditionally referred to in the framework of international human rights law.

6 Conclusion

In this chapter, through an analysis of the Appeals Chamber's decision in the *Lubanga* case, I have examined the structure of the ICC's victim reparation procedure in this case and whether it can be evaluated as giving more weight to the demand for restorative justice or the demand for the redress of victims' rights. First, the reparation procedure in this case ensured the participation of both the victim and the accused in the reparation process. Second, emphasis was placed on clearly indicating the harm suffered by the victim and the extent of the responsibility of the accused. Third, the structure of the reparation procedure has adopted a restitution order type. Moreover, the structure of the reparation procedure in the present case was designed mainly to meet the demands of restorative justice.

In turn, it became clear that the reparation procedure in the case would not operate as an ancillary private action in which the victims themselves would be able to bring civil claims to the international organization, the ICC. Therefore, the reparation procedure in this case cannot be regarded as a development of the system of international law concerning civil claims by individuals for international crimes. However, the application of the reparations framework set out in this judgment was limited to this case, and there is still a possibility that the incidental private action type framework will be adopted in future cases where the number of victims is smaller.[57] Indeed, in the subsequent *Katanga* case, in addition to four collective reparations for all victims, the accused was ordered to provide €250 to each of 297 victims as

[57] For example, in the ICC's *Banda* case concerning the murder of 12 peacekeepers in Sudan, as well as attacks on troops and looting of equipment, it would be practicable to identify the family members of the murdered persons and the eight persons subjected to attempted murder as victims and make an award of compensation based on their individual claims. ICC-02/05-03/09-121 (7 March 2011).

symbolic reparations.[58] It was also decided in the *Ntaganda* case that individual and collective reparations would be used together.[59]

The theoretically important point in the present case is the implication of the distinction between the context of international criminal trials and the context of international human rights trials. That is, the issue of the relationship between the procedural system for the pursuit of individual criminal responsibility and the procedural system for the pursuit of reparations in the ICC's procedural law. The ICC's RPE Rule 85 defines a victim as a person who has suffered harm as a result of the commission of a crime within the ICC's jurisdiction. Many acts overlap with acts prohibited by international humanitarian law and international human rights law, and the commission of crimes under the ICC jurisdiction often simultaneously involves violations of international humanitarian law and international human rights law. Therefore, criminal liability under the ICC Statute arises based on the commission of core crimes, but at the same time, civil liability based on violations of international humanitarian law and international human rights law will also often be considered to have arisen. As mentioned above, since the procedural system to realize the latter liability has not been developed in conventional international law, the framework to pursue the liability under the ICC Statute was the framework of the ICC reparation system of the ancillary private action type. However, liability under the ICC Statute theoretically does not arise from violations of international humanitarian law or international human rights law, but from the commission of criminal acts under the ICC Statute.[60] Therefore, liability for reparations associated with an individual's criminal responsibility for committing ICC jurisdiction crimes and liability for violations of international humanitarian law and international human rights law would need to be pursued under different procedural systems.

---

[58] *Prosecutor v. Katanga*, Order for Reparations pursuant to Article 75 of the Statute (ICC-01/04-01/07-3728-tENG) Trial Chamber II (24 March 2017); *Prosecutor v. Katanga*, Judgment on the appeals against the order of Trial Chamber II of 24 March 2017 entitled "Order for Reparations pursuant to Article 75 of the Statute" (ICC-01/04-01/07-3778-Red) Appeals Chamber (8 March 2018).

[59] *Prosecutor v. Ntaganda, Reparation Order* (ICC-01/04-02/06-2659) Trial Chamber VI (8 March 2021).

[60] If a crime under the ICC's jurisdiction is committed outside the scope of international humanitarian law or international human rights law, or if such crime is committed for an act that is not prohibited by international humanitarian law or international human rights law, a conviction may be handed down at the ICC even if no violation of international humanitarian law or international human rights law can be found. It may be debatable, as in the *Lubanga* case, what violations of international humanitarian law or international human rights law constitute the recruitment and incorporation of children under 15 years of age in a non-international armed conflict by members of an insurgent group and their direct use in hostilities in the first place.

The next question is on what basis of attribution the ICC's liability for reparations would arise if it were divorced from international humanitarian law and international human rights law. In this sense, given the adoption of a restitution order type reparation procedure in this case, it seems appropriate to view liability for reparations for the commission of crimes under ICC jurisdiction as part of the content of an individual's criminal responsibility. However, if we move away from the interpretation of the Statute and assume the argument that the commission by an individual of an act exemplified in the ICC Statute constitutes an internationally wrongful act in itself, there may be room for a different understanding of the ancillary private action-type framework.[61]

[61] On 3 November 2015, the TFV submitted a proposed implementation plan that did not provide the requisite estimated amount requested by the Appeals Chamber, but instead stated that it would "supplement" the amount of Lubanga's reparations award in a broad sense in accordance with TFV Rule 56, and that it would include the amount of funds in the reparations reserve that the TFV Board had approved for use to supplement the reparations in the *Lubanga* case (€1 million) and the reparations program, including rehabilitation. *Prosecutor v. Lubanga*, Redaction of Filing on Reparations and Draft Implementation Plan (ICC-01/04-01/06-3177-Red) Trial Chamber II (3 November 2015); *Prosecutor v. Lubanga*, Annex A to Filing on Reparations and Draft Implementation Plan (ICC-01/04-01/06-3177-AnxA) Trial Chamber II (3 November 2015). The draft plan is more of an administrative compensation type aimed at supplementing the needs of victims to the extent possible, rather than reflecting the nature of restorative reparations between perpetrators and victims and communities as indicated by the Appeals Chamber, perhaps because of the difficulties of damage calculation and the practical limitations of assets.

Chapter 8
Concluding Discussion

Abstract In this book, I have conducted a comparative analysis of various general principles of international criminal procedure with corresponding principles that are valid domestically and in general international law, and to identified special premises in the procedural law of the ICC. With regards to the procedural principles covered in the chapters of the book, several premises have been revealed. This book disclosed the four points that have not been identified in previous studies. These elements can be broadly classified into two categories, and each has two branches of premises. First, (A) the fact that the value of international criminal procedure frequently mentioned in previous studies has not actually had much of an impact: (i) the premise of "seriousness of the core crime" has little influence at the procedural level; and (ii) the premise of deterring illegal investigations has had little impact. Second, (B) the factors that have not been recognized as circumstances or values on which international criminal procedure is premised in previous research significantly influence international criminal procedure: (iii) the entire procedure is based on the primitive premise of speed and "first come, first served"; and (iv) the impact of the premise of consideration for national sovereignty, which is associated with the fact that the ICC is an international organization based on a treaty, is critical. The ICC's institutional premises of the value of expeditiousness and lacking centralized control over its "limbs" have had a significant impact on the various aspects of international criminal procedure.

1 Introduction

In this book, I have conducted a compataive analysis of various general principles of international criminal procedure with corresponding principles that are valid domestically and in general international law, and identified specific premises in the procedural law of the ICC. In this concluding discussion, I will review the various premises of international criminal procedure that have been identified in the chapters

M. Ochi, *The Premises of International Criminal Procedure*,
https://doi.org/10.1007/978-981-97-6786-1_8

of this book, and then discuss the principles and challenges inherent to international criminal procedure, as well as the future prospects for international criminal procedure.

2 Results of Analysis

This book has examined the general principles governing the various issues that arise when proceedings are brought before the ICC along the timeline of international criminal proceedings. With regards to the topics covered in the chapters of the book, the premises that have revealed through the analysis can be summarized as follows.

2.1 Parallel Investigations and Parallel Prosecutions

The principles of international criminal justice are based on the premises of international cooperation, and since multiple criminal justice agencies work together to investigate the same criminal cases, various principles have developed based on the premise of parallel investigations. Although there is an awareness of the adverse effects of parallel investigations in domestic and inter-state relations, the merits of joint investigations in international criminal justice tend to be prioritized. With regards to parallel prosecution, norms for the allocation of jurisdiction were adopted, which were influenced by the institutional characteristics of International Criminal Justice Institutions. The issue of parallel prosecution is generally regarded as a problem to be avoided as in the domestic plane, and the principle of complementarity has been devised and incorporated in the ICC in particular. However, the content of the norms also indicates that the basic principle is that "first come, first served"—the institution that prosecuted the case first is prioritized—.

Thus, the principles concerning parallel investigation and parallel prosecution take into consideration the necessity and effectiveness of prosecution, and concerns about dispersion of evidence and information and duplication of procedures from the viewpoint of litigation economy. In addition, with regards to the prosecution stage, the *burden on the accused* and the adverse effects of duplication of procedures due to parallel prosecution, such as double sentencing, are also taken into consideration. However, it can be confirmed that there is a special premise that it is *necessary to decide in advance which of the International Criminal Justice Institutions or the State has priority and which of them is complementary.* However, as long as "prioritizing" is appropriate, it suggests that the perspective of the *litigation economy of the international community as a whole is becoming apparent.* Furthermore, in addition to this, there is a normative premise of the demand for *speed*—the sooner justice is done, the better—.

2.2 *Priority of Extradition*

There are several situations in which priority is given to extradition/surrender for core crimes as international criminal justice efforts, when there are extradition requests for different crimes. First, with regards to genocide, the Genocide Convention, which obliges the Parties to extradite and has no coordination provisions, basically establishes that, even if there are competing extradition requests for other crimes, priority is given to extradition for genocide. This is applicable even in the case of competing extradition requests against other crimes. However, it is difficult to see how such a principle could be justified, since in none of the extradition regimes, except for the Genocide Convention, was there any rule that priority be given on the basis that the subject offence was a core crime. It is also clear that the seriousness of the offence is not a consideration in relation to competing extradition requests for the same conduct, even between surrender to the ICC and mandatory extradition to a State not party to the Statute. On the other hand, it was found that, in general, in the cases of competing extradition requests for different offences, there are many provisions that give priority or consideration to extradition to the more serious offence, suggesting the possibility of such principle. Seriousness/gravity can be either the gravity of the criminal conduct or the seriousness of the nature of the crime concept itself, and the seriousness of the core crimes can be considered when considering seriousness in the latter sense.

Although it is difficult to prove the existence of a principle on the issue of priority of extradition/surrender, the tendency regarding the content of the treaties indicates that there is a premise of the need to *give priority to the pursuit of justice for serious crimes*. However, given that many treaties do not contain coordination provisions but only discretionary provisions, it may be necessary to consider *political factors among States* other than the pure motive of prosecuting serious crimes in the selection of extradition destinations. In addition, although the framework of the ICC included the norm of giving priority to surrender to the ICC, this is naturally limited to States Parties to the Statute, and the discretionary provision in the case of an extradition request to a State Party to the Statute from a non-State Party under the Statute is, on the contrary, meaning that it was bound by the *principles of treaty law because the ICC is multilateral treaty-based organization* and failed to establish itself as an absolutely overriding regime.

2.3 *Prohibition of Trial* in Absentia

As to whether trial *in absentia* is permissible, even without waiting for the accused to be secured, there could be a premise of international criminal justice of "prevention of impunity" and thoroughness of criminal justice, but the impact of these on the current principle of prohibition of trial *in absentia* was not observed. However, the presence of the accused in international criminal justice is related to the issue of the significance of punishment in international criminal justice. International criminal justice has developed based on the principle of "prevention of impunity", but the question is whether "punishment" in this context refers to retribution or prevention through physical confinement, or whether the "punitive performance" at the international level is more important. However, this performance of punishment is significant in that it provides the international community with official recognition of the harm done to the victim community and is the beginning of a financial and substantive compensation mechanism. Furthermore, that the facts are confirmed by judicial precedents establishes historical awareness of the core crimes that affect the international community as a whole, which can serve as a basis for international reparations lawsuits.

On the other hand, a one-sided trial that violates the rights of the suspect/accused is not justified. Recent ICC precedents and other precedents have recognized the assertion of the principle of presence as the *accused's right to a fair trial.* It is also considered that a court without *legitimacy* would not be able to complete the significance of punitive performance. On the other hand, exceptions to the principle of no trial *in absentia* have tended to expand in recent ICC precedents, and future trends need to be closely monitored.

2.4 Redress for the Rights of the Accused

The ICC clarified that the attribution-required- and comparative-balance-approach is adopted in determining the provision of redress for violations of rights of individuals by State authorities, which requires attribution of the infringing acts to the ICC and that redress is selected on the basis of a comparative balance with other interests. The reason for taking the need for attribution approach is that it emphasizes *procedural justification rather than substantive justification of the redress.* In other words, it is pointed out that the ICC is a treaty body and that this may be a result of reflecting the *legitimacy of the use of contributions by States Parties* in the case of monetary compensation and the concern that the ICC's original purpose of *ensuring the prohibition of impunity* in the case of reduction of sentence or stay of proceedings would be impeded by an act by one State Party. In addition, the absolute approach takes into account the fact that monetary compensation in cases of fine, commutation of sentence or release may have aspects that impede the realization of the *societal interest in punishing the perpetrator of the core crime* and incorporates these considerations into the determination of the content of the redress. From the perspectives of the two objectives of redress in criminal justice—restoration of rights and deterrence of illegal investigations—, it runs counter to the recent development of the concept of the individual's right to compensation, and the vertical regime of the ICC itself cannot escape criticism for potentially facilitating violations of rights.

Meanwhile, the ICC's exercise of its jurisdiction as a preventive and substantive remedy was possible but limited. The complementary regime is essentially a system in which the ICC "cedes" the proceedings if a State's domestic proceedings are validly commenced before the ICC's trial begins. In a sense, it is based on the premise that "first come, first served" in terms of the timing of the commencement of criminal proceedings, and thus has the potential to promote hasty and arbitrary detention by States. Thus, the complementary regime is a system that *responds to the level of development of the domestic criminal justice system* but attempts to strike a balance between the realization of the premise of the *priority of invoking State sovereignty.*

2.5 Admissibility of Evidence

The premises of international criminal justice as incorporated in the ICC's evidentiary rules include the followings. First, the use of video-link has been made available whenever necessary as a facilitator of live testimony rather than an exception to the orality principle, taking into account the ICC's premise that the *crime scene is remote.* It can also be said that the use of previously recorded statements has been greatly expanded, as *witnesses are often unavailable or subject to interference.* Secondly, with regards to the exclusionary rule, it requires balancing while emphasizing compliance with internationally recognized human rights standards, in which the *seriousness of the core crimes* itself does not affect the consideration. Since violations of, or compliance with, national laws are not considered in the application of the exclusionary rule, it presupposes a collective assessment by the ICC Statute and international human rights standards against *investigative disciplines that vary from State to State.*

As described above, exceptions have been devised with regards to the orality principle and the exclusionary rule, considering the wide variety of special circumstances of international criminal justice, but the direction of the impact of these special circumstances on these principles is different. With regard to the orality principle, importance is placed on ensuring the *protection of witnesses* and *speed* by allowing numerous exceptions while maintaining the application of the orality in principle. Meanwhile, with regards to the exclusionary rule, the relatively high threshold of the double test is first used as a criterion for the application of the principle, and a wide range of exceptions are allowed so that even evidence illegally collected through actors other than the ICC can be used. Moreover, since the exclusion of evidence at the ICC does not have any deterrent effect on other actors cooperating with the ICC, the deterrence of illegal searches plays only a limited role as a theoretical basis for the exclusionary rule at the ICC. Furthermore, it was also characteristic that there was no discussion on the use of the system as a remedy for the infringement that occurred in the process of investigation.

2.6 Reparation for Victims

The ICC's reparation procedure is a framework in which the system of punitive restitution orders has been modified to a restorative one. The reasons for this are: the participation of both the victim and the offender in the reparation process was ensured; emphasis was placed on clearly indicating the harm suffered by the victim and the extent of the convict's responsibility; and the structure of the reparation procedure has adopted the restitution order type, where consideration was given to fairness and reparation was awarded even to those who did not apply for it. From these points, at the very least, the reparation procedure in the *Lubanga* case was constructed with the aim of *satisfying the demands of restorative justice* rather than remedying the rights of the victims.

The circumstances behind such a decision may be based on the assumption that *the ICC is not a forum for pursuing reparations for violations of international human rights law or international humanitarian law*. Although the idea of the ICC as such was in the drafting stage, this idea was eliminated in the Principles on Reparations. More to the point, this could be premised on the fact that *the ICC Statute does not cover all violations of international humanitarian law or international human rights law*, that *not all victims are eligible to participate in the ICC, and the issue of the ICC's resources.*

3 Implication of the Premises of International Criminal Procedure

3.1 Checking Against Mégret's List

Among the various premises of international criminal procedure that emerged from the analysis in this book, those identified in Mégret's previous research are as follows.

Among the elements of the circumstances of international criminal procedure ("environment"): (i) With regards to *difficulties such as ensuring State cooperation and access to evidence*, in relation to the admissibility of evidence, the premise that *witnesses may not be available* or *subject to interference* and that the *crime scene is remote* were considered. (ii) With regards to *cultural diversity and value pluralism*, in relation to the admissibility of evidence, it was seen that it was not possible to respond to each *State's different investigative discipline one by one*. (iii) Regarding *exceptionalities such as deviations from human rights and normal rules*, in relation to the redress for the rights of suspects, the choice of a limited and relative approach was seen due to the premise of *thoroughness in prohibiting impunity and the realization of the social interest of punishing those who commit crimes*. Similarly, in relation to the law of evidence, the *relative approach in the application of the exclusion of illegally collected evidence* is also an example of this.

Next, among the elements of various values ("ambition") on which the international criminal procedure is premised, (ix) with regards to the *protection of victims*, various exceptions were placed on the orality principle from the *importance of witness protection* in relation to the evidentiary rules. (xi) In relation to *fair trial*, the *burden on the accused* regarding the rules of parallel investigation and parallel prosecution, and the *defendant's right to a fair trial* in relation to the prohibition of trial *in absentia* were seen to be a premise of criminal human rights. Finally, (xiv) with regards to *alignment with the objectives of transitional justice*, there were examples of the ICC's victim reparation system being premised on the value of *meeting the demands of restorative justice.*

As mentioned above, to a certain extent, the circumstances and values mentioned in Mégret's list have been confirmed by empirical analysis. Of course, due to the limitation of the types of principles discussed in this book, I have not been able to provide examples for all of Mégret's list, and for that reason this book cannot and is not intended to provide a comprehensive defence of them.

3.2 Premises of the ICC Procedure

From the premises of the various principles of international criminal procedure, the following elements can be pointed out as inherent premises of international criminal justice. In particular, this book disclosed the four points that have not been identified in previous studies. These elements can be broadly classified into two two-fold categories as follows.

(A) **The values of international criminal procedure that are frequently mentioned in previous studies do not have much impact.**

  (1) The premise of "seriousness of the core crime" has little influence at the procedural level.
  (2) The premise of deterring illegal investigations has little impact.

(B) **The factors that have not been recognized as circumstances or valued on which international criminal procedure is premised in previous research significantly influence international criminal procedure.**

  (3) The entire procedure is based not on deliberation and prudence, but on the primitive premise of speed and "first come, first served".
  (4) The premise of consideration for national sovereignty has enormous influence, which is associated with the fact that it is an international organization based on a treaty.

The following is an organized presentation of the results of the analysis in this book of these four factors.

3.2.1 The Premise of "Seriousness of the Core Crime" Has Little Influence at the Procedural Level

The allowance of "exceptionality", whereby human rights guarantees are affected and limited in international criminal justice because of the seriousness of core crimes, has long been noted as a trend, or risk, in international criminal procedure.[1] However, the rhetoric that core crimes are more serious than other crimes has actually had little impact on the content of procedural law.

For example, although the substantive law on the priority of extradition assumes the need to give priority to the pursuit of justice for serious crimes, the actual coordination provisions that incorporate them are limited. In addition, in relation to the redress of the rights of the accused, although the relationship with the realization of the social interest of the thoroughness of the prohibition of impunity and the punishment of the perpetrator of the crime was taken into account in the provision of redress for the violation of the rights of the accused, it only affected the choice of the review approach and did not exclude the possibility of the stay of proceedings. Furthermore, with regards to the exclusion of illegally collected evidence, the same approach was taken in the case of the exclusion of evidence of human rights violations from the prosecution of core crimes, but the possibility of excluding evidence of human rights violations at the expense of prosecution of core crimes remained, and the gravity of the human rights violated in such a case itself was not an issue. In addition to these, there was no indication that the seriousness of the core crime made the procedural rules more lenient or provided for more exceptions in the domestic context, for example with regards to the principle of no trial *in absentia.*

The attempt to establish and put into practice an international criminal justice framework is in itself an attempt by the international community to set up a new system of punishment in addition to national penal powers, which is undoubtedly a powerful restriction on the rights of the individual. However, the rules governing its operation, namely international criminal procedure, do not endorse the lowering of standards of human rights guarantees on the grounds of the seriousness of the crimes they deal with. This is one important inherent premise of international criminal justice.

3.2.2 The Premise of Deterring Illegal Investigations Has Little Impact

Although the ICC ensures a human rights standard, procedural restrictions and sanctions aimed at deterring illegal investigations are rarely found against the primary use of coercive force by States in an international cooperative regime. The ICC was not expected to serve as a model for domestic criminal justice systems, which had been anticipated in previous studies but was virtually absent within the scope of this book. In list (xii), Mégret noted the prevention of harm by the international court itself as one of its "ambitions". Indeed, that the ICC itself would not harm can be seen as a

[1] Mégret [123], pp. 95; 96, Davidson [37], Stephen [204], p. 64.

premise of international criminal justice—for example, in relation to violations of suspects' rights, the ICC adopted an approach that requires attribution of violations to the ICC in its early cases—. However, there were no cases in which the premise of preventing some form of illegal investigation for the punishment of core crimes by the various actors working with the ICC was considered.

International criminal courts have been called "limbless giants" since their inception.[2] Although they have established prosecutorial bureaus, they have no international version of a police force, which usually conduct investigations in a domestic setting. Among the penal powers, the executive power basically resides only in the territorial State, and the evidence and information necessary for the investigation, as well as for securing the perpetrators, is basically provided by the State or other international actors that are authorized to investigate or gather intelligence as a function—*e.g.*, UN peacekeeping forces—.

The "limbless" ICC does not make it an important premise of its procedural law to deter illegality in the activities of the various actors that are crucial to its activities. This may be due, in part, to the fact that it is structurally difficult. However, the ICC's attitude is in contrast to the corresponding principles in domestic law, for example, in relation to the redress for violations of the rights of suspects during arrest and detention procedures before the ICC and the exclusion of evidence illegally collected by domestic police. This may be due to an excessive reliance on the assumption that the ICC is an international organization, that its procedures will be carried out fairly by officials with high moral standards, and that the ICC has an international "conscience."

3.2.3 The Entire Procedure is Based not on Deliberation and Prudence, but on the Primitive Premise of Speed and "First Come, First Served"

There is a long standing debate as to which criminal jurisdiction is the best to prosecute core crimes.[3] The prevailing view has been that the exercise of jurisdiction in the place where the crime was committed or the State of the victim's nationality should prevail, based on the premise that the appropriate punishment forum must be chosen according to certain criteria.[4] Therefore, the norm has seemed to be that even if a suspect is detained, a more appropriate venue should be considered and the determination of venue should be made through extradition. In addition, in international criminal justice, which is achieved through international cooperation, many factors

---

[2] See, Cassese [30], p. 13, Maogoto [117].

[3] This is also linked to the substantive law-level question of "whose law should we follow"? See, e.g., Gallant [65].

[4] For example, it has been argued that Article 6 of the Genocide Convention presupposes that the State in which the crime is committed exercises jurisdiction, and that the exercise of jurisdiction under the doctrine of territoriality and protectionism should prevail. See Feller [51].

that delay the process are assumed, such as monitoring by international organizations and deliberation by many stakeholders.

However, in the actual procedural law, it became clear that, on the contrary, the principle of "first come, first served" and the principle of expeditiousness basically prevailed. The "first come, first served" principle can be seen in examples where, for example, when there are parallel prosecutions, priority of jurisdiction is given to the earlier procedure, or where trials *in absentia* are not permitted no matter how serious the core crime, and cases are kept "on hold" until a suspect is apprehended, and where, as a rule, proceedings are carried out in the criminal jurisdiction which apprehended a suspect first. Thus, the principle of coordination is underdeveloped in the international community with regards to the allocation of jurisdiction.

In addition to the discipline of parallel investigations and prosecutions, there were many occasions where the principle of expeditiousness ran throughout the procedural rules, such as the provision of previously recorded testimony and testimony by video-link. This may be due to the importance placed on the speedy conduct of the trial as a right of the accused.[5] It also seems to be that the perspective that the sooner justice is done, the better, and that "justice too late is justice denied" has been rather recognized as a particularly important value in international criminal justice.[6]

3.2.4 The Premise of Consideration for National Sovereignty Has Enourmous Influence, Which is Associated with the Fact that it is an International Organization Based on a Treaty

Another important implication of the analysis in this book is that the ICC is designed as a treaty-based—consent-based—institution, and that the fact that many major actors in the international community have not ratified the ICC Statute influences the content of many of its procedural rules.

For example, in relation to the rules on parallel investigations and parallel prosecutions, a system of complementarity was devised and introduced to determine in advance which of the International Criminal Justice Institution or the State would have priority, and which would be complementary. In relation to the priority of extradition/surrender, since the ICC is based on a multilateral treaty, the system was not designed to give priority to the ICC in the event of a conflict between an extradition request from a State that is not a party to the ICC Statute and a request for cooperation from the ICC. This also reflects the consideration of the need for a margin of discretion in determining extradition destinations due to political factors among States.

---

[5] Farrell [48].

[6] See e.g., ICC, *Statement of the ICC Prosecutor to the United Nations Security Council on the Situation in Libya, pursuant to UNSCR 1970* (2011), at https://www.icc-cpi.int/Pages/item.aspx?name=210517-otp-statement-unsc-libya (accessed 6 February 2022), para. 35. On the other hand, in international criminal justice, the effective pursuit of justice requires a certain period of time in terms of evidence collection, etc. Whiting [244].

There were also glimpses of situations where procedural law is premised on the fact that the ICC is an international organization, on the need to secure more States Parties, and on the need to maintain procedural legitimacy in the application of ICC procedural rules in order to avoid being "sidelined" by existing States Parties. For example, regarding prohibition of trial *in absentia*, the need to maintain the legitimacy of ICC proceedings was noted as a precondition. Similarly, regarding the stay of proceedings as a redress for the rights of the accused, analysis showed that consideration of procedural legitimacy—the justification of the use of contributions by the State Party—, rather than the substantive legitimacy of the redress, influenced the decision. In relation to the principle of complementarity, as long as it is necessary to secure the trust by the State Party, there are circumstances in which the admissibility of a case must be examined with uniform examination criteria, even if the domestic criminal justice system is not yet developed and maintained. Furthermore, as for victim reparation, the background to the selection of the restitution order type was that the ICC Statute was a treaty and defined some of the violations of international humanitarian law and international human rights law as core crimes through discussions when drafting the treaty, and that the crimes under its jurisdiction by no means covered all of them. Even in relation to the limitation of the scope of domestic recourse, the premise is that it did not make it mandatory to criminalize the core crimes in domestic legislation with uniform wording.

Thus, there are clear differences in the criminal procedures at the ICC between States Parties and non-States Parties to the ICC Statute, that there is an awareness of procedural legitimacy rather than substantive legitimacy, and that there are many "external" considerations such as accountability to the financiers.

4 Conclusion: Premises and Challenges Inherent in International Criminal Procedure

Premises refers to "various circumstances and values that are premised on the field of law that seeks to apply the principles." However, since these are the premise of the general principles that permeate the legal system, premises indicate a part of the principles that are specific to that field of law. From the examination of this book, which focuses on the ICC's procedural law, at least the premises that are specific to the ICC's procedural law system have been clarified. In fact, these premises are different in nature from the preamble to the ICC Statute. The aims and objectives of the ICC mentioned in the preamble to the ICC Statute can be broadly divided into, first, the seriousness of the core crimes and the importance of "preventing impunity," the need for all states to exercise criminal jurisdiction to prevent these crimes and to make this possible through international cooperation, and second, that the ICC is complementary to national sovereignty and does not interfere in domestic affairs. However, it seems that the second element has a stronger influence on the premises of the ICC's procedural law than the first element.

This could be seen as the result of the ICC's search for a position that is in harmony with the existing framework for the exercise of penal powers under national sovereignty, based on the premise of international cooperation. Although it has been pointed out that the ICC is a balancing act between the pursuit of justice for core crimes and the human rights value of fair procedure, the need to work with autonomous actors, each with their own sovereignty, has been rather more influential in the content of the procedural law. The institutional feature of the ICC, which is the lack of centralized control over the "limbs", has had a considerable impact on the content of various procedural laws.

In response to the question of what the inherent premises of international criminal procedure are, this book partially outlines the unique system of international criminal procedure that is established on the new premises identified through case law analysis, rather than the premises that have been conventionally identified ideologically. However, it does not provide a normative evaluation of the ICC's procedural law that has been revealed through this analysis. It is difficult to say that it has fully considered the reason why international criminal procedure does not have the seriousness of the core crime or the deterrence of illegal investigations as its premises. In addition, it only presents a certain hypothesis as to why the principles of speed and "first come, first served" are given priority and why the ICC tries to comply with the restrictions of treaty law to such an extent. Furthermore, this book only clarifies which premises the ICC has chosen but does not answer the question of why it has chosen those premises. Whether a normative explanation can be given for the ICC's choices, and the methodology for doing so, are presumably based on an analysis of the judges' internal perspectives when approving individual principles.

However, the multiple premises identified in this book can be seen as a list of candidates for the choice of premises and can be used as a resource for consideration of the issue of choice between premises that will be required in the future. Building on the ICC's procedural premises identified in this book and some of the premises inherent in international criminal procedure that they imply, an assessment of the state of international criminal procedure and a consideration of the reasons for such a state of affairs will be the subject of future work.

Addendum: The Premises in the Formation of an International Cooperative Framework for International Criminal Justice for the Russian-Ukrainian Situation

Abstract

This chapter examines how the state of formation and practice of the international criminal justice framework at the present time, six months after the Russian invasion (15 August 2022) is a pivotal moment, using the framework of the premises of the principles of international criminal procedure. Although practice and research on the establishment of an international cooperative system of international criminal justice for this situation has just begun, I provide a tentative analysis from the perspective of the four elements of the premises of international criminal procedure given in the conclusion of this book. First, the response to this situation itself has been strongly influenced by the axial premise of international criminal justice, namely, the seriousness of the core crimes. Second, on the other hand, there is a growing awareness of the importance of preventing rights violations and excessive burdens on individuals that may arise in this context. Third, it seems to highlight that the entire international criminal justice system is based on the premise of speed and "first come, first served". Fourth, the impact of the premise of consideration for national sovereignty that the ICC is an international mechanism based on treaties has been a problem so far. In this situation as well, Ukraine's cooperation has been a matter of life and death for the ICC. How the fight against impunity for core crimes in Ukraine progresses in the future will, in this sense, depend on Ukraine's willingness and ability to work for justice.

Introduction

The full-scale invasion of Ukraine by Russian forces, which began on 24 February 2022, in itself and during the armed conflict that followed, appears to have resulted in a number of crimes under international law (all dates hereafters are 2022 unless otherwise indicated). The act of invasion itself was declared to constitute aggression in the

M. Ochi, *The Premises of International Criminal Procedure*,
https://doi.org/10.1007/978-981-97-6786-1

United Nations General Assembly resolution on 1 March.[1] In addition, war crimes and crimes against humanity that took place during the Russian military invasion, such as the killing of civilians not taking part in hostilities, the destruction of civilian objects not being used for military purposes, rape, and the looting of residents' property, have been pointed out by many international organizations, including the ICC. Ukraine, the aggressed State, has begun prosecuting and punishing these crimes. One catalyst for the acceleration of international criminal justice efforts came on 3 April, when Russian troops withdrew from the capital Kyiv and the north, and the "crime scene" left behind after the military occupation was reported internationally.[2] The massacre of hundreds of people, documented as the "Bucha massacre", together with images of numerous bodies with hands tied behind their backs, executed and left on the roadside, provoked strong condemnation by States for the possible commission of genocide.[3] Crimes of aggression, war crimes, crimes against humanity and genocide are serious international crimes of concern to the international community as a whole—core crimes—, and many actors, including the ICC, have begun to formulate frameworks for international cooperation on an unprecedented scale. However, the consistency of these frameworks with the principles of international criminal justice needs to be examined in terms of what are the inherent premises[4]—circumstances and values—of international criminal justice.

This chapter examines the state of formation and practice of the international criminal justice framework at the present time, six months after the Russian invasion (15 August 2022), using the framework of the premises of international criminal procedure. To this end, I will first provide an overview of the formation and practice of the framework from 24 February to 25 August, divided into investigations and prosecutions. Then, I will analyse the six areas dealt with in this book, namely, the regulation of parallel investigation and parallel prosecution, the regulation of priority of extradition, the prohibition of trial *in absentia*, the redress of the rights of the accused, the admissibility of evidence, and victim reparation, along the timeline of international criminal proceedings.

I will not go into the substantive issues and establishment of the core crimes, as I will examine only the procedural aspects of international criminal justice. I will also

---

[1] UN Doc. A/ES-11/L.1 (1 March 2022).

[2] "'*Ukuraina ha Hanzai Genbada' Kokusai Keiji Saibansho no Shunin Kensatsukan ga Bucha Homon* ['Ukraine is a crime scene,' International Criminal Court Chief Prosecutor Visits Bucha]", (*Asahi Shimbun*, 14 April 2022).

[3] On April 3, Ukrainian President Volodymyr Zelenskyy noted that the crime in Bucha was "genocide". "Ukuraina Daitoryo 'Jenosaidoda' Kiu Kinko Bucha no Shimin Gisei' [Ukrainian President "It's Genocide," Civilian Victims in Bucha near Kiev]," (*Asahi Shimbun*, 5 April 2022). On 13 April, US President Joe Biden expressed the view that "this appears to be genocide". See also, "*Baiden Amerika Daitoryo, Hajimete 'Jenosaido' to Hinan Ukuraina deno Roshiagun Koi* [U.S. President Biden condemns 'genocide' for the first time, Russian military action in Ukraine]" (Jiji.com, 13 April 2022); See also, "Latvian and Estonian parliaments say Russia committed genocide in Ukraine" (*Reuters*, 21 April 2022).

[4] For more on the "premise" concept, see. Megumi Ochi, *Kokusai Keiji Tetsuzukihō no Taikei—'Puremisu Riron' to Ichiji Fusairi Gensoku* [*A System of International Criminal Procedure: 'Premise Theory' and the Principle of ne bis in idem*]", (Shinzansha, 2020), Chap. 3.

not cover support to the ICC in terms of money and personnel.[5] Furthermore, due to the lack of cooperation with the ICC and insufficient information, I do not cover the prosecution of core crimes by Russia and the so-called Donetsk People's Republic ("DPR") and Lugansk People's Republic ("LPR") in eastern Ukraine, which Russia recognized as States on 22 February.[6]

Current Status of Investigation and Prosecution Activities

New Practices in Investigation Through International Collaboration

Investigations by the ICC

(a) Request for authorisation to investigate and referral of the situation

The ICC prosecutor has been conducting a preliminary examination since 25 April 2014 of the situation in Ukraine since 21 November 2013.[7] Following the full-scale invasion of Ukraine by Russian forces, the ICC Prosecutor's Office requested a decision to allow the Pre-Trial Chamber to investigate on 28 April.[8]

---

[5] In Japan's case, on 15 April, Prime Minister Fumio Kishida announced that he had brought forward the payment of dues, which amounted to around 10% of the ICC budget. "*Kishida Shusho Kokusai Keiji Saibansho no Shien ni Buntankin no Shiharai Maedaoshi* [Prime Minister Kishida brought forward the payment of dues to support the International Criminal Court]" (NHK, 15 April 15, 2022). Also on April 27, three of Japan's top prosecutors entered the ICC to provide advice on criminal justice cooperation. "*Kokusai Keiji Saibansho de Katsudo Kaishi 'Senso Hanzai' Sosa, Shien Kyoka e—Seifu* [Activities at the International Criminal Court to Begin: 'War Crimes' Investigations, Support to be Strengthened—Government]" (Jiji.com, 28 April 2022).

[6] On July 25, the Russian Federal Investigative Committee said it had begun prosecution. "*Roshia, Ukurainahei 92 Nin o Kiso 'Jinrui no Heiwa to Anzen ni Taisuru Hanzai' ni Kanyo to* [Russia indicts 92 Ukrainian soldiers for involvement in 'crimes against the peace and security of mankind']" (BBC, 22 July 2022). The DPR Court has also sentenced three foreigners serving in the Ukrainian army to death for being mercenaries, among other things, and the European Court of Human Rights has taken urgent measures. "European Court grants urgent measures in case of prisoner of war sentenced to death in the so-called 'Donetsk People's Republic'" (European Court of Human Rights, 16 July 2022).

[7] See, "Report on Preliminary Examination Activities (2020)" (ICC, 14 December 2020), 68.

[8] The ICC prosecutor conducts an investigation when there is a referral of the situation by a State Party to the ICC Statute or by the UNSC or when the prosecutor initiates the investigation on his own initiative (ICC Statute, Articles 12 and 13). In the case of an investigation conducted by the prosecutor on his own initiative, i.e. without a situation referral from a State Party or the UNSC, permission to investigate is required from the Pre-Trial Chamber (ICC Statute, Art. 15). The request for a decision to authorize an investigation is itself made when the ICC prosecutor himself concludes, on the basis of the evidence in his possession, that there is a "reasonable basis for proceeding with the investigation" (Article 3). For more information on the ICC's authorization system, see the following. Megumi Ochi, "*Kokusai Keiji Saibansho Kensatsukan no Sotsui Sairyo*

What is unique about the investigation into this situation is that the ICC prosecutor requested a decision to authorize the investigation and a referral of the situation by the States Parties took place during the deliberation of the motion. On 2 March, 39 States Parties—38 joint referrals and a referral by Lithuania-referred the Ukraine situation to the ICC.[9] Subsequently, on 6 March, North Macedonia declared its intention to join this joint referral.[10] On 9 March, Japan also made a separate referral.[11] On 21 March, Montenegro[12] and on 1 April, Chile joined the joint referral.[13]

There is a question of the temporal and subject matter scope of what is referred to this time. The joint referral of 38 States says that what is referred to as "any acts of war crimes, crimes against humanity and genocide alleged to have occurred on the territory of Ukraine from 21 November 2013 onwards, including any allegations of current and ongoing crimes occurring throughout the territory of Ukraine." On the other hand, the Lithuanian document is ambiguous, but this is in the form of a "refers to Article 14 of the Rome Statute for launching an investigation" rather than "referring the situation" (Article 14).

With regards to the temporal scope of the situation referrals, both referrals were made not only after the February invasion, but also after 21 November 2013, when the ICC prosecutor had requested permission to investigate the situation. This is consistent with the scope of the ICC prosecutor's investigation.

Two issues remain concerning the scope of subject matter jurisdiction. First, there is the question of the crime of aggression. The ICC does not have jurisdiction over this crime in the present context. Article 5 of the ICC Statute provides that the crime of aggression is a jurisdictional crime, but its definition and scope were decided in the 2010 resolution amending the ICC Statute ("Kampala Resolution").[14] At that time,

ni Taisuru Saibanbu niyoru Tosei no Hani—Afuganisutan Jitai ni Taisuru Sosa Kyoka ni Kansuru Jososhin Kettei (2020 Nen 3 Gatsu 5 Nichi) [The Scope of Control by the Trial Chamber over the Prosecutor's Prosecution Discretion at the International Criminal Court: Appeals Chamber Decision on Authorizatrion to Investigate the Afghanistan Situation (March 5, 2020)]", *Kokusaiho Kenkyu [International Law Studies]* 9 (2021): 190–199. Pending the decision by the Preliminary Trial Chamber to authorize an investigation, the ICC prosecutor will conduct a preliminary examination.

[9] "Ukraine" (ICC, N. D.) at https://www.icc-cpi.int/ukraine.

[10] *Ibid.*

[11] *Ibid.* First time for Japan to be referred to a situation.

[12] *Ibid.*

[13] *Ibid.* Thus, the present case is the first in which a State Party referral and self-initiated investigation by the prosecutor run side by side. In the case of a State Party referral, the procedure is in a sense the reverse of that in the case of a prosecutor's referral. That is, the prosecutor must initiate the investigation unless he/she decides there is no "reasonable basis for proceeding" or that other criteria, such as seriousness, have not been met (Article 53(1)). In this case, the prosecutor has already requested a decision to allow the investigation, which means that the prosecutor has confirmed that a "reasonable basis for proceeding with the investigation" and other criteria are met. Since the prosecutor has determined that a "reasonable basis for proceeding with an investigation" and other criteria are met, procedurally, the earlier request for an investigation authorization decision is rejected, the procedure for cases referred to a State Party (Article 53 procedure) takes precedence, and the prosecutor must begin an investigation.

[14] RC/Res.6 (11 June 2010).

a provision was established limiting the conditions under which jurisdiction may be exercised with respect to the crime of aggression.[15] It states that the ICC cannot exercise jurisdiction if the State of nationality of the aggressor or the territorial State in which the aggression took place has not accepted the amended resolution (Article 121(5) of the ICC Statute, Article 15bis, Activation Resolution, main text 2).[16] In the present situation, neither Ukraine nor Russia is a State Party to the ICC Statute and therefore cannot accept the Kampala Resolution in the first place. However, Ukraine has accepted the exercise of ICC jurisdiction (Article 12(3)), so it may also be able to accept the exercise of jurisdiction over the crime of aggression through this procedure. Even in that case, however, jurisdiction cannot be exercised because the State of nationality of the alleged aggressor—in this case, Russia—is not a State Party and has not accepted the Kampala Resolution. On this basis, the crime of aggression is excluded from all State Party referral documents. Although the ICC prosecutor is not bound by the specification of the crimes or persons to be covered by the referral,[17] in any event, the crime of aggression is excluded from jurisdiction because neither Ukraine nor Russia is a State Party to the ICC in relation to the crime of aggression and therefore naturally have not ratified the 2010 Amended Resolution which confers jurisdiction over the crime of aggression. Therefore, the crime of aggression is outside the jurisdiction of the ICC.

Second, there is the question of exemptions for crimes other than the crime of aggression. This can be seen in the Japanese referral. The joint referral specifies three crimes other than the crime of aggression: genocide, crimes against humanity, and war crimes. On the other hand, the Japanese referral stated that it "decides to refer the Situation in Ukraine …for the purpose of requesting the Prosecutor to investigate that Situation under which war crimes appear to have been committed on the territory of Ukraine." Thus, Japan's referral is limited to war crimes, with no mention of genocide or crimes against humanity. In effect, however, as limiting the content of the referral to specific crimes does not have the effect of limiting ICC jurisdiction, the ICC need not take it into account.[18]

(b) Status of the investigation by the ICC

On 7 March, the ICC prosecutor informed the Pre-Trial Chamber that he had informed the President of the Court on 2 March about the report of the referrals by the State Parties and the commencement of the investigation.[19] Subsequently, Karim A. A.

[15] For more information, see. Akira Mayama, "*Shinryaku Hanzai ni Kansuru Kokusai Keiji Saibansho Kitei Kanpara Kaisei: Heiwa Oyobi Anzen no Iji Seido no Fukanzensei to Serekutibu Justice* [Kampala amendment to the Statute of the International Criminal Court on the Crime of Aggression: imperfections in the peace and security maintenance system and selective justice]", *Kokusaiho Gaiko Zasshi [The Journal of International Law and Diplomacy]* 114, No. 2 (2015): 111–134.

[16] ICC-ASP/16/Res.5 (14 December 2017).

[17] ICC-02/04–01/05–68, paras 4–5.

[18] *Ibid.*

[19] At the same time, it also confirms that permission to open an investigation is not required. ICC-01/22–2, para. 1.

Khan, the ICC chief prosecutor, has visited Ukraine on three occasions up to the time of writing—16 March (Western part), 13 April (Bucha) and 15 June (Kharkiv)—. On 16 May, the ICC announced that it would send 42 investigators to Ukraine.[20] This is the largest deployment ever, 30 of which are officials already temporarily deployed by the Netherlands.[21]

During the Chief Prosecutor's third visit to Ukraine, he announced the opening of an ICC liaison office in Ukraine to increase staff working on the ground and to accelerate the investigation by working more closely with all parties in Ukraine.[22]

Establish a System of Collaboration Between ICC and Other Entities

(a) Cooperation with Ukraine

Ukraine, which was the victim of aggression and the State where many of the core crimes were committed, is not a State Party to the ICC Statute. However, it has made a Declaration of Acceptance of Jurisdiction in accordance with Article 12(3) of the ICC Statute. The Declaration of Acceptance of Jurisdiction by Ukraine was originally limited to the period from 21 November 2013 to 22 February 2014.[23] Subsequently, Ukraine made declarations expanding the scope of its jurisdictional acceptance, and in its 2015 declaration it made an unrestricted jurisdictional acceptance for the future, from 20 February 2014 onwards.[24]

On 3 May, the Verkhovna Rada of Ukraine adopted the "On Amendments to the Criminal Procedure Code of Ukraine and Other legislative Acts of Ukraine Concerning Cooperation with the International Criminal Court" ("Ukrainian ICC Cooperation Act").[25] Chapter 9 of the Code of Criminal Procedure, newly added by the law, contains provisions for coordination in view of the particularities of cooperation with the ICC, designating the Prosecutor's Office as the department responsible for cooperation with the ICC and for coordination with the ICC and for filing objections, and the Ministry of Justice as the corresponding department with respect to cooperation in the execution of sentences (Article 618). Amendments to existing provisions allow Ukraine to apply its national laws on custody of the subject in the event of an ICC request for arrest and extradition, and at the same time extend

---

[20] "ICC Prosecutor Karim A.A. Khan QC announces deployment of forensics and investigative team to Ukraine, welcomes strong cooperation with the Government of the Netherlands" (ICC, 17 May 2022).

[21] *Ibid*.

[22] "*Kokusai Keiji Saibansho, Ukuraina ni Jimusho Kaisetsu he Senso Hanzai no Sosa Susumeru* [International Criminal Court to Open Office in Ukraine to Advance Investigation of War Crimes]" (*Asahi Shimbun*, 18 June 2022).

[23] "Ukraine" (ICC, N. D.) at https://www.icc-cpi.int/ukraine.

[24] *Ibid*. See also, Iryna Marchuk, "Ukraine and the International Criminal Court: the implications of the ad hoc jurisdiction acceptance and beyond", *Vanderbilt Journal of Transnational Law* 49, No. 2 (March 2016): 323–370.

[25] Law No. 2236-IX (3 May 2022).

provisions on the rights of the suspect in the case of proceedings before the ICC (Articles 8 and 51 of the Criminal Code of Ukraine, Articles 183 and 208 of the Code of Criminal Procedure, etc.). The Law on the Security of Persons in Relation to Criminal Proceedings was also amended to apply measures for the protection of witnesses and victims in relation to ICC proceedings (Articles 2 and 20).

(b) Eurojust Joint Investigation Team (JIT)

On 25 April, the ICC prosecutor announced that he would join the Joint Investigative Team ("JIT") formed by Ukraine, Poland and Lithuania and supported by Eurojust, the EU's body on criminal justice cooperation.[26] On 1 June, a meeting between the JIT and the ICC was held in The Hague, and the following day it was announced that Estonia, Latvia and Slovakia would join the ICC and JIT.[27]

The six participating States are "members" and Eurojust and the ICC are considered "participants".[28] This is the first time the ICC has participated in this form of investigative cooperation framework, and it will draw attention if the ICC has any additional powers.

(c) Political Declaration by 45 States

The ICC also participated in the conclusion of political guidelines for multilateral joint investigations. On 14 July, in The Hague, the Political Declaration of the Ministerial Ukraine Accountability Conference was adopted by 45 States ("Political Declaration").[29] In addition to Ukraine, the signatories include all members of the EU, the US, the UK, Canada, Mexico, Australia, New Zealand, Colombia and the Nordic States.

It condemns aggression by Russia and seeks to promote accountabilities for all international crimes committed in Ukraine—which the document refers to as war crimes and crimes against humanity—and to facilitate coordination and effective efforts by common efforts, including those of the ICC (paras 1–4). It contains innovative content that anticipates the adverse effects of the involvement of multiple States in investigations, such as warning against excessive burdens on witnesses and re-traumatization due to duplicate investigations (paras 16–17). It also actually decided to establish a Dialogue Group on Accountability for Ukraine ("the Dialogue Group"), which aims to promote dialogue between national, European and international attempts to pursue and record responsibility (para. 25). Japan attended the meeting itself but did not sign the document.

---

[26] "Statement by ICC Prosecutor, Karim A.A. Khan QC: Office of the Prosecutor joins national authorities in Joint Investigation Team on international crimes committed in Ukraine" (ICC, 25 April 2022).

[27] "Estonia, Latvia and Slovakia become members of joint investigation team on alleged core international crimes in Ukraine" (*Eurojust*, 31 May 2022).

[28] "Eurojust and the War in Ukraine" (*Eurojust*, N. D.) at https://www.eurojust.europa.eu/eurojust-and-the-war-in-ukraine (as of 15 August 2022).

[29] Political Declaration of the Ministerial Ukraine Accountability Conference, The Hague, 14 July 2022.

Investigations by Ukraine

Ukrainian judicial officers who had been evacuated from the war zone since April, when the partial withdrawal of Russian troops began, have returned to their workplaces and first started core crime investigations in the area around the capital Kyiv and in the northern regions. Iryna Venediktova, then prosecutor general of Ukraine, entered Bucha on 12 April to conduct autopsies together with forensic experts from the French gendarmerie.[30] At this point, she was already in contact with Beth Van Schaack, the US ambassador for Global Criminal Justice.[31] As of 26 April, the Prosecutor's Office of Ukraine announced that it was preparing indictments against seven Russian servicemen, including the pilot of a downed fighter jet.[32] It announced that it had identified 7,600 cases of suspected war crimes as of the same date and 8,600 cases as of 28 April.[33] At this point, it said that 8,000 people were engaged in evidence gathering, including security services, police and foreign investigators, in addition to the War Crimes Bureau of the Prosecutor's Office, but it was unable to conduct field investigations in places under Russian military occupation and was gathering information mainly through interviews with displaced people.[34] In addition, on 30 April, investigations were launched against 10 Russian soldiers on war crimes charges in Bucha.[35] Since then, the number of criminal cases due to the Russian invasion has soared to 28,350—27,258 war crimes, 73 crimes of aggression, 28 war propaganda and 991 other cases—as of 15 August.[36]

Former Prosecutor General Venediktova, who had been actively building a system of cooperation with international actors since the invasion and disseminating information on social networking sites and other media, was dismissed on 19 July for her failure to respond to corruption issues involving her subordinates.[37] Oleksiy Yuriyovych Simonenko was then acting, but on 27 July, Andriy Kostin, a member of the ruling party, was appointed prosecutor general.[38]

Kostin held an online meeting with the ICC chief prosecutor on 10 August to discuss investigative cooperation and the opening of an office in Ukraine, but the ICC noted that the law needs to be amended to allow ICC officials to conduct investigative activities on Ukrainian territory.[39]

---

[30] Alessandra Prentice, "French forensic experts in Bucha to help Ukraine investigate possible war crimes" (*Reuters*, 13 April 2022).

[31] Anthony Deutsch, "Ukraine prepares war crimes charges against Russian military personnel, including pilots" (*Reuters*, 26 April 2022).

[32] *Ibid.* It is believed that this pilot returned to Russia for the exchange of prisoners of war.

[33] *Ibid.* "Ukraine identifies 8,600 suspected war crimes" (AFP, 29 April 2022).

[34] *Ibid.*

[35] "*Ukuraina, Bucha deno Senso Hanzai Yogi de Roshiahei 10 Nin no Sosa Kaishi* [Ukraine launches investigation of 10 Russian soldiers for war crimes in Bucha]" (BBC, 1 May 2022).

[36] [Prosecutor General's Office of Ukraine], at https://www.gp.gov.ua/ (as of 15 August 2022).

[37] "Venediktova dismissed as Prosecutor General of Ukraine" (*Ukrinform*, 19 July 2022).

[38] "President appoints Andriy Kostin as Prosecutor General" (*Ukrinform*, 28 July 2022).

[39] [Andriy Costin in conversation with Karim Khan, prosecutor at the International Criminal Court] (*Ukrinform*, 10 August 2022).

Investigation by a Third State

(a) Investigations by the States

This situation has resulted in large-scale and brutal core crime cases, and in addition to the movement of many displaced people to neighbouring States, foreign journalists and humanitarian aid staff have entered the region, and there have been many cases in which third State nationals have been killed, not only in neighbouring States. At least 18 States have launched their own investigations as of 28 May,[40] and many third States, mainly European States, are cooperating with Ukraine in the investigation.

Poland, which is hosting displaced persons from Ukraine, announced that it had already collected war crimes testimonies from 300 people as of 17 March.[41] Lithuania launched a war crimes investigation on 3 March,[42] and sent a team of law enforcement officers to assist in the investigation in Ukraine on 5 May.[43] Romania launched a war crimes investigation only on 11 July.[44]

In addition to a forensic investigation in Bucha in April, the French Gendarmerie's Institute for Criminal Investigations has experts on explosives and drones investigating shelling by Russian forces in Chernihiv, northern Ukraine.[45] Also in July, a French "mobile DNA laboratory" was sent to Kyiv.[46] Following the death of a French journalist on 30 May, France's "Central Office to Combat Crimes against Humanity, Genocide and War Crimes" has also launched a war crimes investigation.[47]

The US established a War Crimes Investigation Team within the Department of Justice on 21 June to ensure direct investigative cooperation between the two States, and the Minister of Justice and Ambassador Van Schaak visited Ukraine.[48] The US has also made clear this year the usefulness of the ICC and the US willingness to cooperate with the ICC, even though it is not a party to the ICC.[49]

---

[40] "An 'unprecedented' effort to document war crimes in Ukraine. but what chance of justice?" (*The Washington Post*, 25 May 2022).

[41] "Poland say it has collected more than 300 witness statements on war in Ukraine" (*Reuters*, 17 March 2022).

[42] "Lithuania prosecutors launch Ukraine war crimes investigation" (*Reuters*, 3 March 2022).

[43] "Lithuanian team arrives in Ukraine to help investigate war crimes" (Lithuanian National Radio and Television, 5 May 2022).

[44] "*Rzboiul din Ucraina-sesizare din oficiu cu privire la svârirea unor infraciuni contra umanitii, prev. de art. 439 din Codul penal* [War in Ukraine—Ex officio notice on the commission of crimes against humanity, art. 439 of the Criminal Code]" (Romanian Public Prosecutor's Office, 11 July 2022).

[45] "French experts collect evidence of possible war crimes in Ukraine's Chernihiv" (*Reuters*, 11 June 2022).

[46] "France sends mobile DNA lab to Kyiv, as countries coordinate war crimes investigations" (*Euronews*, 15 July 2022).

[47] "French prosecutors to probe death of BFMTV journalist in Ukraine as war crime" (*Ukrinform*, 31 May 2022).

[48] "Justice News" (The United States Department of Justice, 21 June 2022).

[49] See e.g., "Remarks by U.S. Ambassador Beth Van Schaack on Strengthening the ICC" (U.S. Mission to the Organization of American States, 16 June 2022).

Elsewhere, the UK announced on 4 March that Scotland Yard's war crimes unit would begin an investigation, and on 29 April announced that it would send a war crimes expert to Ukraine in May.[50] In Germany, two former ministers filed war crimes charges in Ukraine with the Federal Prosecutor's Office on 8 March, which led to the opening of an investigation under universal jurisdiction.[51] Switzerland announced on 22 May that the Federal Prosecutor's Office will set up a task force on war crimes.[52]

(b) Multi-State groups
(1) Accountability Friendly Group (GoF)

On 25 March, six States—Albania, Colombia, Denmark, the Marshall Islands, the Netherlands and Ukraine—opened the Group of Friends of Accountability ("GoF") in New York and Geneva.[53] It aims to share information among States, international organizations and with civil society, and to involve small States that do not have sufficient accountability capacity in the development of accountability measures.

(2) Atrocity Crime Advisory Group (ACA)

The EU, the US, and the UK launched the Atrocity Crimes Advisory Group ("ACA") on 25 May.[54] This will support efforts of the War Crimes Bureau within the Prosecutor's Office of Ukraine to seek accountability for "atrocity crimes"—synonymous with core crimes—that arise in the context of Russia's invasion of Ukraine during its aggression. The ACA is composed of the Advisory Group to the Prosecutor General's Office ("OPG"), which is composed of practitioners, including prosecutors, investigators, military analysts and coroners with experience in investigating and prosecuting atrocity crimes, and the Mobile Justice Teams, which is composed of international experts who aim to improve the capacity of Ukrainian prosecutors and local prosecutors to conduct field investigations.

Investigations by Other International Organizations and Non-Governmental Organizations

On 13 March, the Organization for Security and Cooperation in Europe ("OECE") appointed three experts to a special mission of the Moscow Mechanism to investigate. On 13 April, it became the first international organization to issue a report on the

[50] "UK dispatches war crimes experts to help Ukraine with investigations" (Gov.UK, 29 April 2022).

[51] "Former German ministers file war crimes complaint on Russia" (AP News, 8 April 2022).

[52] "*Ukuraina deno Senso Hanzai Giwaku, Suisu mo Shoko Shushu ni Honso* [Alleged war crimes in Ukraine, Switzerland scrambles to gather evidence]" (Swissingo.ch, June 3, 2022).

[53] "High-Level Launch Meeting of the Group of Friends of Accountability Following the Aggression Against Ukraine". (International Peace Institute, 25 March 2022).

[54] See e.g., "Ukraine: The European Union, the United States, and the United Kingdom establish the Atrocity Crimes Advisory Group (ACA) for Ukraine" (European Union External Action, 25 May 2022).

various illegal acts that accompanied the invasion of Ukraine, declaring the attacks on the participating hospitals and theatres to be war crimes.[55]

The Human Rights Monitoring Mission ("HRMMU") of the Office of the United Nations High Commissioner for Human Rights ("OHCHR") has been monitoring and reporting on the human rights situation in Ukraine and Donetsk, Luhansk and Crimea since 2014.[56] In addition to this work, on 4 March, the UN Human Rights Council decided to establish an independent international commission of inquiry.[57] On 12 May, it adopted a new resolution directing it to investigate incidents in certain regions within Ukraine.[58] The first field investigation took place between 7 and 16 June.

Several other non-governmental organizations, including international human rights organizations, are monitoring and reporting on core crimes. Also receiving attention this time around was the use of digital open sources for investigation and evidence collection and preservation. Organizations such as Bellingcat and Truth Hounds are contributing to the sorting out of the vast amount of information that has been muddled together by fact-checking publicly available footage and documents and clarifying that the Bucha Massacre was not fake news. They are contributing to the sorting out of the vast amount of information.

Prosecution Practices by Each Actor

Prosecution by the ICC

As of 15 August, no prosecution by the ICC regarding the Ukrainian situation has been initiated. However, on 30 June, the ICC issued three arrest warrants against Russia, which is believed to have a number of war crimes suspects in the case, related to the Georgia situation in 2008, which it had already started investigating.[59] As there are many similarities in the structure and methods of the case in the Georgia situation, as well as in the actions of the Russian military and information inside the organization, it is likely that many of the criminal procedures will be followed as well.[60]

---

[55] Wolfgang Benedek, Veronika Bílková and Marco Sassòli, "Report on Violations of International Humanitarian and Human Rights Law, War Crimes and Crimes Against Humanity Committed In Ukraine Since 24 February 2022", OSCE Doc. ODIHR.GAL/26/22/Rev.1 (13 April 2022).

[56] A total of 57 personnel sent. The transfer from the DPR to Ukraine of 400 detainees is taking place. UN Human Rights in Ukraine, https://www.ohchr.org/en/countries/ukraine/our-presence#:~:text=The%20UN%20Human%20Rights%20Monitoring,occupied%20by%20the%20Russian%20Federation.

[57] UN Doc. A/HRC/RES/49/1 (7 March 2022).

[58] UN Doc. A/HRC/RES/S-34/1 (16 May 2022).

[59] "Situation in Georgia: ICC Pre-Trial Chamber delivers three arrest warrants" (ICC, 30 June 2022).

[60] See, "Georgia, the ICC's testing ground for Ukraine" (Justiceinfo.net, 31 March 2022).

Prosecution by Ukraine

The first trial in the war crimes trial in Ukraine began on 13 May at the Solomiansky District Court in Kyiv.[61] The sight of defendant Vadim Shishimarin, a 21-year-old Russian Army sergeant, being brought into the small courtroom was broadcasted to the world through the press, including many foreign media outlets packed outside the glass-fronted booth. The defendant was charged under Article 438(2) of the Criminal Code of Ukraine (Violation of the Laws of War) for allegedly firing on and killing an unarmed 62-year-old civilian man in a village in northeastern Ukraine's Sumy Oblast on 28 February.[62]

According to Article 438 of the Criminal Code of Ukraine, the statutory penalties for the crime of violation of the laws of war differ depending on whether the crime involves intentional killing or not. Paragraph 1 of the same article provides that "Cruel treatment of prisoners of war or civilians, deportation of civilian population for forced labour, pillage of national treasures on occupied territories, use of methods of warfare prohibited by international instruments, or any other violations of rules of warfare recognized by international instruments consented to by binding by the Verkhovna Rada of Ukraine, and also giving an order to commit any such actions shall be punishable by imprisonment for a term of eight to twelve years." On the other hand, paragraph 2 states that "The same acts accompanied with a murder,—shall be punishable by imprisonment for a term of ten to fifteen years, or life imprisonment." Thus, the Criminal Code of Ukraine conforms to international law with regards to the specifics of violations of the laws of war, while the statutory penalties differ in terms of the amount of punishment, depending on whether the intentional killing was intentional or not.

The trial against Shishimarin is assessed to have been conducted fairly, with an interpreter and defence counsel provided free of charge and the defendant present in all proceedings.[63] The accused admitted his guilt during the interrogation, and the court heard testimony from another Russian soldier who was a passenger in the car in which the accused was riding at the time of the incident, the victim's wife, who saw the car immediately after the incident, and other witnesses. At trial, the defence argued, among other things, that the shooting was in accordance with the order of a senior soldier—who was not a direct superior officer—. The prosecutor sought a life sentence, the maximum penalty under Article 438(2).

[61] On the abolition of the military justice system in 2010 through judicial centralization in Ukraine, see Mindia Vashakmadze, *Military Justice in Ukraine: A Guidance Note* (The Geneva Centre for the Democratic Control of Armed Forces (DCAF), 2018).

[62] Case No. 760/5257/22, Judgment of the Solomiansky District Court of Ukraine, 24 May 2022 (hereinafter Sicimarin Judgment). For more on the trial and testimony, see also Irina Salii, "Ukraine Opens First War Crime Trial of a Russian Soldier" (Justiceinfo.net, 17 May 2022); Irina Salii, "First Ukraine War Crime Trial Through the Eyes of a Local Court Reporter" (Justiceinfo.net, 24 May 2022).

[63] Gaiane Nuridzhanian, "Prosecuting war crimes: are Ukrainian courts fit to do it?" (EJIL Talk!, August 11, 2022), https://www.ejiltalk.org/prosecuting-war-crimes-are-ukrainian-courts-fit-to-do-it/.

On 23 May, the Court found Shishimarin guilty and sentenced him to life in prison as sought. In full recognition of the facts of the crimes alleged by the prosecutor, the reasons given for the life sentence instead of a fixed-term sentence were that the war crimes were "crimes against the security and peace of mankind and against international law", that the international community strongly condemned aggression and war, and that they were "a danger to the world order and the peaceful coexistence of mankind on this planet". The defence appealed against the sentence, and the Kyiv Appeals Court on 29 July, reduced the sentence to 15 years' confinement on the grounds that there was no prior conspiracy.[64]

Since then, as shown in the table, several court cases are underway. All of them are violations of Article 438 of the Criminal Code of Ukraine, but only the first one resulted in loss of human life.

[Table] War crimes trials of Russian soldiers against Russian prisoners of war in Ukraine (as of 12 August 2022)

Trial	Case name	The charge	Procedure
	Shishimarin case	Killing civilian	May 23: Guilty (life sentence) July 29: Guilty (appeal) (reduced to a 15-year imprisonment)
	Bobbikin-Ivanov case	Destruction of civilian objects	May 31: Guilty (11 years and 6 months imprisonment)
	Kulikov case	Destruction of civilian objects	August 8: Guilty (10 years imprisonment)
	Zakharov case	Pillage	August 3: Guilty (12 years imprisonment)
Pretrial Hearing	Steiner case	Destruction and pillage of private property	May 30: Preliminaries begin (*in absentia*)
	Romanov case	Rape	June 24: Trial begins (*in absentia*)
	Zuravlev case	Destruction of civilian objects	August 9: Preliminaries begin

*For more information, see: "Ukraine War Crimes Trial Database" by Megumi Ochi, at https://alkaline-lantana-adf.notion.site/Ukraine-War-Crimes-Trial-Database-66fada9c1e9f416185ac180562814e86?pvs=4 (as of a August 2024)

[64] [Appeals court sentences Russian military officer Shishimarin to 15 years instead of life in prison]" (*Court Reporter*, 29 July 2022).

An Analysis from the Perspective of International Criminal Procedure

Parallel Investigations and Parallel Prosecutions

Establishment of a Multilateral International Cooperative Investigation System

This international criminal justice effort has four distinctive features. First, the ICC prosecutor acted with unprecedented speed. Even though the ICC had been conducting a preliminary examination of the situation since November 2013, it requested an atuhorization to initiate an investigation on 28 February 2022, four days after the start of the Russian full-scale invasion, without waiting for a UN resolution. The ICC has never commenced an investigation at such an early stage of an international armed conflict. It is also unprecedented that the ICC prosecutor himself conducted frequent visits to the places where crimes were committed. The fact that the ICC dispatched its largest-ever contingent of staff to the region is also unique.

Second, many States referred situations to the ICC on an unprecedented scale. In the past, the mainstream of referrals to the ICC was self-referral by the State where the crime was committed or referral to the UN Security Council, perhaps because of concerns about the political repercussions of referring another State's case to the ICC. In this case, however, the 43 States wanted the ICC to investigate and exercise jurisdiction over the core crimes, even at the risk of political friction with the aggressor, Russia.

Third, a number of investigative cooperation groups have been set up. The practices of the GoF, formed by Ukraine and five other States, and the ACA, formed by the EU, the US and the UK, are new. The ICC's participation in the JIT, originally run as a Eurojust project, is also unprecedented. The primary objective for such a group was to build capacity in Ukraine, as the State lacks resources, knowledge and experience in investigating core crimes. This was possible largely because of Ukraine's earlier participation in European democracy assistance projects.[65] It was also likely premised on the post-2019 extradition issue between Ukraine and the US.[66]

Fourth, technical guidelines were developed on the premise of parallel investigations. The Political Declarations by 45 States addressed issues such as the possible dispersion of evidence and undue burden on providers of evidence that could arise from conducting parallel investigations and provided general guidelines. This was the first time that such guidelines for multilateral investigative cooperation for a specific situation had been developed.

---

[65] See, e.g., Silviya Nitsova, Gripore Pop-Eleches, and Graeme Robertson, "Revolution and Reform in Ukraine: Evaluating Four Years of Reform" (*PONARS Eurasia*, 18 July 2018).

[66] See, e.g., "U.S. Prosecutors Call Him a Murderer. To Ukraine He's an Asylum Seeker" (*The New York Times*, 3 March 2021).

How to Discipline Parallel Investigations

In the case of domestic investigations, duplicate investigations by multiple investigative agencies are undesirable from the perspective of judicial economy and effective prosecution and are therefore subject to discipline based on norms such as the principle of prosecutorial unity.[67] However, it has been further clarified that these rationales are not valid in international criminal justice, which is based on international cooperation. The move to establish a multifaceted international cooperative system in response to this situation was also an indication that the international community is moving in the direction of establishing a system of necessary overlapping coordination, while giving full priority to the merits of parallel investigations. The perspective of effective prosecution is of paramount importance, where a cooperative system is being set up in accordance with the necessity and effectiveness of the investigations.

Discipline for Parallel Prosecution

With regards to parallel prosecutions in international criminal justice, norms for the allocation of jurisdiction have been adopted, influenced by the institutional characteristics of International Criminal Justice Institutions. In particular, the ICC has devised and adopted the principle of complementarity for States (ICC Statute, Articles 1 and 17). However, from the specific content of the norm, it is basically a "first come, first served" principle the prosecution of the institution that prosecuted the case first takes precedence.[68] However, at present, it appears that careful adjustments are being made at the practical level to avoid duplication of procedures that would bring up the principle of complementarity.

However, there is a strong demand for expeditious action, as the fighting is still ongoing. In particular, there is a risk that the collection and preservation of evidence may become difficult in areas occupied by the Russian side, which is not cooperative in international criminal justice. Depending on the war situation, access to certain areas may become impossible. In addition, the need to record testimonies quickly has arisen as witnesses have become displaced persons and are on the move.

With regards to prosecution, duplication of proceedings on the same case is considered to be an undue burden. Moreover, because core crimes prosecutions are, by their nature, theoretically conducted by one State on behalf of the international community as a whole, they need to be fair and satisfactory to all States in terms of procedure and outcome. Otherwise, a request may arise for a different sentence to be issued by another criminal jurisdiction that does not accept the content of the initial judgment. In light of these considerations, it seems necessary that duplicate proceedings

---

[67] See Chap. 1 of this book.

[68] See below. Megumi Ochi, "*Kensatsukan Tai Saifu Aru =Isuramu Kadafi Jiken (Kokusai Keiji Saibansho (Dai Ichi Yoshin Saibanbu) Juri Kyoyo-Sei ni Kansuru Kettei, 2013 Nen 5 gatsu 31 Nichi)* [The Prosecutor v. Saif al-Islam Gaddafi (Decision on admissibility of the International Criminal Court (Pre-Trial Chamber I), 31 May 2013)]", *Osaka Hogaku [Osaka Law Review]* 64, No. 1 (2014): 237–250.

and judgments on the same matter should be governed by general principles such as jurisdictional rules and the prohibition of double prosecution.

At present, there is no overlap in prosecution between the ICC and Ukraine or any other State. In addition, if the ICC initiates a prosecution in the future, the rules of Part IX of the ICC Statute will apply, at least as between Ukraine and the ICC, because Ukraine has made a declaration of acceptance of jurisdiction, even though it is not a State Party (Article 12(3) of the ICC Statute). However, it seems debatable whether this extends to the jurisdiction and admissibility rules of Part II of the Statute. Ukraine has recently enacted a cooperation law with the ICC, but whether the content of the law adequately reflects the standards under the ICC Statute requires careful analysis.

Priority of Extradition

Extradition Between States

Ukraine and Russia have ratified the European Convention on Extradition.[69] Ukraine can request Russia to extradite criminal suspects in accordance with the Convention. However, as the European Extradition Convention recognizes the right not to extradite one's own nationals, extradition can be refused if the suspect is a Russian national (Article 6(1)(a) of the European Extradition Convention). This reason cannot be used to refuse extradition of foreign war crimes suspects who are located in Russia. However, at the time of ratification of the Convention, Russia made a reservation to the effect that "...the Russian Federation shall reserve the right not to extradite the persons whose extradition can affect its sovereignty, security, public order or other essential interests."

However, since the obligation to "prosecute or extradite" is applicable to war crimes (e.g., Article 49(2) of the First Geneva Convention), if there is an extradition request for war crimes but the suspects are not extradited, the obligation to initiate criminal proceedings against these persons for war crimes in their own State arises.

In addition, when a third State makes an extradition request to Ukraine or Russia, there are the same barriers to extradition in the case of a State Party to the European Convention on Extradition as there are in the case of an extradition request between Ukraine and Russia. However, if a third State Party to the European Convention on Extradition detains a Ukrainian or Russian suspect and Ukraine or Russia makes an extradition request to that third State, an extradition obligation may arise. If there are competing extradition requests from several States, the European Convention on Extradition has discretionary provisions, which means that the requesting State can decide at its discretion which of the two States to extradite to. However, in making

[69] "Chart of signatures and ratifications of Treaty 024" (Council of Europe Portal, N. D.). https://www.coe.int/en/web/conventions/full-list?module=signatures-by-treaty&treatynum=024 (as of 15 August 2022).

such a decision, the relative gravity and place of commission of the crime, the date of each request, the nationality of the subject person, and the possibility of subsequent extradition to another State must be taken into account (Article 17). In the case of a competing extradition request involving Russian military personnel, the requested State is required to make a political decision as to whether to extradite them to Ukraine, where the crime was committed, or to Russia, the land of their nationality.

Between Ukraine and the ICC

A State Party to the ICC Statute is obliged to surrender a suspect if an surrender request is made by the ICC (ICC Statute, Articles 89 *et seq.*). If a surrender/extradition request is made by the ICC and another State simultaneously, the scope of the obligation depends on conditions such as whether the requesting State is a State Party to the ICC Statute and whether the surrender/extradition is for the same crime.[70] Although Ukraine is not a State Party to the ICC Statute, it has made a declaration of acceptance of jurisdiction in accordance with Article 12(3) of the ICC Statute and is therefore obliged to comply with the provisions of Part IX of the ICC Statute concerning the obligation to cooperate in extradition and other matters.

Ukraine prohibits the extradition of its citizens to other States under Article 25 of its Constitution, and in a 2001 Constitutional Court decision, referring to the fact that the ICC is not synonymous with other States but applies international standards agreed by States and the principle of complementarity of the ICC, the Constitutional Court held that the non-extradition of citizens does not apply to surrender requests from the ICC.[71]

With regards to surrender/extradition, while there is a need to give priority to the pursuit of justice for core crimes, there is a difficulty in taking into account political factors between States when other States have an interest in prosecuting other extra crimes. In addition, since the ICC is based on a multilateral treaty, priority is not necessarily given in cases of conflicting extradition requests from non-ICC Member States (ICC Statute, Article 90).

[70] With respect to the priority of delivery to the ICC, see below for further details. See Chap. 2 of this book.

[71] Ukraine, Constitutional Court, Opinion of the Constitutional Court of Ukraine in the case of a constitutional submission by the President of Ukraine on issuing opinion related to compliance of the Rome Statute of the International Criminal Court to the Constitution of Ukraine, Case No 1–35/2001, 11 July 2001, paras 2.3–3.3.

Prohibition of Trial in Absentia

Discussion on Trial *in Absentia* at the ICC

Because of the importance of guaranteeing the accused's human right to be present in court and ensuring the legitimacy of the trial, the ICC does not, in principle, allow trials in the absence of the accused under its Statute.[72] On the other hand, due to the importance of the prosecution of core crimes and the difficulty of securing suspects, the significance of allowing trials *in absentia* has also been argued at the ICC.

With regards to the situation in Ukraine, there is growing interest in the prosecution of not only the perpetrators who actually entered Ukraine and committed core crimes, but also the Russian upper echelons who planned and executed the invasion. On the other hand, given Russia's lack of cooperation with international criminal justice, it remains to be seen what impact this will have on the theory of admissibility of trials *in absentia* as a method of pursuing the responsibility of senior figures within Russia.

Trial *in Absentia* Allowed in Ukraine

In January 2015 and April 2021, amendments were made to Article 323 of the Ukrainian Code of Criminal Procedure, which prohibits trials *in absentia* as a general rule. As a result, trial *in absentia* is now permissible for crimes under paragraph 2 of Article 297–1 of the Code—e.g., Actions aimed at take-over of government against suspects who is hiding in the temporarily occupied territory of Ukraine or on the territory of an aggressor state—.

The right to be in court is one of the rights to a fair trial for defendants under criminal prosecution. Therefore, it is necessary to secure the custody of the accused in order to ensure a fairer trial. On the other hand, the current situation raises the issue of non-prosecution due to the fact that many war crimes suspects are returned to Russia in exchange for prisoners of war with members of the Ukrainian military.[73] Within Ukraine, there is an awareness that the legitimacy of trials *in absentia* is reduced, while on the other hand there is a conflict with the strong demand for prosecution.

---

[72] For more information on the ICC's ban on absentee trials, see Chap. 3 of this book.

[73] For an example, refer to the following: "*Kurozu Appu Gendai Zen Kiroku 'Senso Hanzai' ha Sabakeru noka Ukuraina Kensatsu Shirarezaru Tatakai* [Close-up of Contemporary Records: Will the "War Crimes" Be Brought to Justice? The Unknown Struggle of the Ukrainian Prosecutors] (NHK, 1 August 2022), at https://www.nhk.or.jp/gendai/articles/4692/ (as of 15 August 2022).

Redress for the Rights of the Accused

With regards to this situation, the violation of the rights of the accused in the criminal justice process is not an issue at this time, as far as we can see. However, doubts have been raised as to the fairness of a trial by Ukraine, a party to the conflict, in the context of ongoing combat operations.[74] In particular, if the trial is to be positioned as a core crimes trial representing the interests of the international community as a whole, it is required of Ukraine, which will conduct the trial, to provide international standards of rights guarantees to suspects and accused persons.

As for the ICC, only about 40 officers are on the ground in Ukraine, and basically the judicial authorities in Ukraine and other States will use coercive force, such as detaining people and seizing evidence and materials in the field, and hand them over to the ICC. The ICC is the only authority that can take action against violations of rights by national judicial authorities. For violations of rights by national judicial authorities, the ICC has so far focused on procedural rather than substantive legitimacy of the redress provided by the ICC.[75] This is because the ICC has to take into account the legitimacy of the use of contributions by States Parties when providing monetary compensation, and the aspects of the ICC's original purpose of ensuring the prohibition of impunity and the realization of the social interest of punishing those who perpetrate crimes when providing relief through measures such as commuting sentences or suspending proceedings.

If, in exercising coercive force, due process is not guaranteed, such as informing suspects of their rights in a language they understand and taking measures to prevent arbitrary detention, it will be interesting to see how the ICC responds to such violations of their rights. In particular, this time, as in the Political Declaration by 45 States, a number of States have shown their willingness to cooperate, and investigators from European States have been dispatched to Ukraine. However, if at some point in the proceedings there is a case of inadequate protection of rights, the ICC itself will need to be prepared to provide remedies.

Admissibility of Evidence

Evidence Sharing

One of the features of the multilateral joint investigation framework development that has attracted attention is the use of a shared evidence database. The Eurojust Joint Investigation Team has amended the relevant rules to make the evidence database operational and expanded its powers to store, analyse and archive evidence relating

[74] See, e.g., Robert Goldman, "War crimes trial of Russian soldier was perfectly legal—but that doesn't make it wise", (*The Conversation*, 23 May 2022).

[75] For more information on the ICC's remedies for the rights of accused persons, see Chap. 4 of this book.

to core crimes.[76] Specifically, it was empowered to use automated management and storage facilities for the evidence provided and to provide the information obtained from the analysis to other investigative entities. The database essentially only receives evidence submitted by national authorities, while information collected by private entities such as non-governmental organizations and civil society organizations is evaluated by national and international judicial authorities before being stored.

New Forms of Evidence

This time, witnesses to the core crimes in various parts of Ukraine, in many cases, recorded the crime scenes with their handheld camera phones and disseminated the information on SNS. On the other hand, fabricated data and discourses abound on the internet claiming to have recorded criminal acts that did not actually take place, and the importance of fact-checking has been reaffirmed. Therefore, in relation to the collection of information and evidence on core crimes, the use of open-source intelligence ("OSINT") attracted attention this time. OSINT is a method of examining and comparing open materials that can be legally obtained, and by comparing official documents, photos and video data on SNS from various perspectives, it is possible for private organizations to obtain detailed information. By comparing official documents, photos and videos on SNS from various angles, private organizations can analyse the details and authenticity of information.

At the ICC, too, many digital open sources have been presented in court as evidence,[77] but in the face of such a vast flood of data as in this case, a framework for their use is being explored. For example, the Leiden Guidelines on Digitally Derived Evidence in International Criminal Courts and Tribunals project has created the Leiden DDE Database to provide a framework for the use of digitally derived evidence ("DDE"), with references to cases where DDE has been used in the past.[78]

---

[76] "Regulation (EU) 2022/838 of the European Parliament and of the Council of 30 May 2022" (*Eurojust*, 31 May 2022).

[77] See, Sam Dubberley, Alexa Koenig, and Daragh Murray, eds., *Digital Witness: Using Open Source Information for Human Rights Investigation, Documentation, and Accountability* (Oxford University Press, 2020).

[78] Leiden Guidelines on the Use of Digitally Derived Evidence, at https://leiden-guidelines.com/ (as of 25 August 2022).

Use of Evidence at the ICC

In this situation, the quality and quantity of information has increased overwhelmingly compared to previous core crimes cases.[79] There are issues regarding the admissibility of evidence in trials, including the digital open source itself and whether information analysed through OSINT can be used directly as evidence. In addition, there could be an increase in the number of cases in trials during ongoing combat, where the person who provided testimony has died and only recorded statements from his or her lifetime are available. It is also possible that witnesses may be threatened or interfered with in the future by internal witnesses within the Russian military, when prosecution reaches those responsible at higher levels. To address these, the use of previously recorded statements used by the ICC will become even more important.[80]

Originally, the use of evidence at the ICC was accompanied by the remote location of the crime, but with the recent admission of video-link testimony, it is expected that measures to reduce the burden on witnesses will continue to be used.[81]

In addition, the current situation where evidence collection is dispersed by many different entities raises issues such as the problem of investigative discipline, which differs from State to State, and ensuring standards of witness protection and promptness. In addition, in relation to the exclusion of illegally collected evidence at the ICC, it is necessary to disseminate the method of evidence collection in a manner that complies with the standards at the ICC and to have the relevant entities comply with them.[82] The fact that this point was included in the Political Declaration by 45 States indicates that the need for measures was recognized (Political Declaration, para. 12).

Reparation for Victims

The road to victim reparations with respect to this situation is a long one. The Law of Armed Conflict envisages post-war reparations between States as a post-processing of international armed conflict.[83] However, since it is unclear whether this situation

---

[79] For example, the investigation at the International Criminal Tribunal for the former Yugoslavia (ICTY) took years just to collect satellite images and intercept records to locate mass graves. Hiroto Fujiwara, "*ICTY ni yoru Kokusai Keiji Sousa to Sureburenitsua* [International Criminal Investigation by ICTY and Srebrenica]", in Yukie Osa, ed., *Sureburenitsua Jenosaido: 25-Nenme no Kyokun to Kadai [The Srebrenica Genocide: Lessons and Challenges from 25 years],* (Toshindo, 2020): 119–138.

[80] For more information on the exceptions to the orality principle at the ICC, see Chap. 5 of this book.

[81] *Ibid.*

[82] On the exclusion of illegally collected evidence at the ICC, see *ibid.* for details.

[83] Article 3 of the Hague Rules of Land Warfare, Article 91 of Geneva Additional Protocol I, etc. The State responsibility under these rules refers to the responsibility for monetary compensation for damages other than those known to the State for damages arising from illegal acts of

will come to an end in the form of the conclusion of a peace treaty, there has been very little discussion of the issue of post-conflict reparations.[84] On the other hand, in the framework of international criminal justice, which pursues the criminal responsibility of individuals, there is the possibility of victim reparations in the event of a conviction, which could be realized earlier than post-war reparations between States.

The ICC's reparations system consists of direct reparation orders against convicted persons for the harm caused by their crimes, and general support from the ICC's TFV for situations subject to ICC investigation. For the former system, it was built to meet the demands of restorative justice to provide healing and reconciliation for victims and perpetrators, as well as communities, beyond reactive and preventive criminal justice.[85] However, it has also been confirmed that the ICC Statute does not cover violations of international humanitarian law or international human rights law, that not all victims are eligible to participate in the ICC, and that the ICC is not a forum to pursue reparations for violations of international human rights law or international humanitarian law, due in part to ICC resources.[86]

The ICC has not undertaken any specific activities on reparations at this time, but the TFV Board of Directors on 9 March expressed its deep concern about this situation and called for voluntary contributions from States for victims' reparations.[87]

Conclusion

Although practice and research on the establishment of an international cooperative system of international criminal justice for this situation has just begun, I would like to make a tentative analysis from the perspective of the four premises of international criminal procedure given in the conclusion of this book.

First, it must be said that the response to this situation itself has been strongly influenced by the axial premise of international criminal justice, namely, the seriousness of the core crimes. Although the special nature of the core crimes in the individual procedural laws remains to be verified, at the very least, never before has an international cooperative system been established so quickly and on such a large scale.

---

war, and after the end of hostilities. In practice, many of them make the defeated State liable for comprehensive payment for all damages suffered by the victorious State due to the war. Hisakazu Fujita, *Shinpan Kokusai Jindoho (Sai Zoho)* [New Edition of International Humanitarian Law (Re-enlarged)] (Yushindokobunsha, 2003), 195–196.

[84] See, e.g., Chiara Giorgetti, Markiyan Kliuchkovskyi and Patrick W Pearsall (EJIL Talk!, 20 May 2022), at https://www.ejiltalk.org/launching-an-international-claims-commission-for-ukraine/ (as of 31 August 2022); Laurie Blank, "War Reparations for Ukraine: Key Issues" (Just Security, 2 May 2022).

[85] See below for more information on the ICC's victim compensation system. See Chap. 6 of this book.

[86] *Ibid.*

[87] "Statement TFV Board of Directors on the situation in Ukraine" (ICC, 9 March 2022).

Second, on the other hand, there is a growing awareness of the importance of preventing rights violations and excessive burdens on individuals that may arise in this context. It remains to be seen how the premise of deterring illegal investigations will be reflected in the law governing the international cooperative system.

Third, it seems to highlight that the entire international criminal justice system is based on the premise of speed and "first come, first served". Perhaps the most important aspect from now on will be the jurisdictional alignment between the ICC and Ukraine, and specifically the question of which Party will be responsible for the prosecution of which person. It is assumed that the ICC, Ukraine, and third States will coordinate their jurisdictions in the future, and it will draw attention how this will turn out.

Fourth, the impact of the premise of consideration for national sovereignty that the ICC is an international organization based on a treaty has been a problem so far. In this situation as well, Ukraine's cooperation has been a matter of life and death for the ICC. Ukraine has not ratified the ICC Statute for many years despite domestic and international requests,[88] and if Ukraine withdraws its declaration of acceptance of jurisdiction, the cooperation system that has been established so far will collapse at once. It is important to recognize the fact that it is Ukraine that holds the decision-making authority in the international cooperative regime that is now being built. And this means that the significance of the international cooperation system as a whole will be affected by how Ukraine, as a State, responds to the future extension of justice to Ukrainian nationals. Ukraine's attitude towards cooperation with international criminal justice is also closely linked to the evolution of the war situation. How the fight against impunity for core crimes in Ukraine progresses in the future will, in this sense, depend on Ukraine's willingness and ability to work for justice.

[88] "Ukraine" (Coalition for the International Criminal Court, N. D.), at https://www.coalitionforthe icc.org/country/ukraine (as of 15 August 2022).

Bibliography

1. Abtahi H (2020) The international criminal court during the COVID-19 pandemic. J Int Crim Just 18(5):1069–1076
2. Ambos K, Stephani B (2012) Procedural regimes. In: Reydams L, Wouters J, Ryngaert C (eds) International prosecutors. Oxford University Press, pp 488–541
3. Ambos K (2003) International criminal procedure: "adversarial", "inquisitorial" or mixed? Int Crimi Law Rev 3:1–37
4. Antkowiak TM (2011) An emerging mandate for international courts: victim-centered remedies and restorative justice. Stanford J Int Law 47(2):279–332
5. Aptel C (2007) Some innovations in the statute of the special tribunal for Lebanon. J Int Crim Just 5(5):1107–1124
6. Aust A (2013) Modern treaty law and practice, 3rd edn. Cambridge University Press
7. Banzai H (2015) Kokusai Iho Koi Sekinin no Kenkyu—Kokka Sekininron no Kihonmondai [A study of the responsibility for internationally wrongful act : basic issues in the theory of state responsibility]. Seibundo
8. Barnett RE (1977) Restitution: a new paradigm of criminal justice. Ethics 87(4):279–301
9. Bassiouni MC (1995) Aut Dedere Aut Judicare: the duty to extradite or prosecute in international law. Martinus Nijhoff Publishers
10. Bassiouni MC (2007) International extradition: United States law and practice, 5th edn. Oxford University Press
11. Bassiouni MC (2012) Introduction to the international criminal law, 2nd Revised edn. Martinus Nijhoff Publishers
12. Beresford S (2002) Redressing the wrongs of the international justice system: compensation for persons eroneously detained, prosecuted, or convicted by the ad hoc tribunals. Am J Int Law 96(3):628–646
13. Beulke W (2014) Doitsu Keiji Soshoho (2) [Strafprozessrecht], trans. Katsuyoshi Kato and Norio Tsujimoto, *Kinkidaigaku hogaku* 62(1):196–197
14. Bitzilekis N (2015) The violation of mankind's multiculturalism: another approach to the definition of international crimes. Int Crim Law Rev 15(6):1040–1068
15. Boas G (2001) Developments in the law of procedure and evidence at the international criminal tribunal for the former Yugoslavia and the international criminal court. Crim Law Forum 12:167–183
16. Bodin J (2017) Les six livres de la République avec l'Apologie de R. Herpin. Texte édition 1576. Myriel, Paris
17. Boister N, Gless S, Jeßberger F (eds) (2021) Histories of transnational criminal law. Oxford University Press

M. Ochi, *The Premises of International Criminal Procedure*,
https://doi.org/10.1007/978-981-97-6786-1

18. Bose M (2011) Harmonizing procedural rights indirectly: the framework decision on trials in absentia. North Carolina J Int Law Comm Regul 37(2):489–510
19. Bouloc B, Matsopoulou H (2009) Droit pénal général et procédure pénale, 17 edn. Sirey
20. Braithwaite J (2002) Restorative justice & responsive regulation. Oxford University Press
21. Brown B (1998) Primacy or complementarity: reconciling the jurisdiction of national courts and international criminal tribunals. Yale J Int Law 23:383–436
22. Brown DJ (1999) The international criminal court and trial in absentia. Brooklyn J Int Law 24(3):763–796
23. Brown DK, Turner JI, Weisser B (eds) (2019) Oxford handbook of criminal process. Oxford University Press
24. Bucerius SM, Tonry MH (eds) (2014) The oxford handbook of ethnicity, crime, and immigration. Oxford University Press
25. Khan KA, Buisman C, Gosnell C (2010) Principles of civil law. In Khan K, Buisman C, Gosnell C (eds) Principles of evidence in international criminal justice. Oxford University Press, pp 7–20
26. Caianiello M (2010) Law of Evidence at the international criminal court: blending accusatorial and inquisitorial models. North Carol J Int Law 36(2):287–318
27. Carter L, Pocar F (eds) International criminal procedure: the interface of civil law and common law legal systems. Edward Elgar
28. Cassese A, Gaeta P (2013) Cassese's international criminal law, 3rd edn. Oxford University Press
29. Cassese A, Gaeta P, Jones JRWD (eds) (2002) The Rome statute of the international criminal court: a commentary. Oxford University Press
30. Cassese A (1998) On the current trends towards criminal prosecution and punishment of breaches of international humanitarian law. Eur J Int Law 9:2–17
31. Cassese A (2008) International criminal law, 2nd edn. Oxford University Press
32. Chouliaras A (2015) A strategic choice: the state policy requirement in core international crimes. Leiden J Int Law 28(4):953–975
33. Clamp K (2015) Restorative justice in transition. Routledge
34. Crane DM, Sadat LN, Scharf MP (eds) (2018) The founders: four pioneering individuals who launched the first modern-era international criminal tribunals. Cambridge University Press
35. Cunneen C (2014) Colonial processes, indigenous peoples, and criminal justice systems. In: Bucerius SM, Tonry MH (eds) (2014) The oxford handbook of ethnicity, crime, and immigration. Oxford University Press, pp 386–407
36. Currie RJ (2007) Abducted fugitives before the international criminal court: problems and prospects. Crim Law Forum 18:349–393
37. Davidson A (2016) Human rights protection before the international criminal court: assessing the scope and application of article 21(3) of the Rome statute. Int Commun Law Rev 18:72–101
38. de Brouwer AM (2005) Supranational criminal prosecution of sexual violence: the ICC and the practice of the ICTY and the ICTR. Intersentia
39. De la Cuesta, L J (2001) Current national and international jurisdiction and the principle 'Ne bis in idem. Revue Internationale de Droit Pénal 72:753–764
40. DeGuzman MM (2012) How serious are international crimes? The gravity problem in international criminal law. Columbia J Trans Law 51(1):18–68
41. del Carmen VR (1994) Amerika Keiji Tetsuzukiho Gaisetsu—Sosa, Saiban ni Okeru Kenpo Shihai no Kantetsu [Criminal procedure law and practice, 2nd edn], trans. Masanori Kabashima and Kanae Hiroyuki. Daiichi Hoki
42. Donat-Cattin D (2016) Article 75 reparations to victims. In: Triffterer O, Ambos K (eds) Commentary on the Rome statute of the International Criminal Court: observers' notes, article by article, 3rd edn. Hart Publishing, pp 1853–1870
43. Dubberley S, Koenig A, Murray D (eds) (2020) Digital witness: using open source information for human rights investigation, documentation, and accountability. Oxford University Press
44. Dwertmann E (2010) The reparation system of the international criminal court: its implementation, possibilities and limitations. Publishers

45. Dworkin R (1986) Law's empire. Hart Publishing, 1998; Fontana Press
46. Elberling B (2008) The next step in history-writing through criminal law: exactly how tailor-made is the special tribunal for Lebanon? Leiden J Int Law 21:529–538
47. Evans C (2012) The right to reparation in international law for victims of armed conflict. Cambridge University Press
48. Farrell B (2003) The right to a speedy trial before international criminal tribunals. South Afr J Hum Rights 19(1):98–117
49. Fedorova MI (2012) The principle of equality of arms in international criminal proceedings. Intersentia
50. Feeney F, Herrmann J (2010) Hitotsu no Jiken Futatsu no Seido—Beikoku to Doitsu no Keiji Tetsuzuki [One case—two systems: a comparative view of American and German criminal justice systems], Taguchi M (trans). Seibundo
51. Feller SZ (1981) Current criminal jurisdiction in the international sphere. Israel Law Rev 16(1):40–74
52. Findlay M (2001) Synthesis in trial procedures? The experience of international criminal tribunals. Int Comp Law Q 50(1):26–53
53. Fischer H, Kreß C, Lüder SR (eds) (2001) International and national prosecution of crimes under international law: current developments. Berlin. Verlag A, Spitz
54. Friman H, Lewis P (2001) Reparations to victims. In: Lee RS (ed) The international criminal court: elements of crimes and rules of procedure and evidence. Transnational Publisher, pp 474–492
55. Friman H, Brady H, Costi M, Guariglia F, Stuckenberg CF (2013) Charges, confirmation, res judicata, Lis Pendens, Iura Novit Curia. In: Sluiter G, Friman H, Linton S, Vasiliev S, Zappalà S (eds) International criminal procedure: principles and rules. Oxford University Press, pp 381–488
56. Friman H (1999) Rights of persons suspected or accused of a crime. In: Lee RS (ed) The international criminal court: the making of the Rome statute, issues, negotiations, results. Kluwer Law International, pp 247–261
57. Fujimoto T, Senzu M (2002) Nyujirando ni okeru Shufukuteki Shiho no Ichi Shudan to Shite no Baisho Meirei [Reparation order as a means of restorative justice in New Zealand]. Hogaku Shimpo [Chuo Law Rev] 109(3):47-77
58. Fujita H (2003) Shinpan Kokusai Jindoho (Sai Zoho) [New edition of international humanitarian law (re-enlarged)]. Yushindokobunsha
59. Fujiwara H (2020) ICTY ni yoru Kokusai Keiji Sousa to Sureburenitsua [International criminal investigation by ICTY and Srebrenica]. In: Osa Y (ed) Sureburenitsua Jenosaido: 25-Nenme no Kyokun to Kadai [The Srebrenica genocide: lessons and challenges fat the 25 years anniversary]. Toshindo, pp 119–138
60. Furuya S (2005) Kokusai Jindoho Ihan to Higaisha ni Taisuru Hosho—Kokusai-Teki Seido no Tenkai [Violation of international humanitarian law and compensation for victims: development of international institutions]. Juristo [Jurist] 1299:64–72
61. Furuya S (2008) Kokusai Keiji Saiban Seido ni Okeru Higaisha e no Baisho [Reparations for Victims in the international criminal court system]. Waseda Hogaku [Waseda Law Rev] 83(3):155-181
62. Furuya S (1999) Kyu Yugo Kokusai Keiji Saibansho ni Taisuru Kyoryoku Gimu no Seikaku—Kokunai Jisshi Rippo no Kento o Chushin ni [The nature of the duty to cooperate with the international criminal tribunal for the former Yugoslavia: focusing on the examination of domestic implementation legislation]. Waseda Hogaku [Waseda Law Rev] 74(3):189–209
63. Gaeta P (2007) To be (present) or not to be (present) trials in absentia before the special tribunal for Lebanon. J Int Crim Just 5(5):1165–1174
64. Gaeta P (ed) (2013) The UN genocide convention: a commentary. Oxford University Press
65. Gallant KS (2022) International criminal jurisdiction: whose law must we obey? Oxford University Press
66. Gewirtz P (1983) Remedies and resistance. Yale Law J 92(4):585–590
67. Guilfoyle D (2016) International criminal law. Oxford University Press

68. Hart HM Jr (1958) The aims of the criminal law. Law Contemp Prob 23:401–441
69. Heller KJ (2006) The shadow side of complementarity: the effect of article 17 of the Rome statute on the national due process. Crim Law Forum 17:255–280
70. Heller KJ (2017) What is an international crime? (A revisionist history). Harv Int Law J 58(2):353–420
71. Henckaerts J-M, Doswald-Beck L (2005) Customary international humanitarian law. Cambridge University Press
72. Henzelin M, Heiskanen V, Mettraux G (2006) Reparations to victims before the international criminal court: lessons from international criminal court. Crim Law Forum 17(3):317–344
73. Hiéramente M (2011) The myth of 'international crimes': dialectics and international criminal law. Goettingen J Int Law 3:551–588
74. Higashizawa Y (2011) Kokusai Keiji Saibansho (ICC) ni Okeru 'Koseina Saiban': Rubanga Jiken o Furikaette ['Fair trial' at the International Criminal Court (ICC): looking back on the Lubanga case]. Meiji Gakuin Daigaku Hoka Daigakuin Rorebyu [Meiji Gakuin Univ Law School Law Rev] 15:91-110
75. Higashizawa Y (2007) Kokusai Keiji Saibansho—Ho to Jitsumu [The international criminal court: law and practice]. Akashi Shoten
76. Higashizawa Y (2013) Kokusai Keiji Saibansho to Jinken Hosho [International criminal court and human rights guarantee]. Shinzansha
77. Hirano R (1968) Keiji Soshoho Gaisetsu [Outline of the code of criminal procedure]. University of Tokyo Press
78. Holmes JT (2002) Complementarity: national courts versus the ICC. In: Cassese A, Gaeta P, Jones JRWD (eds) The Rome statute of the international criminal court: a commentary. Oxford University Press, pp 667–686
79. Inazumi M (2021) Kokusai Keiji Saiban ni Okeru Kesseki Saiban: Kokusai Keiji Saibansho (ICC) to Rebanon Tokubetsu Hotei no Saikin no Doko [Trial in absentia in international criminal tribunals: recent trends in the International Criminal Court (ICC) and the special tribunal for Lebanon]. Kanazawa Hogaku [Kanazawa Law Rev] 63(2):13-39
80. Inazumi M (2014) Kokusai Keiji Saibansho (ICC) to Afurika Shokoku tono Kakushitsu [The feud between the International Criminal Court (ICC) and African States]. Kanazawa Hogaku [Kanazawa Law Rev] 56(2):71–97
81. Inazumi M (2006) Ruwanda Kokusai Keiji Saibansho (ICTR) to Higisha no Jinken: Tetsuzuki Ihan no Kyusai ni Tsuite [The international criminal tribunal for Rwanda (ICTR) and human rights of suspects: remedies for violation of procedures]. Kanazawa Hogaku [Kanazawa Law Rev] 48(2):39-70
82. Inazumi M (2007) Kokusai Keiji Saibansho ni okeru Higaisha no Kenri Hosho [Guaranteeing victims' rights at the international criminal court]. Horitsu Jiho 79(4):48-53
83. Inoue M (1985) Keiji Sosho ni Okeru Shoko Haijo [Exclusion of evidence in criminal procedure]. Kobundo
84. Ishihara T (2015) Ruwanda Jenosaido Go no Komyuniti deno Wakai Jissen: NGO Richi Ruwanda no Katsudo kara [Reconciliation practices in communities after the rwandan genocide: from the activities of NGO reach Rwanda]. Kumamoto Daigaku Shakai Bunka Kenkyu [Kumamoto Univ Stud Soc Cult Sci] 13:135–156
85. Jalloh CC (2013) Self-representation and the use of assigned, standby and amicus counsel. In: Carter LE, Pocar F (eds) International criminal procedure: the interface of civil law and the common law legal system. Edward Elgar Publishing, pp 125–165
86. Jenks CW (1951) The conflict of law-making treaties. Br Yearb Int Law 20:401–453
87. Jenks C (2009) Notice otherwise given: will in absentia trials at the special tribunal for lebanon violate human rights. Fordham Int Law J 33(1):57–100
88. Jennings M (2008) Article 78: determination of the sentence. In Triffterer O (ed) Commentary on the Rome statute of the international criminal court: observers' notes, article by article, 2nd edn. Hart Publishing, pp 1433–1437
89. Jessberger F, Werle G (2014) Principles of international criminal law, 3rd edn. Oxford University Press

90. Johnstone G (2011) Restorative justice: ideas, values, debates, 2nd edn. Routledge
91. Jorda C, Hemptinne J (2002) The status and role of the victim. In: Cassese A, Gaeta P, Jones JRWD (eds) The Rome statute of the international criminal court: a commentary. Oxford University Press, pp 1387–1420
92. Jordash W, Parker T (2010) Trials in absentia at the special tribunals for lebanon: incompatibility with international human rights laws. J Int Crim Just 8(2):487–509
93. Kaku S (2021) Kokusai Keiji Tetsuzukiho no Taikei—'Puremisu Riron' to Ichiji Fusairi Gensoku [The system of international criminal procedure': 'premises theory' and the principle of ne bis in idem]. Kokusaiho Gaiko Zasshi [J Int Law Dipl] 120(3): 474-478
94. Kaku S (2020) The promise of the premise thesis. In: The book review meeting of Megumi Ochi '*Kokusai Keizi Tetsuzukihō no Taikei* [A System of international criminal procedure law]', online, 19 Sept 2020
95. Kalshoven F (1991) State responsibility for warlike acts of the armed forces. Int Comp Law Q 40(4):827–858
96. Karemaker R, Don Taylor III B, Pittman TW (2008) Witness proofing in international criminal tribunals: a critical analysis of widening procedural divergence. Leiden J Int Law 21(3):683–698
97. Kawai K (2021) Who enforces an arrest warrant of the international criminal court? Surrogation of jurisdiction theory from the perspective of international organizations law. J Int Crim Just 19(3):3–26 and 543–564
98. Keen PC (2004) Tempered adversariality: the judicial role and trial theory in the international criminal tribunals. Leiden J Int Law 17(4):767–814
99. Khan KA (2016) Article 78: determination of the sentence. In: Triffterer O, Ambos K (eds) Commentary on the Rome statute of the international criminal court: observers' notes, article by article, 3rd edn. Hart Publishing, pp 1891–1900
100. Khan K, Buisman C, Gosnell C (eds) (2010) Principles of evidence in international criminal justice. Oxford University Press
101. Kim S et al (2015) Doitsu Keijiho Nyumon [Introduction to German criminal law]. Horitsubunkasha
102. Kitano Y (2008) Kokusai Keiji Saibansho ni Yoru Kankatsuken Koshi no Kokusaihojo no Konkyo-zuke (1)~(3) Saibansho Kitei no Kiso Katei no Kento o Chushin ni [The legal basis for the exercise of jurisdiction by the International Criminal Court (1)-(3) An analysis based on the preparatory work of the Rome statute]. Hogakuronso [Kyoto Law Rev] 163(3):116–137; 5:173–187; 6:173–187
103. Kleffner JK (2008) Complementarity in the Rome Statute and national criminal jurisdictions. Oxford University Press
104. Ko K (2012) Ikoki no Seigi (Transitional Justice) to Kokusai Keiji Saiban—Kokusai Keiji Saiban no Kino Henka to Kadai [Transitional justice and international criminal jurisdiction : contemporary challenges]. Kokusaiho Gaiko Zasshi [J Int Law Dipl] 111(2):217-242
105. Ko K (1998, 1999) Kokusai Shiho Kyoryoku toshite no 'Hikiwatashi' no Hoteki Seishitsu (1) (2) Surrender Gainen no Seibi ni Mukete [The legal nature of 'extradition' as international judicial cooperation (1) (2) toward the development of the surrender concept]. Jochi Hogaku Ronshu [Sophia Law Rev] 42(2): 271–299, and 3 and 4:329–370
106. Kojima J (2000) Niju no Kiken no Seiritsu Katei [The formulation of the principle against double jeopardy]. Waseda Hogaku [Waseda Law Rev] 76(2):267-308
107. Kojo T (1972) Illinois v. Allen, 397U.S. 337 (1970)—*Hoteinai no Futona Gendo niyori Shinri o Bogai Suru Hikokunin ha Zaiteiken o Ushinau* [Illinois v. Allen, 397U.S. 337 (1970)—A defendant who interferes with a trial by unreasonable in-court conduct loses the right to be in court]. Americaho (1):126–130
108. Kress C, Prost K (2016) Article 90 competing requests. In: Triffterer O, Ambos K (eds) Commentary on the Rome statute of the international criminal court: observers' notes, article by article, 3rd rdn. Hart Publishing, pp 2059–2067
109. Kress C (2003) The procedural law of the international criminal court in outline: anatomy of a unique compromise. J Int Crim Just 1(3):603–617

110. Kuc O (2012) The Rome statute and legal limitations to the international surrender regime. New England J Int Comp Law 18(1):265–282
111. Kumagai T (2013) Kokusai Terorizumu to Joyaku no Yakuwari: Hikiwatashi matawa Sotsui no Kitei o Chushin ni [The conventional obligation to extradite or prosecute (aut dedere aut judicare) in the fight against international terrorism]. Nigata Kokusai Johodaigaku Joho Bunka Gakubu Kiyo [Bull Niigata Univ Int Inf Stud Department of Information Culture] 16:65-80
112. Langbein JH (1977) Comparative criminal procedure: Germany. West Publishing Company
113. Lee RS (ed) (1999) The international criminal court: the making of the Rome statute, issues, negotiations, results. Kluwer Law International
114. Lube S, Reed JS (1986) Extradition of Nazis from the United States to Israel: a survey of issues in transnational criminal. Stanford J Int Law 22(1):1–65
115. Machochoko P (1999) International cooperation and judicial assistance. In: Lee RS (ed) The making of the Rome Statute, issues, negotiations, results. kluwer law international, pp 305–318
116. Mansfield DY (2019) Kokusai Keiji Saibansho (ICC) ni Okeru Baisho Meirei no Ho Kozo—Kokusaiho no Kojin ni Taisuru Chokusetsu no Keijiteki Kiritsu no Shin Tenkai to Sono Genkai [The legal structure of the reparation orders of the international criminal court: new dimensions to international law's direct penal control of individuals and its limits]. Kokkagakkai Zasshi [J Assoc Polit Soc Sci] 132(7, 8):756–684
117. Maogoto JN (2004) A giant without limbs: the international criminal court's state-centric cooperation regime. Univ Queensland Law Journal 23(1):102–133
118. Matsuo K et al (2009) Jokai Keiji Soshoho (dai 4 han) [Criminal procedure law, article-by-article, 4th edn)]. Kobundo
119. Mayama A (2007) Kokusai Keiji Saibansho no Taisho Hanzai to Kokunaiteki Taio [The subject crimes of the international criminal court and domestic responses]. Horitsu Jiho 79(4):31–36
120. Mayama A (2015) Shinryaku Hanzai ni Kansuru Kokusai Keiji Saibansho Kitei Kanpara Kaisei: Heiwa Oyobi Anzen no Iji Seido no Fukanzensei to Selective Justice [Kampala amendment to the Statute of the international criminal court on the crime of aggression: imperfections in the peace and security maintenance system and selective justice]. Kokusaiho Gaiko Zasshi [J Int Law Dipl] 114(2):111–134
121. McCarthy C (2012) Reparation and victim support in the international criminal court. Cambridge University Press
122. Mégret F (2009) Beyond 'fairness': understanding the determinants of international criminal procedure. UCLA J Int Law Foreign Aff 14(1):37–76
123. Mégret F (2015) What sort of global justice is 'international criminal justice'? J Int Crim Just 13(1):77–96
124. Menkel-Meadow C (2007) Restorative justice: what is it and does it work? Ann Rev Law Soc Sci 3:161–187
125. Michels JD (2010) Compensating acquitted defendants for detention before international criminal courts. J Int Crim Just 8(2):407–424
126. Minow M (1998) Between vengeance and forgiveness; facing history after genocides and mass violence. Beacon Press
127. Miyamoto Y (1971) Kesseki Saiban no Yokoten to 'Saiban no Keni' [The principle of in absentia and 'trial authority']. Houritsu Jihou 43(12):40-47
128. Mizuno Y (2013) Iho Shushu Shoko Haijo Hosoku ni Kansuru Ichikosatsu—Gasshukoku ni okeru Giron o Sanko ni [A study on the law of exclusion of illegally collected evidence: with reference to the discussions in the United States]." Hiroshima Hogaku [Hiroshima Law J] 37(2)
129. Morishita T (1999) Kokuren no Hanzainin Hikiwatashi Moderu Joyaku [The United Nations Model Treaty on Extradition]. Keisatsugaku Ronshu [J Police Sci] 52(6):68–69
130. Morita C (2020) Iho Shushu Shoko Haijo Hosoku ni okeru Iho no Judaisei Handan to Shukanteki Jijo [Judgment of the severity of illegality and subjective circumstances in the law of exclusion of illegally collected evidence]. Tsukuba Hosei [Tsukuba Univ J Law Polit] 83:270-231

131. Murai N (2007) Hanrei Shokai Kokusai Keiji Saibansho (ICC) ni Taisuru Ihona Taiho Koryu ni Motozuku Tetsuzuki Chushi Shinsei—Rubanga Diro Jiken (Kokusai Keiji Saibansho 2006. 10. 3 Yoshinbu Kettei Donen 12. 14 Josobu Hanketsu) [Judicial precedents: Prosecutor v. Thomas Lubanga Dyilo; challenge to jurisdiction by reason of alleged unlawful arrest and detention (International Criminal Court, decision by the Pre-Trial Chamber 1 of 3 Oct. 2006; judgment by the Appeals Chamber of 14 Dec. 2006)]. Kokusai Jinken [Human Rights Int] 18:133-135
132. Murai N (2015) Kokusai Keiji Saibansho (ICC) no Jitai Sentei Kijun to Shite no Judaisei no Kijun [Gravity as a standard for selection of situations at the International Criminal Court]. Ryukoku Hogaku [Ryukoku Law Rev] 48(1):445–499
133. Muttukumaru C (199) Reparation to victims. In: Lee RS (ed) The international criminal court: the making of the Rome statute, issues, negotiations, results. Kluwer Law International, pp 262–269
134. Nagata K (2013) Zaisanteki Keiji Seisai no Kenkyu—Omoni Bakkinkei to Higai Bensho Meirei ni Shoten o Atete [A study of property criminal sanctions: focusing mainly on fines and orders to compensate for damages]. Kansaidaigaku Shuppanbu
135. Nakazawa Y (2018) Kokusai Keiji Saibansho (ICC) Kensatsu-Kyoku no Sotsui Senryaku no Henyo: Kankatsuken Koushi ni Okeru Shototsu no Kozu/Kyodo no Kozu [Changing strategies of prosecution by the international criminal court—between collision and cooperation]. Waseda-Hogakkaishi 69(1):303–352
136. Naruse G (2018) Kokusai Keiji Saibansho ni Okeru Shoukoho—Kakkoku no Shoukoho tono Hikaku Bunseki [Evidence law at the international criminal court: comparative analysis with evidence law of each state]. Horitsu Jiho 90(10):16–22
137. Naymark D (2008) Violation of the rights of the accused at international criminal tribunals: the problem of remedy. J Int Law Int Relat 4:1–18
138. Nishii M (1974) Seiji Hanzainin Fuhikiwatashi Gensoku no Keisei Katei (1) (2) [The formation process of the principle of non-extradition of political offenders (1) (2)]. Hogaku Ronso [Kyoto Law Rev] 94(2):18–39, and 95(3):33–64
139. Nishimura H (2015) Nihon ni okeru Shuhukuteki Shiho no Genryu o Tazunete—Hikaku Nendaishiteki Kentou [Inquiry into the origin of restorative justice in Japan—a comparative chronological study]. In: Nishimura H, Norio T (eds) Shufukuteki Seigi no Shoso: Hosoi Yoko Sensei Koki Shukuga [Aspects of restorative justice: in honour of professor Yoko Hosoi]. Seibundo, pp 1-114
140. Noguchi M (2014) Higaisha Shintaku Kikin to Sono Katsudo [The Trust Fund for Victims and its activities]. In: Murase S, Keiko K (eds) Kokusai Keiji Saibansho—Mottomo Judai na Kokusai Hanzai o Sabaku (dai 2 han〕 [International criminal court—judging the most serious international crimes, 2nd edn]. Toshindo, pp 339–354
141. Nsereko DDN (2008) The abuse of process doctrine in the administration of criminal justice before national courts and international tribunals. Univ Botswana Law J 7:29–72
142. O'Keefe R (2015) International criminal law. Oxford University Press
143. Ochi M (2016) Gravity threshold before the international criminal court: an overview of the court's practice. ICD Brief 19:1–16
144. Ochi M (2021) Hanrei: Kokusai Keizi Saibansho Kensatsukan no Sotsui Sairyo ni taisuru Saibanbu niyoru Tousei no Hani: Afuganisutan Zitai ni taisuru Sousaku Kyoka ni kansuru Zyososhin Kettei (3/5/2020) [Case review: the scope of regulation by the trial chamber of the ICC: appeal decision on authorisation of investigation into the Afghanistan situation]. Kokusaiho Kenkyu [Tokyo Rev Int Law] 9:190–199
145. Ochi M (2014) Kensatsukan Tai Saifu Aru = Isuramu Kadafi Jiken (Kokusai Keiji Saibansho (Dai Ichi Yoshin Saibanbu) Juri Kyoyo-Sei ni Kansuru Kettei, 2013 Nen 5 gatsu 31 Nichi) [The prosecutor v. Saif al-Islam Gaddafi (Decision on Admissibility of the international criminal court (pre-trial chamber I), 31 May 2013)]. Osaka Hogaku [Osaka Law Rev] 64(1):237–250
146. Ochi M (2016) Kokusai Keiji Shiho ni Okeru Niju Saiban Kinshi no Hani: Ippan Kokusaiho toshite no Ichiji Fusairi no Kihan Naiyo ni Kansuru Ichikosatsu [The scope of ouble trial prohibition in international criminal justice : A research on the contents of Ne Bis In Idem as a general international law]. Nomos 39:117–152

147. Ochi M (2018) Kokusai Keiji Shiho ni okeru Onsha to Ichiji Fusairi no Tekiyo Reigai—'Fushobatsu tono Tatakai' Koso no Gutaika no Hanei toshite [Amnesty and the exception of ne bis in idem in international criminal justice : Reflecting the concretization of 'combating impunity']. Kokusai Kokyo Seisaku Kenkyu [Int Public Policy Stud] 23(1):75–96
148. Ochi M (2022) The new recipe for a general principle of law: premise theory to 'fill in the gaps'. Asian J Int Law, pp 1–19
149. Ochi M (2020) Kokusai Keiji Tetsuzukihō no Taikei-'Puremisu Riron' to Ichiji Fusairi Gensoku [A system of international criminal procedure: 'premise theory' and the principle of *ne bis in idem*]. Shinzansha
150. Ohlin JD (2013) Goals of international criminal justice and international criminal procedure. In: Sluiter G, Friman H, Linton S, Vasiliev S, Zappalà S (eds) International criminal procedure: principles and rules. Oxford University Press, pp 55–68
151. Okada Y (2021) Koteki Shikaku wa Mukankei ka: Genshoku Kokka Genshu ni Taisuru Taihojo Happu ni Miru Kokusai Keiji Saibansho to Kokuren Anzen Hosho Rijikai no Kankei [Are official qualifications irrelevant?: the relationship between the International Criminal Court and the UN security council in issuing arrest warrants against incumbent heads of state]. Horitsu Jiho 93(7):34–40
152. Okubo T (2005) Saibanin Seido ni Okeru 'Shoko no Toriatsukai' to Sosa heno Eikyo—'Chokusetsu Shugi/Koto Shugi' o Megutte [Influence of the new trial system on investigation and evidence]. Hiroshima Hoka Daigakuin Ronshu [Hiroshima Law Rev] 1:113–147
153. Okumura M (2015) Hanzai Higai Kyufu Seido no Genjo to Kadai [The current state of and challenges for the crime victimization benefit system]. Higaishagaku Kenkyu [J Victimol] 25(1):131-147
154. Okumura M (2007) Nyujirando ni okeru Hanzai Higaisha to Keiji Shiho [Crime victims and criminal justice in New Zealand]. Doshisha Hogaku [Doshisha Law Rev] 59(1):1-18
155. Oya M (1977) Higaisha no Hosho [Compensation for victims]. Gakuyo Shobo
156. Ozaki K (2021) Kokusai Keiji Saibansho ni Okeru Higaisha no Chii [Status of victims before the International Criminal Court]. In: Yuji I, Masataka O (eds) Kokusai Kankei to Ho no Shihai—Owada Hisashi Kokusai Shiho Saibansho Saibankan Tainin Kinen [International relations and the rule of law: in commemoration of the retirement of judge Hisashi Owada from the international court of justice]. Shinzansha, pp 637–666
157. Ozaki K (2021) Kokusai Jinken Keiji ho Gairon (Dai 2 Han) [Introduction to international human rights criminal law, 2nd edn]. Shinzansha
158. Placha M (2001) The Lockerbie case: the role of the security council in enforcing the principle Aut Dedere Aut Judicare. Eur J Int Law 12:125–140
159. Pocar F, Carter LE (2013) The challenge of shaping procedures in international criminal courts. In: Carter LE, Pocar P (eds) International criminal procedure: the interface of civil law and common law legal systems. Edward Elgar, pp 1–33
160. Pons N (2010) Some remarks on in absentia proceedings before the special tribunal for Lebanon in the Case of a state's failure or refusal to hand over the accused. J Int Crim Just 8(5):1307–1321
161. Radosavljevic D (2008) Mala Captus Bene Detentus and the right to challenge the legality of arrests under the ICC statute. Liverpool Law Rev 29:269–285
162. Randelzhofer A, Tomuschat C (eds) (1999) State responsibility and the individual: reparation in instances of grave violations of human rights. Martinus Nijhoff Publishers
163. Raub L (2009) Positioning hybrid tribunals in international criminal justice. New York Univ J Int Law Polit 41:1013–1053
164. Roark RM, Masahito I, Megumi Y (1987) Amerika no Keiji Tetsuzuki [American criminal procedure]. Yuhikaku
165. Reydams L, Wouters J, Ryngaert C (eds) (2012) International prosecutors. Oxford University Press
166. Richardson L (2017) Offences against the administration of justice at the international criminal court: robbing Peter to Pay Paul? J Int Crim Just 15(4):741–774

167. Roht-Arriaza N (2004) Reparations in the aftermath of repression and mass violence. In: Stover E, Weinstein HM (eds) My neighbor, my enemy: justice and community in the aftermath of mass atrocity. Cambridge University Press, pp 121–140
168. Roth R (2013) The extradition of génocidaires. In: Gaeta P (ed) The UN genocide convention: a commentary. Oxford University Press, pp 278–309
169. Roxin C (1992) Doitsu Keijitetsuzukiho [Strafverfahrensrecht {German code of criminal procedure}]. In: Shinya E, Yoshida N (trans.). Daiichi Hoki 1992.
170. Sadoff DA (2016) Bringing international fugitives to justice: extradition and its alternatives. Cambridge University Press
171. Safferling CJM (2001) Towards an international criminal procedure. Oxford University Press
172. Safferling C (2012) International criminal procedure. Oxford University Press
173. Sakamaki T (2015) Keiji Soshoho [Criminal procedure law]. Yuhikaku
174. Sakamoto K (2021) Megumi Ochi: Kokusai Keiji Tetsuzuki-Hō no Taikei—'Puremisu Riron' to Ichiji Fusairi Gensoku [Book Review: Megumi Ochi, The system of international criminal procedure: 'premise theory' and the principle of ne bis in idem]. Kokusai Jinken [Int Human Rights] 32: 130-132
175. Sakamoto K (2000) Kokusai Hanzai ni Kansuru Joronteki Kosatsu—Kokusai Keiji Saibansho no Taisho Hanzai no Bunseki kara [An introduction to international crimes: an analysis of the target crimes of the international criminal court]. Kyushu Kokusai Daigaku Hogaku Ronshu [Kyushu Int Univ Law J] 6(3):27–65
176. Sarkin J (2012) Enhancing the legitimacy, status and role of the international criminal court by using transitional justice or restorative justice strategies. Interdisc J Human Rights Law 6:83–102
177. Sasayama F (2018) Igirisu ni Okeru 'Shijin ni yoru Wana' no Tetsuzukihoteki Koka [The legal consequences of 'private entrapment' in England and Wales]. Doshisha Hogaku [Doshisha Law Rev] 69(7):3369-3400
178. Sato M (2019) Yoroppa Jinken Saibansho Hanketsu ni Okeru Iho Shushu Shoko no Kyoyo Sei Handan—Iburahimu Hoka Tai Igirisu 2016 Nen 9 gatsu 13 Nichi Dai Hotei Hanketsu o Chushin ni [Judgments on the Admissibility of illegally collected evidence in European Court of human rights judgments: focusing on the Ibrahim et al. v. the United Kingdom, 13 September 2016 grand chamber decision]. Kanazawa Hogaku [Kanazawa Law Rev] 62(1):61-86
179. Schabas WA (2000) Barayagwiza v. Prosecutor (decision, and decision (prosecutor's request for review or reconsideration)) Case No. ICTR-97-19-AR72. Am J Int Law 94(3):563–571
180. Schabas WA, Caruana V (2016) Article 63 trial in the presence of the accused. In: Triffterer O, Ambos K (eds) Commentary on the Rome Statute of the international criminal court: observers' notes, article by article, 3rd edn. Hart Publishing, pp 1563–1587
181. Schabas WA (2010) The International Criminal Court: a commentary on the Rome Statute. Oxford University Press
182. Schiffbauer B (2014) "Article VII". In: Tams CJ, Berster L, Schiffbauer B (eds) Convention on the prevention and punishment of the crime of genocide: a commentary. C. H. Beck/Hart/Nomos, pp 261–269
183. Schuon C (2012) The appeals decision in the ICC's Jean-Pierre Bemba Gombo case on the trial chamber's 'decision on the admission into evidence of materials contained in the prosecution's list of evidence.' Leiden J Int Law 25(2):511–520
184. Schwarz A (2016) The legacy of the Kenyatta case: trials in absentia at the international criminal court and their compatibility with human rights. Afr Human Rights Law J 16(1):99–116
185. Shaw GJ (2012) Convicting Inhumanity in absentia: holding trials in absentia at the international criminal court. George Washington Int Law Rev 44:107–140
186. Shelton D (2006) Remedies in international human rights law, 2nd edn. Oxford University Press
187. Sheppard D (2010) The international criminal court and 'internationally recognized human rights': understanding article 21(3) of the Rome Statute. Int Crim Law Rev 10:43–71

188. Shereshevsky Y (2015) Monetary compensation as a remedy for fair trial violations under international criminal law. New Crim Law Rev 18(1):71–99
189. Shimaoka M et al (2019) Furansu Keijiho Nyumon [Introduction to French criminal law]. Daiichi Hoki
190. Shiratori Y (2011) Furansu no Keiji Shiho [Criminal justice in France]. Nihon Hyoronsha
191. Shiratori Y (2015) Keiji Soshoho (dai 8 han) [Criminal procedure law, 8th edn)]. Nihon Hyoronsha
192. Shukuya A, An S (2010) Shuhukuteki Seigi Joron [An introduction to restorative justice]. Seibundo
193. Simon TW (2015) Genocide, torture, and terrorism: ranking international crimes and justifying humanitarian intervention. Palgrave Macmillan
194. Sloan J (2003) Prosecutor v. Dragan Nikolic: decision on defence motion on illegal capture. Leiden J Int Law 16:541–552
195. Sluiter G, Friman H, Linton S, Vasiliev S, Zappalà S (eds) (2013) International criminal procedure: principles and rules. Oxford University Press
196. Sluiter G (2003) The surrender of war criminals to the international criminal court. Loyola Los Angeles Int Comp Law Rev 25:605–651
197. Stahn C (2015) Reparative justice after the Lubanga appeal judgment: new prospects for expressivism and participatory justice or 'juridified victimhood' by other means? J Int Crim Just 13(4):801–813
198. Stahn C (2012) Libya, the international criminal court and complementarity: a test for 'shared responsibility.' J Int Crim Just 10(2):325–349
199. Stahn C (2019) A critical introduction to international criminal law. Cambridge University Press
200. Staker C, Nerlich V (2016) Article 85: compensation to an arrested and convicted person. In: Triffterer O, Ambos K (eds) Commentary on the Rome statute of the international criminal court: observers' notes, article by article, 3rd edn. Hart Publishing, pp 1998–2002
201. Starr SB (2008) Rethinking 'effective remedies': remedial deterrence in international courts. New York Univ Law Rev 83:693–768
202. Stefani G, Levasseur G, Bourock B (1982) Furansu Keijiho (Keiji Soshho) [Droit pénale {French criminal law}]. In: Sawato Y, Sawato T, Niikura O (trans.) Seibundo
203. Stephen C (2012) International criminal law: wielding the sword of universal criminal justice? Int Comp Law Q 61(1):55–89
204. Stern V (2001) An alternative vision: criminal justice developments in non-western countries. Soc Just 28(3):88–104
205. Stroh D (2001) State cooperation with the international criminal tribunals for the former Yugoslavia and for Rwanda. Max Planck Yearb United Nations Law 5:249–283
206. Suemichi Y (2006) Furansu No Keiji Rippō No Dōkō: Loi Perben II-Hō Ni Tsuite [Trend of Criminal Legislation in France: About the Loi Perben II Law], Nanzan Hogaku, 29(2):123–165
207. Suzuki K (2013) Kokusai Keiji Saiban ni Okeru Shiho Torihiki (1)(2) [Plea bargaining in international criminal trials (1)(2)]. Hikakuho Zasshi [Comp Law Rev] 46 2159–185; 47(1):145–185
208. Swart B (2002) International cooperation and judicial assistance-general problems. In: Cassese A, Gaeta P, Jones JRWD (eds) (2002) The Rome Statute of the International Criminal Court: a commentary, vol 2. Oxford University Press, pp 1589-1606
209. Taguchi M (2011) 338 Jo Koso Kikyaku no Hanketsu [Article 338: judgment of dismissal of public prosecution]. In Kawakami K et al (eds) Dai Konmentaru Keiji Soshoho dai 8 kan (Dai 2 han) [Great commentary on criminal procedure law, vol 8, 2nd edn]. Seirin Shoten, pp 285–286
210. Takahashi N (2003) Shufukuteki Shiho no Tankyu [The quest for restorative justice]. Seibundo
211. Takayama K (2014) ICC no Keiji Tetsuzuki no Tokucho [Characteristics of the ICC's criminal procedures]. In: Murase S, Ko K (eds) Kokusai Keiji Saibansho—Mottomo Judaina Kokusai Hanzai o Sabaku (dai 2 han) [International criminal court: judging the most serious international crimes, 2nd edn]. Toshindo, pp 227-252

212. Takemura H (2011) Hanrei Shōkai: Kokusai Keiji Saibansho Kensatsukan no Jiko no Hatsui Ni Yoru Sosa ni Taisuru Yoshin Saibanbu no Kyoka Kettei: Kenia no Jitai (Kokusai Keiji Saibansho Yoshin Saibanbu (2010. 3. 31 Kettei) [Introduction to precedents: decision of the pre-trial chamber to allow the prosecutor to investigate on their own motive: the situation in Kenya {International criminal court pre-trial chamber, 3.31.2010 Decision}]. Kokusai Jinken [Human Rights Int] 22:168–170
213. Takemura H (2021) Hanrei: Kokusai Keiji Saibansho Kitei Hiteiyaku Koku ni Kansuru Hanzai ni Taisuru Kokusai Keiji Saibansho no Kankatsuken: Banguradeshu/ Myanma no Jitai ni Kansuru Dai 3 Yoshin Saibanbu ni Yoru Sosa Kaishi Kyoka Kettei (November 14, 2019) [Case review: the jurisdiction of the international criminal court for crimes related to states not party to the statute of the international criminal court: decision on permission to commence investigation by pre-trial chamber III on the situation in Bangladesh/Myanmar {November 14, 2019}]." Kokusaiho Kenkyu [Tokyo Rev Int Law] 9:181–189
214. Takemura H (2015) Kokka Genshuto no Gaikoku Keiji Kankatsuken kara no Menjo: Sono Rinkaku to Kokusai Keiji Kankatsuken to no Kankei [Immunity from foreign criminal jurisdiction for heads of state and others: its contours and relationship with international criminal jurisdiction]. Kokusaiho Gaiko Zasshi [J Int Law Diplom] 114(3):251–279
215. Takemura H (2018) Kokusai Keiji Saibansho Kitei Seido no Jikkoteki Jitsugen no Tame no Sotsui Senryaku to Kokka no Gimu [Prosecution strategies and state obligations for the effective implementation of the statute system of the international criminal court]. Kokusaiho Kenkyu [Tokyo Rev Int Law] 6:21–45
216. Takemura H (2015) Kokusai Keiji Saibansho ni Taisuru Kokka no Kyoryoku Gimu no Naiyo to Hoteki Kiso [The content and legal basis of the state's obligation to cooperate with the international criminal court (2)]. Aichikenritsudaigaku Daigakuin Kokusai Bunka Kenkyuka Ronshu [Bull Grad School Int Cult Stud Aichi Prefectural Univ] 16:111–115
217. Takemura H (2009) Nihon to Kokusai Keiji Saibansho ni Okeru Kensatsukan no Sairyo [The prosecutor's discretion in Japan and at the international criminal court]. Kyushu Kokusai Daigaku Hogakuronshu [Kyushu Kokusai Univ Law Rev] 15(3):177–241
218. Takemura H (2013) Lebanon Tokubetsu Hotei o Meguru Kokusai Keijiho-Jo no Sho Ronten [Some legal issues on the Special Tribunal for Lebanon]. Kitakyushu Shiritsu Daigaku Hosei Ronshu [Kitakyushu Shiritsu Daigaku J Law Polit Sci] 40(4):203–231
219. Takizawa M (2001) *Hutai Shiso ni yoru Higaisha no Songai Kaihuku* [Recovery of damages for victims through ancillary private actions]. Hogaku Shimpo [Chuo Law Rev] 107(9/10):141-162
220. Tamiya H (1996) Keiji Soshoho (shinpan) [Criminal procedure law, New edn)]. Yuhikaku
221. Tammelo I (1959) On the Logical openness of legal orders: a modal analysis of the law with special reference to the logical status of non liquet in international law. Am J Comp Law 8(2):187–203
222. Tams CJ, Berster L, Schiffbauer B (2014) Convention on the prevention and punishment of the crime of genocide: a commentary. C. H. Beck/Hart/Nomos
223. Tatsuda R (2015) Kokusai Keiji Saibansho ni okeru Shufukuteki Apurochi Oyobi Higaisha Shien—Rubanga Saiban o Furikaette [Restorative approach and victim support in the International Criminal Court: reflections on the Lubanga trial]. In Nishimura H, Norio T, Seigi S (eds) no Shoso: Hosoi Yoko Sensei Koki Shukuga [Aspects of restorative justice: Dr. Yoko Hosoi's Koki celebration]. Seibundo
224. Tiba FK (2007) The Mengistu genocide trial in Ethiopia. J Int Crim Just 5(2):513–528
225. Timm B (2001) The legal position of victims in the rules of procedure and evidence. In Fischer H, Kress C, Lüder SR (eds) International and national prosecution of crimes under international law: current developments. Verlag A. Spitz, pp 289–308
226. Tomuschat C (1999) Individual reparation claims in instances of grave human rights violations: the position under general international law. In: Randelzhofer A, Tomuschat C (eds) State responsibility and the individual: reparation in instances of grave violations of human rights. Martinus Nijhoff Publishers, pp 1–26
227. Tonry M (ed) The oxford handbook of crime and criminal justice. Oxford University Press

228. Tonry M (2011) Crime and criminal justice. In Tonry M (ed) The oxford handbook of crime and criminal justice. Oxford University Press, pp 1–25
229. Tracogna C (2010) The influence of the ECHR jurisprudence on the national criminal procedure system: the italian perspective: from the Italian perspective: from divergence to realignment. Lex ET Sci Int J XVII-1:84–99
230. Triffterer O, Ambos K (eds) (2016) Commentary on the Rome statute of the International Criminal Court: observers' notes, article by article, 3rd edn. Hart Publishing
231. Triffterer O (ed) (2008) Commentary on the Rome statute of the International Criminal Court: observers. In: Notes, article by article, 2nd edn. Hart Publishing
232. Tulkens F (2011) The paradoxical relationship between criminal law and human rights. J Int Crim Just 9(3):577–595
233. Turner JI (2019) Pluralism in international criminal procedure. In: Brown DK, Turner JI, Weisser B (eds) Oxford handbook of criminal process. Oxford University Press, pp 993–1017
234. Turner JI (2012) Policing international prosecutors. New York Univ J Int Law Polit 45:175–258
235. Uto T, Takeshi M, Shinji H (2012) Keiji Soshoho [Criminal procedure law]. Yuhikaku
236. Van Den Wyngaert C, Ongena T (2002) Ne bis in idem principle, including the Issue of amnesty. In: Cassese A, Gaeta P, Jones JRWD (eds) The Rome Statute of the International Criminal Court: a commentary. Oxford University Press, pp 705–730
237. Van den Wyngaert C (2011) Victims before International Criminal Courts: some views and concerns of an ICC trial judge. Case Western Res J Int Law 44:475–496
238. Van N, Daniel W, Strong KH (2014) Restoring justice: an introduction to restorative justice, 5th edn. Anderson
239. Viebig P (2016) Illicitly obtained evidence at the international criminal court. Asser Press
240. Wagatsuma H (2013) Furansu ni Okeru Koso Juzaiin [The court of appeal felony in France]. Hosei Riron [J Law Polit] 45(4):184-229
241. Walgrave L (2000) How pure can a maximalist approach to restorative justice remain? Or can a purist model of restorative justice become maximalist? Contemp Just Rev 3(4):415–432
242. Wheeler CH (2017) Right or duty? Is the accused's presence at trial a right or a duty under international criminal law? Crim Law For 28:99–127
243. Wheeler CH (2021) Shifting priorities: are attitudes changing at the international criminal court about trials in absentia? Int Crim Law Rev, published online (22 Jan 2021), pp 1–29
244. Whiting A (2009) In international criminal prosecutions, justice delayed can be justice delivered. Harv Int Law J 50(2):323–364
245. Willey P (2014) Trials in absentia and the cuts to criminal legal aid: a deadly combination? J Crim Law 78(6):486–510
246. Yamaguchi K (2008) Kokusai Keiji Saiban Kikan ni Okeru Shonin—Shonin no Hogo to Hikokunin no Kenri no Hazama de [Witness under the international criminal justice system: in search of the appropriate balance between the protection of witnesses and the right of the accused to a fair trial]. Law Pract 2:217–251
247. Yamamoto K (2010) Hanrei Kenkyu: Shokyokuteki Sosho Joken to Shite no Nijukiso to Sono Hosei (Tokyo Chisai Heisei 20. 5. 22 Hanketsu) [Case study: double indictment as a negative process requirement and its amendment (Tokyo District Court Decision on May 22, 2008)]. Senshu Rojanaru [Senshu Law Rev] 5:190–191
248. Yamamoto M et al (2007) Purimeru Keiji Soshoho [A primer of criminal procedure law]. Horitsubunkasha
249. Yamamoto S (1985) Hanzainin Hikiwatashi Seido ni Okeru Seijisei no Henshitsu [The transformation of politics in the extradition system]. Hogaku [J Law Polit Sci] 49(3):355-391
250. Yamamoto S (1991) Kokusai Keijiho [International criminal law]. Sanseido
251. Yamanaka K (2017) Kindai Keiho no Shiteki Tenkai [The historical development of modern criminal law]. Shinzansha
252. Yanagawa S (2006) Hanzainin Hikiwatashi Seido no Rekishiteki Hatten to Konnichi no Kokusaiteki Doukou: Kokusai Keiji Shihou Kyozyo to Kokusai Jinkenho no Ichi Danmen [The historical development of the criminal extradition system and today's international trends: a

cross section of international criminal legal assistance and international human rights law]. Meiji Gakuin Daigaku Hoka Daigakuin Rorebyu [Meiji Gakuin Univ Law Rev] 5:37–47
253. Yee S, Wang T (eds) (2001) International law in the post-cold war world: essays in memory of Li Haopei. Routledge
254. Terasaki, Y (1994) Sosho Jokenron no saikosei—Kosoken Ranyoron no Saisei no Tameni [Reconstruction of the theory of process requirement: for the rehabilitation of the theory of abuse of the right to prosecute]. Seibundo
255. Zakerhossein MH, De Brouwer A-M (2015) Diverse approaches to total and partial in absentia trials by international criminal tribunals. Crim Law Forum 26:181–224
256. Zanotti I (2006) Extradition in multilateral treaties and conventions. Martinus Nijhoff Publishers
257. Zappalá S (2003) Human rights in international criminal proceedings. Oxford University Press
258. Zegveld L (2010) Victims' Reparations claims and international criminal courts. J Int Crim Just 8(1):79–111
259. Zehr H (2015) Changing lenses: restorative justice for our times. Herald Press

The manufacturer's authorised representative in the EU is Springer Nature Customer Service Centre GmbH, Europaplatz 3, 69115 Heidelberg, Germany. If you have any concerns regarding our products, please contact ProductSafety@springernature.com

Printed and bound by CPI Group (UK) Ltd, Croydon, CR0 4YY
01/10/2026
02225849-0005